Hypogrif in Bubbaville

*A Memoir of
Race, Class and Ego*

Grif Stockley

Books by Grif Stockley

FICTION

Expert Testimony

Probable Cause

Religious Conviction

Illegal Motion

Blind Judgment

Salted With Fire

NON-FICTION

Blood in Their Eyes: The Elaine Race Massacres of 1919

Daisy Bates: Civil Rights Crusader from Arkansas

Race Relations in the Natural State

Ruled by Race: Black/White Relations in Arkansas From Slavery to the Present

Black Boys Burning: The 1959 Fire at the Arkansas Negro Boys Industrial School

Blood in Their Eyes: The Elaine Massacre of 1919, Second Edition, with Brian K. Mitchell and Guy Lancaster

Figure 1: Grif Stockley, Greenville, Mississippi, c.1997. Photo by Lynn Pence.

GRIF STOCKLEY is an author, historian, and attorney known for his dedication to advancing civil rights after coming of age in the Jim Crow South. His Gideon Page series of legal mystery novels became popular in the 1990s. His non-fiction titles exploring the history of race relations in Arkansas have earned him widespread acclaim. Stockley has been awarded the Porter Prize, the Booker Worthen Literary Prize (twice), and the Lifetime Achievement Award from the Arkansas Historical Association.

Hypogrif in Bubbaville

Copyright © 2020 by Grif Stockley.

All rights reserved. Subject to the fair use exception of Section 107 of the U.S. Copyright Act, reproduction of this publication by any means, in any format, in whole or in part, is prohibited without written permission from the author.

ISBN 979-8-6349-2556-1

For my long-time friends
Lee Brown and Teresa Marks

Contents

Chapter 1: One of the "Ten Hardest Places" 9

Chapter 2: Looking for a Family Hero 37

Chapter 3: The "White" American Century 63

Chapter 4: "The All-Pervading Doctrine" 95

Photographs 113

Chapter 5: College—Let Me Out of There! 121

Chapter 6: Me Not Talk Pretty, EVER 141

Chapter 7: No Strings to Pull 165

Chapter 8: Talk, Talk, Talk 189

Chapter 9: Sexism and Racism—the Law School Way 201

Chapter 10: Legal Services 211

Chapter 11: Due Process 231

Chapter 12: *Hypogrif* 247

Acknowlegments 255

Notes 257

CHAPTER 1

One of the "Ten Hardest Places"

"We have the genius of make-believe here, and of not seeing...There is a culture of repression here."

— Political scientist Dr. Flavien Koudawo, commenting in the *New York Times* on June 28, 2009, on the violence in his native African country of Guinea-Bissau

"We were taken care of by Negroes... "

— Sally Stockley Johnson, *The Seasons of My Life* (unpublished), in possession of the author

"[T]he wound won't close till its existence is spoken aloud, but no person dares to."

— Yvonne Adhiambo Owuor, *Dust*, (New York: Knopf, 2014)

TRUTH MATTERS. Even when exaggerated. When we get together now, my sisters, Sally and Harriet (Figure 16, p.119), will rather gleefully recount how "rotten-spoiled" I was—that I didn't learn to walk or talk until I was two, because all I needed to do was point. Their mission in life was to wait on me hand and foot. How they had time to get dressed, eat or go to the bathroom they have no idea. "Rotten-spoiled," with teeth-clenched emphasis on the word "rotten," is a redundant descriptor borrowed from my mother. Temple, a life-long, two-pack-a-day Camel smoker (until it killed her), who, with as much drama as she could muster, entertained me and herself by magically transmogrifying the word "rotten" into a sound as raspy and nasty as a cough that has dredged mucus from the rawest and deepest recess of an abscessing throat. *Rotten!*

Don't be fooled. Temple, when the occasion called for it, was the quintessential, white Southern lady, who, when my father Jake died, had the connections to find genteel employment as a housemother for a sorority at the University of Mississippi. An excerpt of a letter from one of her "girls" to the Alpha Delta Pi brass after her death in 1970, asking permission to buy a chair from her room, pinpoints Temple's strengths:

> "...She was my mother away from home as she was for so many ADP's. When I thought of Ole Miss, I thought of her...I am writing to ask you a very great favor. Mrs. Stockley had a red velvet covered chair in her bedroom that I believe is part of the housemother's quarters at the ADPi house. She always sat in that chair when she was in that room alone, I believe, or when we came to ask her advice or just to talk. That chair has her personality, for it was a part of her. I would like to know if there is any chance of my buying that chair...At this moment I—like everybody else—would like to preserve all things that were Mrs. Stockley's or a part of her. Her chair is so much a part of her, and she is so vivid to me now as I picture her sitting there. I miss her, as we all do, and I will always treasure our memories that we have together..."[1]

Forty-four years after making this request, Janelle Cranford Arnold remembered Temple as "kind and loving and a beautiful lady who helped us to be young ladies in her image."[2]

Some people have concrete slabs erected in their honor; a red velvet chair purchased by a thoughtful and grateful sorority girl symbolized Temple's particular gifts. One could do a lot worse and many have: me, for one, but it took a long time to figure that out. Of course, it was Temple who was overseeing the spoiling of the long hoped-for boy-king. Sally, seven years older, and Harriet (whom we have always called "Boo"), my senior by five years, could only go along with it. My parents had lost a set of twins after having my two sisters, and I was Temple's last chance. As the baby I could do no wrong, and my childhood would mostly stay that way. Even when Temple got mad and threatened to "spank all three of us," I am alleged to have made her laugh by saying, "Mama, I'm not three; I'm two." Cute, but not that cute; however, spoiling is not the worst thing that can happen to a child. At best, it means I was loved, and Temple and Jake, too, loved me—in the lyrics of Paul Simon, one of my generation's musical geniuses and my personal all-time favorite—"like a rock."

The advantages and consequences of Southern white male heterosexual privilege have dramatically affected how I have interacted with the rest of the planet. True, I am hardly the "Lone Ranger" in this regard, but no one at the time took me aside and said, "Son, you are not as wonderful as you think!" Those lessons have come later.

The man Temple would marry, and stay married to for a lifetime, adored her and she adored him. From his cotton plantation, Whitehall in the Arkansas Delta (Figure 9, p.116), Griffin Jasper Stockley wrote in 1934:

> *Temple — for an hour I have been trying to work on my books but instead of figures I seem to see a pair of dark blue eyes looking up at me, a dimpled smile, and I go off into a reverie — living again some of the precious moments I have spent with you. Yesterday already seems a year ago, and yet memories of it are so vivid in my mind, that I seem to be with you again, to hear your voice, to feel your touch. Sundays pass to [sic] quick, weekdays so slow, and Thursdays seem to never, never come.*

> *Nights here are ones of solitude, some times [sic] I have hated them, now I am glad, for in my loneliness there is nothing to distract my thoughts from you, and I have them all to myself, loving them as I love the one whom they are of.* — Jake

Maybe not poetry, but not bad for a man who liked to tell the story that he hadn't actually stuck around the last day of class to get his diploma from high school in Memphis. Whether he had or not was not his point. This man wanted her. She wanted him, but did she really want to move from her hometown of Marianna to a 5,000 acre flood-prone plantation powered by mules and black sharecroppers 20 miles out in the county during the middle of the Great Depression?

This was decidedly not going to be Tara before the Civil War in "Gone With the Wind," and Jake was no Clark Gable, but, on the other hand, Temple, who could get herself up in pearls and white gloves when the occasion called for it, was no Vivienne Leigh. Nor was she brilliant and elegant like her older sister, Harriet (whose nickname in the family was "Tissie"); neither was she beautiful and unforgettably sweet like her younger sister, Sarah Hope. Though Temple delighted in making me snicker with her sardonic brand of humor, she wasn't "LOL" funny like her younger brother David Wall, Jr. And if she had a scientific bent like her physician father, Enoch David, Sr., she kept it to herself. Finally, neither was she a writer and historian like her mother, Effie, who in 1907 had made and probably regretted a similar decision to live for a time in the wilds of Lee County. As would be demonstrated repeatedly, Temple's long suit was her personality, her warmth and genuine interest if she decided to like you. Sally and I were admittedly "pleasers," and she favored us over our middle sister, Harriet, who had a more independent streak.

But it is my college-educated grandmother's life and literary output where I begin the effort to make sense of the Arkansas/

Mississippi River Delta, its effect on me, my family and friends, and others who lived in this region. Not only did Effie Allison Wall personify many of the values and attitudes that initially shaped our lives and attitudes, she exercised considerable influence over her husband, their four children and a few of her older grandchildren. At the same time, her recorded successes, hopes, and fears were a window on the dominant white culture in eastern Arkansas, an agricultural paradise or hell, depending on your perspective.

As I wrote these words in the early morning hours on America's official Independence Day in 2014, I took note that the *New York Times* magazine has characterized the county where I grew up in the Arkansas Delta (Lee County—named after you know who) as statistically one of the "ten hardest places to live in the U.S."[3] Through the magic of technology I will never come close to understanding, I can place my cursor over a digital map in the article and learn just how wretched conditions are today for many in the Delta county where I spent 15 of my first 17 years. Having lived in Little Rock in the center of the state since 1972 (roughly a hundred miles from the county seat of Marianna), hearing bad news about Lee County has become routine. As measured by "education (percentage of residents with at least a bachelor's degree), median household income, unemployment rate, disability rate, life expectancy and obesity," according to the *Times* we have been outed once again.

It is no longer merely a case of Yankees muttering "tut-tut" and looking down their noses at us. As a state, we are not quite so defensive about our seemingly intractable poverty since some parts of Arkansas are doing quite well, thank you very much. On Christmas morning in 2013, the *Arkansas Democrat-Gazette* reported on its first page that in Lee County "only one in 16 adults 25 and older have a four year [college] degree."[4] Not only is that statistic the worst in the state, according to the paper, it is worse now than in 1990. For those unfamiliar with the Arkansas Delta (pretty much the world), this fact alone suggests that in a country as rich as the United States, something was and is seriously out of kilter.

Why not note quietly that I was born with a white skin and escaped the Delta, thus minimizing any embarrassment and controversy and distill my life with a reference? See the entry for "Grif Stockley" in the on-line Arkansas Encyclopedia of History and Culture[5] for background on this privileged Arkansas Delta white boy who was once described by his legal adversaries in a Little Rock newspaper column as "arrogant as all get-out" and that was written by someone who described herself as a friend!

Now that time is seriously running out, the desire to look in the mirror and probe beneath the surface and say what my life was all about has become a compulsion. For my Gideon Page novels and short stories, I have mined my life for material, but those characters aren't quite me or projections of me. I pulled my punches in the service of making most of them somewhat likable white Southerners who weren't perfect, but whom ultimately the generous reader may want to cut some slack. Additionally, I show up occasionally in the five books of non-fiction about the history of race relations in Arkansas, but in the guise of a helpless observer, which is the luxury of writing history. I haven't always been so helpless.

Despite its relentless fecundity, the English language, I presume to judge, will benefit from a modicum of help to encompass not only the world I grew up in but also a description of myself: hence, the nonsensical words in the title, "Hypogrif" and "Bubbaville," the meanings of which are intended to edify the reader in due course.

Some of my grandmother's interests would be similar to mine—history and writing.

Born in 1883, Effie's heyday as a published writer began in the 1920s when her articles about Lee County history were welcomed by the publisher of Marianna's weekly newspaper, *The Courier Index*. Like her daughter Temple, she also died in 1970, five years before I unsuccessfully began to try to get my first manuscript published. Now, after twelve books, this memoir my thirteenth, I get to have the last word, suspecting that it might be painful to know how many people would have declined to give birth if they could have known what their "loved ones" would say about them.

As she did with most of her grandchildren, "Nannie," as we unoriginally called her, read books to me as a child—my favorite was a highly romanticized child's version of the military exploits of U.S. Calvary officer George Armstrong "Autie" Custer, who, in fact, bravely but recklessly lost his life and the lives of his troops (including two brothers) at the Battle of the Little Big Horn River in the Territory of Montana in June of 1876.

Obviously, little did I know or care in the 1950s (I was born in 1944) that *Custer's Last Stand*, published by Random House as part of the popular "Landmark" history series for children, celebrated, subliminally or otherwise, "Manifest Destiny," or what is termed today "American Exceptionalism." It was an American "boy book" populated with accounts of slaughter, the Americana of the Old West. Did Effie know the Landmark series was part of an enculturation process which taught that we white Europeans were entitled to march from coast to coast at whatever cost to those peoples, Native Americans and Mexicans, who had come before us? Of course, she did. Would she be surprised today that parents who today home-school their children are avid collectors of this now out-of-print series? She wouldn't bat an eye.

Nannie was an avid subscriber to the tenets of Bubbaville, not a state or region to be equated with the Southern stereotype, but rather the preferred state-of-mind for a healthy percentage of Americans of European descent who to this day maintain an abiding certainty that we are absolutely deserving of our wealth and prosperity, however modestly and charmingly we dismiss our good fortune. A flesh-and-blood product of this worldview, a *hypogrif* is one who professes to be skeptical of this mythology but whose actions have, from time to time, called into question his or her sincerity.

If only I'd had enough sense or curiosity to talk to Nannie about her life! In my twenties when she died, I had plenty of chances. I didn't know I would become a writer, and the windows of opportunity opened and closed until they finally slammed shut for good with her senility. I was too busy "individuating" or less charitably, perfecting an almost total self-absorption that had no room for the stories of an old woman (probably about my age now when her mind and emotional state began to deteriorate), even if she was the only grandparent I ever knew. It was my loss and a profound one. Given what I would one day be most interested in—writing about the racial history of Arkansas—"Miss Effie," as our father and others called her, could have immeasurably enriched the books I would write about race, class and ego.

And it is in this vein I consciously and no doubt controversially employ the pronouns "we," "our," and "us" to describe behavior that occurred long before I was born. As a self-described white, once upper-middle-class heterosexual male, I am not the only one to have directly and indirectly benefited in significant ways from having been born and raised in the South with a white skin, and that is where the story must begin. But, in my view, we not only have paid but also have enacted a high price for the privilege.

As to our location, GPS computer maps to the rescue! Zero in on Memphis and pan to the surrounding states, but instead of looking southeast into Mississippi, peer southwest across the Mississippi River bridges into Arkansas. My roots are in both, but from the age of two, I have lived in what is now called by

Arkansas Parks and Tourism, "The Natural State." For years, Arkansas license plates advertised the "Land of Opportunity," but given our bottom-feeder national poverty and education statistics, our branding department understood that tourists were smirking and not squinting when they pulled up behind a dirty pick-up with a gun-rack brandishing a deer rifle. Thus far, we have been much more successful marketing "The Natural State" than hoping somehow to be Silicone Valley South or even a haven for low wage industry.

Many of us whites had come to this so-called "Mid-South" area of the Mississippi River Delta from older southern states before the Civil War to farm the incomparable bottom soil, an area arguably richer than the Nile River Valley. The irony, of course, was that the climate and geography which made the potential wealth in the soil possible also made it nigh impossible to get at without the right kind of help. Disease, including malaria, intolerable heat and humidity, seemingly impenetrable swamps and forests, turned the enterprise into a hellish nightmare. There seemed to be only one solution, and for a time it succeeded splendidly from our economic point of view. By 1860 Arkansas was home to over 100,000 enslaved persons, and, after Texas, was the fastest growing slave state in the country. Cotton and the price of human chattel were going through the roof. For the first and only time in our history Arkansas was ranked in the top half (sixteenth out of 34) in per capita income.

Arkansas Governor Henry Rector spilled the beans in his written message to the delegates to the first Arkansas secession convention assembled in Little Rock in 1861:

> "God in his omnipotent wisdom, I believe, created the cotton plant—the African slave—and the lower Mississippi valley, to clothe and feed the world, and, a gallant race of men and women produced upon its soil, to defend it, and execute that decree."[6]

God did it! Did my ancestors believe this, too? How convenient. Just before this sentence the governor had written:

> "The productive portion of the soil of Arkansas is so geographically circumstanced as to preclude the idea that it can be successfully cultivated by white labor."

The operative word was successfully. To make the system really pay, we needed gangs of strong black bodies, men, women and children, and the more land and bodies the better. "There in one sentence was the unvarnished justification for slavery," I wrote in *Ruled by Race: Black/White Relations in Arkansas from Slavery to the Present*, published in 2009 by the University of Arkansas Press. But for reasons that are still disputed, the assignment of guilt or innocence by historians, psychologists, social scientists, theologians, philosophers, writers, and the public for our treatment of black persons, women, and the poor generally, is, after all this time, a highly controversial topic, and not just south of the Mason-Dixon Line.

"Make believe" and "not seeing" have been a specialty of the house not just in Africa but in ole Dixieland as well, and still are. It is awkward, even considered impolite in the 21st century, to ask each other: did your family own other human beings? During a speaking engagement in Columbus, Mississippi, in 2012, I asked to see where the slaves lived and was frostily shown the "servants' quarters" at the lovely restored bed and breakfast antebellum home where my hosts at the local library had arranged for me to stay. Servants? Really? Alice should have skipped over Wonderland and come South. Servants, a far less painful word than slaves. Segregation and "Jim Crow," far less descriptive terms than white supremacy.

Unlike Jake's side of the family, the Walls and Allisons didn't own human beings.

Most Southerners didn't, but either way the moral issue of slavery was not an issue we white Arkansans lost sleep over. An incident Effie wrote about in *The Courier Index* illustrated our mindset in what is now Lee County. After listing the names of Confederate soldiers who served in Company "F" of the Second Arkansas Regiment, Effie writes that in 1869 one of those veterans by the name of Tom Freeman happened to be riding one of four mules hitched to a wagon loaded with cotton in Marianna. Effie explains:

> *He rode one of the mules in order to drive the four. His negro helper rode on the wagon, when they were overtaken by a Mississippian named Tom Slaughter and his cousin Arthur.*
>
> *Tom Slaughter said in a voice loud enough to be heard, "Where I came from the niggers do the driving and the white folks ride. He's taken the nigger's job."*
>
> *Tom Freeman replied, "I'll see you later about that." Moments later when the Slaughters pulled up to a store and dismounted and began talking to friends, Freeman hitched his team, and walked toward the men and with words, "I've got a niggers [sic] job, have I," fired at Tom Slaughter. By the time the shooting was over, all three men were dead.*[7]

Effie writes that Freeman was married with several children and that "it was a fact that Freeman and Slaughter had never laid eyes on each other before that day." Left unsaid by Effie, but understood by her white readers, was that this horrific episode was an extreme demonstration of "honor." Slaughter had insulted Freeman by comparing him to a black person, and his honor had to be upheld. Fightin' words. Fights, duels and murders to defend one's honor were still taking place in many venues in the nineteenth century but found especially fertile ground in frontier states like Arkansas. White men settled questions of their testosterone level (aka "honor") with one's fists, or "Arkansas toothpicks" (Bowie knives) or, as here, with guns.

In this environment Effie grew to maturity in the early twentieth century in the Arkansas Delta during what some historians of the South refer to as the "nadir" in race relations, a period in which white supremacy was unleashed in its most virulent form since slavery. Reconstruction had died an unmourned death by native whites (the final nail in its coffin the withdrawal of federal troops from the South), and by the turn of the century, black males (women, of course, white or black, couldn't vote) were disenfranchised, lynched with increasing frequency, and increasingly segregated by law, "custom," and "tradition," the latter two words first-rate euphemisms for how white supremacy was implemented. It was open season on blacks, who after Reconstruction were increasingly characterized as criminals and rapists, in a word, dangerous.

In Lee County, one of six counties in the state then with a black majority, the nadir got started early. In 1891, in one terrifying episode, fifteen blacks were murdered, nine of whom were hanged summarily during an aborted cotton picker strike. Effie, born and married next door in Phillips County, would have been eight years old at the time. It was open season on black Arkansans. A year later, Malcolm Argyle, an Arkansas black preacher, wrote to a Philadelphian that:

> "All over the state, blacks were being murdered by whites: some being strung up to telephone poles, others burnt at the stake; and still others being shot like dogs. In the last 30 days there have been not less than eight colored persons lynched in this state."[8]

In 1904, 13 blacks were lynched in Arkansas County, also adjacent to Phillips County. No whites were charged. In 1919, the

Elaine Race Massacres occurred in Phillips County. The national office of the NAACP estimated that 250 blacks, including women and children, were murdered. Five whites were killed. No whites were charged, but 12 blacks would be sentenced to die in the electric chair.[9]

The "trouble" in Phillips County brought national attention to Effie's stomping grounds and has spawned several books, including my own. *Blood in Their Eyes: The Elaine Race Massacres of 1919* was published by the University of Arkansas Press in 2000 and received a Certificate of Commendation from the American Association for State and Local History.

Had she written about it, Effie's version would likely have been from the perspective of a woman told stories by whites scared out of their wits that black sharecroppers, who outnumbered whites nine to one in the area around the town of Elaine, were staging what we whites called an "insurrection." From slavery forward, at various times, we feared blacks would "revolt" and would react to rumors and fearful headlines with overwhelming force to "put down uprisings" that have never been documented to be even contemplated, much less attempted in the state. Self-defense was as far as a handful of blacks got during the Elaine "incident," but the memory of and stories about John Brown's raid in Kansas had a long shelf life.

Historians recognize now there were at least two motives for the murder of so many blacks in Phillips County beginning on September 30, 1919. A group of African-Americans had formed a sharecropper's union to demand fair treatment from planters and had begun to meet regularly in the area. It would be wiped out in the next 24 hours after a mob of over 500 white males stormed into the county armed with rifles and shotguns. Within another 24 hours they would be followed by 583 U.S. Army troops, many of whom were veterans of the second battle of the Marne in France, who rolled into Elaine with ten machine guns on a troop train from Camp Pike outside of Little Rock. As indicated, the other motive for such mayhem was sheer panic that the "thing" so dreaded was now wildly rumored to be coming to pass. The evidence that an insurrection was in the offing in Phillips County would prove to be non-existent, but that did not stop us from reacting in our customary tried and true manner, whether it was Arkansas's highly educated and erudite governor, Charles Hillman Brough, or the most brutal redneck in a multistate area, both of whom participated in a "nigger hunt," as the sheriff of Phillips County termed the event. Interest in the "Elaine Massacre" has grown dramatically as the centennial anniversary in 2019 has approached.

It was inevitable that, separated in age by 61 years, my view of the past would be quite different. Effie was dead by the time I began to work on a manuscript which eventually became *Ruled by Race*. If my grandmother came back to life, she would think I have lost my mind.

As a teenager growing up in eastern Arkansas, I didn't know then that psychologists and social scientists had names for the elaborate "make-believe" and "not seeing" that characterized our behavior *vis-à-vis* the black population of Marianna, and may still today. It was Anna Freud, who, standing on her father's shoulders, is given credit for peering further than most others into the unconscious and more fully parsing the subtle psychological mechanisms by which we humans keep fear, anxiety and shame at bay. Sigmund Freud recognized the general concept of "repression," but it was his daughter who initially best described the mental gymnastics our brains employ to shield us from painful emotions and made familiar the concepts we call "defense mechanisms": denial, rationalization, projection, reaction formation, and the other names given to this unconscious process.

In fact, it would be Southern journalist Wilbur J. Cash, who in 1940 with his seminal book *The Mind of the South* (still in print today) so incisively and compellingly applied these psychological processes to our behavior in the South during and after the slave era. It was this book that for many of us whites raised the curtain forever on our "front-stage/back-stage" behavior.

For a region of the country so besotted with our ancestors, the past generally, and the written word, surely it is a puzzle to some why we are still able to hide so much of our history involving race. It wasn't that Effie couldn't write. Her description of that part of Lee County outside of Marianna where she and our grandfather briefly resided comes juicily alive even though she wrote about it 30 years later. At the age of 22, Effie married David Wall, a young doctor who persuaded her to move out to the same general area as Whitehall to build a practice. "Dave," as he was known, had gotten a loan from Hugh Ivy Mixon, a prominent Marianna businessman, that enabled him to get his medical education at Vanderbilt. In gratitude Dave named his only son David Mixon Wall. Our cousin Allison adds that an unnamed riverboat captain set Dave up in practice outside of Marianna in the rural community of Raggio, named for an Italian immigrant.

At Raggio, Dave's patients were primarily sharecroppers and the employees of the lumber camps that dotted the landscape in eastern Arkansas. One assumes that the riverboat captain, who may have been a gambler as well, had some kind of family or proprietary interest in property in the area.

Thus, many years later, Effie wrote about Raggio and her life there for *The Courier Index*:

> *"Rarin' swearin', hard drinkin', rip snortin' crap shootin' guntotin' lawless old Raggio! Steamboats on the rivers; the Harry Lee, the Stacker Lee...Timber camps, east, west, north and south. Great rafts of logs choking the rivers and bayous, logs on great barges,*

logs on the bank of every stream, logs everywhere. No highways, no telephones, no railroads, mail carried to and from Marianna by horseback, the round trip requiring an entire day."[10]

Logging, as long as it lasted, was a cash cow, and Raggio was front and center of the action. The tiny hamlet, she remembered, "consisted of a long row of drab unpainted shacks." She and Dave had a small house built for them on the east bank of Alligator Bayou, and my grandmother wrote glowingly about their picnics, dinners, and celebrations. Effie remembered:

"...*long horseback rides through the caves and forests...a June picnic up the St. Francis on the Hinkley launch, a darling blue-eyed baby in my arms on the cabin roof—Margaret Dozier five years old...A fishfry on Old River...swimming on the sandbars in the St. Francis...Young voices singing 'Rufus Rastus Johnson Brown,' 'Alexander's Ragtime Band'...*"

Only once does she mention the downside of such isolation, but her anguish is telling:

Winter!-cold!-mud!-rain!-tortured with loneliness and fear. Old Magie, Negro blows hand off with a giant firecracker. Doctor [Dave] works hard to save a remnant. A call to Whitehall, the jumping off place to Whiskey Island in the Mississippi. Ride, walk, row, maybe swim, to get there—gone from home days.[11]

Much more friendly an environment in Lee County for Effie was our hometown of Marianna where she and Dave would eventually live out their lives. Crystal clear on the point that location and geography are destiny, in 1857 the "city" fathers had moved the boundaries of the town three miles down-river to a navigable part of the L'Anguille River, but kept the name Marianna. With this decision commerce began to flourish. According to entries in *Lee County History*, three busy sawmills competed at the river's edge and two enormous warehouses were built to store the thousands of bales of cotton that were making some planters wealthy. Like its much better-known sister city Helena in Phillips County, 30 miles to the south and strategically located on the Mississippi River, Marianna was booming. So impressed were journalists in the rest of the state that in 1913 the town was chosen to be the host city for the Arkansas Press Association, which, according to *Lee County History*, gushed that Marianna, "the gem of the St. Francis Valley, has again demonstrated her right to the title of being the most hospitable in eastern Arkansas, if not the state, by entertaining most royally" its members. It didn't hurt that Marianna had "three saloons" open for business to quell the thirst of its admiring visitors. On and on the Association extolled the virtues of "The City Beautiful": the "crowning feature" was the absence of "factions." Business and professional folks "are working for the good of the city."[12]

Typically unmentioned in this story was the explanation of how much of all this wealth was generated and accounts of the people whose backs and status made this hospitality and economic success happen. With her interviews of the early white settlers of Lee County, Effie would fit right in. "The torch of Lee County's history was established by Effie Allison Wall," state the editors in the introduction of *Lee County History*.[13] The book was a "project" of the Lee County Sesquicentennial Committee in recognition of Arkansas's entry into the Union in 1836. Effie's version of our county history appears in four well-written, scholarly Arkansas Historical Quarterly articles but also, as mentioned, in numerous newspaper columns in *The Courier Index*, a number of which were republished in an edited form in 1987 in *Lee County*

History. Additionally, a scrapbook she kept containing some of her original research, articles in which she is mentioned, and her own pieces are guides to what Effie thought about, what she considered important and what she ignored or took for granted over a period of approximately three decades. A copy is in the Lee County Library in Marianna under the name Effie Allison Wall.

But, arguably, Effie was not the "torch" of Lee County history. Rather, she focused primarily on the deeds and achievements of the white minority in Lee County, and when she did not, she minimized or ignored altogether what was occurring in the black community. In so doing, she was no different from other white historians, both "academic" and "local" of her era, including other contributors to *Lee County History*.

Her intention seemed not so much to write about the actual history of Lee County, the early economic success of which was directly and indirectly dependent upon the presence of black people, as it was designed to document the roles of some of the early white power structure. Given the influence and relative economic affluence of her subjects, her interviews and descriptions of early white pioneers in Lee County and the origin of place names were absorbing and important in themselves but without any context could only be misleading if the reader is interested in how the wealth of the county was generated and distributed. Since history has always been written by its winners, Effie's approach was no surprise. She and the early contributors might be considered as having lit candles to illuminate the corners of Lee County history, but what she and others didn't acknowledge about our past was crucial to an understanding of it. What she and others didn't write about was how white supremacy was implemented in Lee County, and for good reason. Again, it must be added that their version was par for the course. The truth, however, was too disturbing to acknowledge.

Among other present-day historians, University of Arkansas at Little Rock professor Carl Moneyhon has shown that Arkansas planters during the long era of sharecropping after slavery often intimidated and stole from their tenants through a variety of methods. The head of the Arkansas Freedmen's Bureau estimated that as much as a third of what was owed to the former slaves, now working on shares, "was not paid." "Men who profess to be honest and honorable cannot understand that there is any moral wrong in robbing and cheating a Negro."[14] That this attitude had not changed in the Arkansas Delta by the twentieth century would be exposed by Reverend Burke Culpepper, an evangelist in Phillips County in 1916. *The Helena World* gave the following account:

> *The evangelist took up another line of spiritual wickedness in high places in this community, in the unfair treatment of labor especially of colored farm labor, on the part of those whose positions as financial and social leaders should make them above such practices. The evangelist evidently knows that some large fortunes in Helena have been founded on unfair and unrighteous treatment of negro farmers and held all men guilty of such action up for the severest condemnation.... At the conclusion of the speaking, another large number of persons, most of them men, and many of them of real worth in the community, went forward and professed conversion.*[15]

Whether these conscience-stricken individuals righted the injustices they had perpetrated on their tenants is unknown; however, one can assume the idea of reparations among whites was even less popular in Effie's time than it is today. Whatever her actual views, there is no overt racism in her articles. While in Raggio, she and the doctor received "[a]n invitation to hear the Negro bishop at the colored church—a masterly address." Right below this entry, she remembers, "[g]iving breathless attention to an account of the Battle of Gettysburg as given by Mr. Charles

Dozier's father." One has to believe, however, that the Bishop's talk was not a call for revolution by black sharecroppers.

Effie doesn't mention in her piece on Raggio, or elsewhere in her published work, her father or mother, yet they were able to see that she got a college education. The older of two sisters, Effie graduated from Ouachita Baptist College in the town of Arkadelphia in the southern part of the state with a major in Music and a minor in English, an accomplishment in turn-of-the-century Arkansas that was neither desired nor thought necessary by most of her contemporaries. Authorized in 1886 by the Arkansas State Baptist Convention, Ouachita took itself seriously as a private Christian institution for up-and-coming white boys and girls, meaning that like all church-related colleges in those days it was steeped in fundamentalism. No one recalls Effie as fixated on religion though she seems to have remained throughout her life a Baptist. As far as life-long influences, she may have been close to her father, who at one time owned a store in Raggio, but Effie in our memory seldom mentioned her parents to her grandchildren in her accounts of yesteryear.

As a writer, Effie had material to spare about Raggio. Violence, incidental and intentional, came with the territory (my cousin Hope says her mother told her that Effie and Dave both kept guns in Raggio), and without the fights, shoot-outs, and accidents, my grandfather's income would have been appreciably less during this period of their lives. Looking back over thirty years, Effie wrote,

> *Ferryman and mailman shoot out an old feud on the ferryboat. Both die. Negro sharecropper shoots to death the Negro schoolteacher. A Saturday Night Free-For-All. Two dead. Five wounded. Hot water, more hot water, more gauze and bandages, all night long...*[16]

It appears from this snippet that Effie acted, at least in this instance, in the capacity of a nurse, not a Florence Nightingale image that has endured in her grandchildren's memories of her. Yet it is her life in Marianna after she and Dave moved into town that also provides some of the best clues to understanding how people like our grandmother navigated the first half of the twentieth century in the Arkansas Delta and influenced those closest to them.

"People like her" were educated white women who were the occupants of the highest social class in Lee County and didn't take their status lightly. They were active in the United Daughters of the Confederacy, the Daughters of the American Revolution and self-improvement clubs. Their husbands were typically planters, and the doctors, lawyers and businessmen who served the plantation economy in Lee County.

Descendants of the "first" families who began to form Marianna society after the Civil War, these were women who presented programs to each other on western culture, art, music and literature. It went without saying that these organizations were for white women only. Women in Effie's class and income bracket managed their black servants who cooked, cleaned and looked after their children.

No photographs of Effie as a young woman in her bloom seem to have survived, and the older ones of an unsmiling matron, her eyes hidden by thick glasses, probably do not do her justice, her figure having thickened after the birth of four children. Before her marriage to Dave, Effie had taught school briefly in the town of Magazine in the western part of the state and even applied to teach in the Philippines, but love apparently aborted those plans. The details of her interest in teaching overseas have been lost. The fact that she would have even wanted to is at odds with our memories of her. I would not think her as the Peace Corps type, but at one time perhaps she was.

In her privileged position as a hardworking doctor's wife, Effie was not content merely to stay at home. One might even argue she was an early feminist and that Lee County and Arkansas history were her path to liberation. Researching and highlighting the exploits of local white pioneers and place names were her ticket to a wider intellectual and emotional experience than ordering about the "help" and waiting for Dave to come home from a hard day of doctoring. And like her author grandson, Effie seemed to enjoy the attention and seeing her name in print.

To join the Daughters of the American Revolution, Effie traced her ancestry back to a North Carolinian officer named John Carruth, a discovery which later paved the way for the memberships of Aunt Harriet and our sister Harriet. Patriotism is one of the DAR's principal reasons for existing, and the exuberant flag-waving nationalism practiced by the L'Anguille Chapter in the early twentieth century perfectly fit the mood of the country, but also the mood of white Southerners who relished being on the winning side of a war. In 1910, the D. C. Govan chapter of the United Daughters of the Confederacy, of which she may well have been a member by then, donated a towering statue of Robert E. Lee to be placed in the new city park in Marianna. Eugenia Rives, who taught me in high school in 1959 and the author of the entry in *Lee County History* titled "Marianna's First 100 Years," called the gift "a beautiful and enduring monument of those noble defenders of the Lost Cause and their Noble Leader."

In the interest of truth, "Miss Eugenia," as we were taught to call her, was careful to note that "[c]ivic pride did not carry over when Marianna had the opportunity to secure a free $25,000 Carnegie Library Grant. When a public meeting was held so few attended" that the project was dropped.[17] Doing so well, the Marianna white power structure obviously concluded it was comfortable with things just the way there were and had all the books it needed.

In fact, many outsiders didn't care for the "Bear State," nor did they care who knew it. As a state where slavery had been practiced and which was still known for its brutality to its black citizens, Arkansas came in for its share of criticism and not merely for its hostility to the principles of the Fourteenth and Fifteenth Amendments. In Effie's era, H. L. Mencken, at the top of his fame, infamously characterized the Southerner in 1921 as "a walking sarcophagus of dead ideas," and Arkansas as containing little more than "miasmatic jungles" that were "trackless and unexplored." Much more would be said by him and others about the state's poverty, educational and cultural deficits, hillbillies, and general backwardness, including its commitment to religious fundamentalism, all of which became known to Arkansans who had more than a passing acquaintance with their daily newspapers. Much has been made by Arkansas's own literary community over the last century and well into the present about the state's notorious inferiority complex. Indeed, it has become a cottage industry all its own; however, it does not appear that Effie paid any attention to what others outside the South said about Arkansas. There is no evidence she joined in the outrageous responses to Mencken's attacks (the editor of *Arkansas Writer* called for efforts to banish him from the United States), but there also is no suggestion she ever questioned the lengths to which her native state went to insure that black Arkansans remained subjugated.[18]

Effie's work as a historian included recording the names of the returning World War I veterans who joined American Legion Post No. 5 in Marianna. Her local chapter held a banquet in their honor at the Marianna Hotel on November 11, 1920, an event that included her husband, "1st Lt. E.D. Wall," who served his country as a surgeon on a troop ship in England. It did not include those black veterans from Lee County who had also served their country in the war.

In fact, we whites had needed black men in support roles to do the dirtiest jobs in the war effort just as we had needed them in the cotton fields and needed them again now that they were back and the war was over. But we needed them to settle down and get back to work as before. The "Red Summer of 1919," with 25 race riots all over the country, had frightened everyone, but surely none more so than blacks and whites in Phillips County and the surrounding area. Believing they had served their country during the war, some blacks had come back home with a militant attitude, and not for the first time we whites believed we needed to put them in their place. Lynching was an extreme way to accomplish this purpose, but it got the point across.

Effie was elected and re-elected both state historian of the Arkansas DAR and historian for the local chapter (L'Anguille) in Lee County, positions of importance in these organizations, given that their purpose was to honor the past. For the latter, Effie co-wrote at least one pageant to be performed by members for each other and invited guests in Marianna. White Southerners like my grandmother moved easily from glorifying the "Lost Cause" to "celebrat[ing] General Washington's birthday" in 1926. Effie's theme for this pageant was "America's Melting Pot," but with a decidedly Old South bias. In a sweeping blank verse poem, our grandmother extols Spanish explorers, French Huguenots, Pilgrims, Cavaliers, Puritans, Quakers, Scots, and the Dutch. She leaves out African-Americans except for a "negro maid suggestive of antebellum days" who "attended...Miss Elizabeth Harrington," who "represented a typical southern girl." Miss Harrington sang, "Carry Me Back to Old Virginny," whose original lyrics tell us, "That's where the old darkey's heart am long'd to go; That's where I labored so hard for Massa."[19]

This ritualized celebration of supposed black loyalty and white benevolence in the Delta toward black Arkansans during slavery co-existed with a reality we white Arkansans preferred to overlook. Included in her scrapbook is a portion of a diary Effie copied in her own hand. It was kept by a Phillips County slave mistress by the name of Mary Sales Edmondson in 1863-64. Written for her children, Mrs. Edmondson's diary entries follow the painful last illness of "Davy," the family's "faithful, beloved" slave who was buried on October 28, 1864.

Davy was the last of a family of faithful upright servants whose ancestors belonged to my ancestors for almost a hundred years... [Her slave] Aunt Chris helped to raise us all—we eight children, having none of her own—she nursed father and mother thru many severe illnesses and was nursed thru many severe attacks by [?] and myself. She, Davy, her niece Martha and John Warner's son are the only ones of all of my father's well-cared for, well taught servants who withstood the temptations, constantly employed by Yankee abolitionists.[20]

As obviously intended by Effie, this slice of a Civil War diary demonstrates affection between slave and mistress, at least from the mistress's viewpoint. Effie quotes at length the efforts of Mary Edmondson's physician husband to relieve the suffering of Davy and the family's stated concern for his soul because he was not a "Christian." The disconnect with this touching portrayal of white Southern paternalism documented by our grandmother is that the overwhelming number of enslaved persons in Arkansas needed no "tempting" by Yankee abolitionists to "desert" us at the first opportunity. In *Ruled by Race*, I again quote Professor Moneyhon who notes that, "Well-treated slaves left [the plantations] as quickly as others." By 1862, Union ships had begun to dominate river traffic in Arkansas, and enslaved persons "merely had to run to the Union boats and camps, and this they did in droves." Instead of admitting that slaves, of course, wanted their freedom, we interpreted their behavior as traitorous and punished them for the unrelenting misery of the Civil War in the state. In the words of Arkansas Freedman's Bureau representative E.W. Gantt: "I saw this sorrowfully of our people, but I know it but to be too true. Their wrath over defeat would be poured upon the hands of the helpless ones once their slaves."[21] One need only to read the unnerving accounts by other Freedman's Bureau agents in Arkansas to grasp the truth of this observation.

Since day one of the slave era, a good bit of the tension between blacks and whites in Lee County (as elsewhere) was sexual, and how it played out in Effie's long life in the state was accompanied by political exploitation at various times all the way through the era of Governor Orval Faubus in the 1950s and 1960s. As slave owners, overseers, sons, uncles, and nephews, a substantial number of us white males raped or coerced the female slaves on our farms and plantations. The percentage of mulattoes in the Arkansas population was as high as 12 percent in 1850 and 10 percent in 1860, the last time these statistics were kept on a national level by the United States Census.

The end of slavery did not mean the end of interracial sex, and it quickly became a political issue in the 1868 Arkansas Constitutional Convention, which was controlled by a coalition of white Republicans and eight black delegates during the brief Reconstruction era. On the convention floor, James White, a black delegate and an Indiana native who had never been a slave, spoke aloud what no native black Arkansan could ever say publicly: "The white men of the South have been for years indulging in illicit intercourse with colored women, and in the dark days of slavery, this intercourse was in a great majority of cases forced upon the innocent victims."

The issue was naturally a ticklish one and designed to split the Republican coalition which managed to keep the issue of miscegenation out of the state constitution, but it was understood by one and all that a prohibition against marriage between blacks and whites would become a part of state law. But as was clear to anyone walking the streets of Marianna, a prohibition against marriage between blacks and whites meant little if the aim was to eliminate the appearance of a light-skinned black caste.

Nor would it end the political rants favored by some Arkansas politicians during Effie's formative years. Once campaigning for governor, Jeff Davis, who was elected to four two-year terms between 1898 and 1906 and then U.S. Senator, promised, "We may have a lot of dead niggers in Arkansas, but we shall never have negro equality, and I want to say that I would rather tear, screaming from her mother's arms my little daughter and bury her alive than to see her arm in arm with the best nigger on earth." We white males had gone from raping black women to claiming there was an epidemic of black men raping white women. Indeed, Governor Davis took the occasion of a visit from the President of the United States to Little Rock on October 25, 1905, to justify lynching. With Theodore Roosevelt at his side, the Democratic governor explained to his audience:

> Charitable and indulgent as we have ever been to an inferior race, cheerfully contributing bountifully of our time and means toward their material and moral betterment, still, if the brutal criminals of that race...lay unholy hands upon our fair daughters, nature is so riven and shocked that the dire compact produces a social cataclysm, often, in its terrible sweep beyond the utmost counter efforts of all civil power.[22]

A southern governor's justification of lynching was not something the President of the United States could allow to go unchallenged, which Roosevelt did in no uncertain terms, but as an Arkansas politician, Davis, as usual, carried the day. With this kind of demagoguery setting the tone for the state, Effie's fears, whatever caused them, can be better understood, and they would arguably affect her life many years later.

The upshot of all of this was that black Arkansans were tolerated so long as they were docile and subservient to whites and accepted exploitation as sharecroppers and laborers without complaint. As Davis ranted more than once on the campaign trail, "Educate a nigger and you ruin a good field hand."[23] At the same time there was an unconscious and sometimes conscious dread of blacks. Despite her fears, quite possibly, Raggio may have been where the couple's best selves were displayed.

Doctors in those days didn't worry about their business plans and seeing 30 patients a day to pay their overhead. Instead, as Effie remembered, there had been "long hard calls to timber camps in every direction; to the cut-off, to the Willows, to Council, to Daylight, to Soudan, to Egypt, to Double Bar Bend, to Red Oak, West Wood, Peters, on horseback, on foot, on skiffs."[24] Dave worked hard for his patients. Effie memorialized his efforts, and for that and for including Effie's contributions, we, their descendants, are grateful to the editors of *Lee County History*.

CHAPTER 2

Looking for a Family Hero

DAVE WALL would have been successful anywhere. A photograph of our maternal grandfather in his World War I officer's uniform reveals a pair of soulful eyes that likely made him irresistible to his patients, family and friends. We know him only through the comments of others, but unlike those about Effie, they are all positive. From all accounts, he was adored by his brothers, his own children and nieces and nephews.

Moving into Marianna from Raggio was surely always my grandparents' intention, but clearly it was the best decision Effie and Dave ever made. Until the Depression, life was good for upper middle-class whites in Lee County, but the population of the county peaked below 30,000 by 1930.[1] It has declined ever since.

How irresistible Dave was to Effie though is another question. My cousin Allison remembers being told by a neighbor that for recreation our grandfather was an enthusiastic poker player once he got out of the house or office. His preferred location was in a garage across from one of Marianna's cemeteries. Our grandmother would not drive except when she was out hunting Dave, who wasn't above taking a drink during his recreational hours. Like a good scientist he wasn't hesitant about experimenting with the brew. During prohibition there was a time in their attic one sweltering day he put together a libation that exploded. A doctor in need of a relaxing drink, not a bomb maker. Both Sally and

Allison remember coming across letters from him to Effie that he had written during World War I. In one letter, Sally writes in her memoir, "he was begging her to love him. It was so personal we didn't read any more and left them in the chest."

The old saw, "familiarity breeds contempt," doesn't apply in Dave's case except perhaps in his relationship with Effie. Why shouldn't she have been jealous of her husband's popularity, his lovable nature, and status as a respected physician in town? Who doesn't get a little weary of someone so wonderful? Dave was a gravitational force all his own. Even now a niece counts among her treasured memories our grandfather doing nothing more than taking her to get an ice cream cone.[2] "Uncle Dave," she sighed, her voice tender at the thought of it. If he'd had a rival for "most popular Wall," it would have been his youngest daughter Sarah Hope, but she was merely sweet and kind, dubious qualities to have in a family whose tongues could turn rapier sharp with or without the right amount of alcohol.

Gossip was a cherished Wall pastime, and I learned it from the masters. With me in tow before I was ten or so, Temple would drive the half-mile or so from North Pearl to my aunt's home on Magnolia Place (I don't remember us ever walking) to visit Effie and Tissie. As often as some of us went to church, one might have expected some of the verses in the Bible about "backbiting" to have struck a chord, but as a leading offender, I confess there is too much pleasure to be gained by discussing others' lack of character, atrocious behavior, unfortunate physical appearance, misfortune, stupidity, bad judgment, betrayals, addictions, hypocrisy, vanity, and undeserved luck to do much more than to hold it in check around my grandchildren. Doubtless there are other reasons for this particular character flaw of mine: a judgmental nature, a desire to be funny or entertaining in order to get attention, jealousy, a lack of something worthwhile to say, a cheap way of trying to create intimacy, and a sleazy way of trading for information (I will tell you about Jimmy and now you have to tell me about Jane.) In my case, I am overly fond of saying to good friends after a particularly productive exchange of verbal assassination, "Animals! We're just animals!" After an exuberant denunciation of our species, I imagine my dogs and/or cats rolling their eyes since presumably they have never uttered an unkind remark about their peers or masters.

Might I chalk up this character flaw as a particularly Southern phenomenon, or is "backbiting" a blood sport equally enjoyed by the entire species? My bias is to spread the blame around, but growing up I thought of it generally as a team sport for women and relatively harmless, since I was outnumbered and not interesting enough or precocious as a child to be included as a bearer of tales or an object of them. My cousin Hope says that her mother told her that when one of the Walls was mad at someone outside the Wall Clan, all family members were supposed to be angry at whoever had offended one of us, which perhaps is a sign the family unit was much closer than I have imagined. Since Temple's generation is gone and we are all dispersed, that kind of gang mentality no longer exists. Now being confronted by the all-too familiar signs of what we rightly fear will not be a "dotage with dignity," the feuds of the remaining Walls are mostly a thing of the past. As our personal contacts with each other and the world dwindle, our ammunition is running dangerously low.

Was Dave really our family's saint? We apparently had a need to exalt somebody in the family who did not threaten us, and Dave, a male and a hard-working doctor, fit the bill. As I write this, I yield to the temptation to make him a tragic figure who was too good for his own good and probably too good for his wife. In most family lore, there is a hero or heroine who routinely displays an effortless ability to make things brighter and better from the moment he or she gets out of bed in the morning. Usually it is a worked-to-the-bone mother who sacrifices all for the good of the children, but Nannie and Tissie had too many black maids to play the role of the family martyr. Instead, Dave filled those requirements, even dying young.

If we can't know what it was Dave had done to upset Effie and can't be absolutely certain about what he died from, it hasn't stopped me from speculating. Somehow, for years I had it in my head that my grandfather may have died from syphilis in the Arkansas State Hospital for Nervous Diseases in Little Rock. As part of the backstory in the five-book Gideon Page novels, published by Simon & Schuster between 1991–1997, I make the hero's father a casualty of mental illness who dies in the hospital. Understandably, but erroneously, I had readers who assumed I was writing about my own father. Though Dave did breathe his last at what was then known as the Arkansas "Insane Asylum," family lore coupled with his death certificate suggests a less salacious chain of causation.

Whatever grievances Effie nursed against her husband, one seems understandable for the times. My cousin Hope says that her mother Sarah Hope told her that Effie and Dave no longer shared a bedroom after our grandmother gave birth to her at the age of 41. Though hardly a foolproof way of preventing pregnancy, it apparently proved effective since Sarah Hope was the baby of the family. At Effie's age, and in those days, it couldn't have been an easy pregnancy, but telling her youngest daughter may have meant that Sarah Hope had not been "wanted." Whether Sarah Hope, everyone's favorite aunt, had her feelings hurt is doubtful. As an adult, she was relentlessly sunny and way too charitable about others' motives and behavior. Her defense mechanisms in this regard were cast iron. As children, we loved for her to visit. She was kind, sympathetic and made excuses for everyone. Her way of coping with reality seemed to work for her, but her mother, sisters and brother were not nearly so optimistic and positive in their assessment of others. Being so inclined myself, I judged them to be not so much tacky as realistic about human nature.

In any case, Effie's last pregnancy didn't slow her down as a writer and local historian. Her greatest claim to fame as a "local historian" was just a few years off. In 1918, a "million dollar fire" destroyed a number of businesses on Poplar Street in downtown Marianna, including Dave's medical office, but the town continued to prosper and Dave along with it. Not satisfied with his income generated from medicine, he, like a number of professionals and businessmen in Marianna, acquired farm land in the county and rented it out, and that was where real money was to be made. The wealth generated from cotton, timber, related businesses and professions, and most critically the coolie wages paid to black labor, can still be seen in the large homes enterprising whites began to have built for themselves in Marianna roughly in the 1880s and continuing until the Great Depression. Though not nearly as grand as the Vicksburg and Natchez antebellum mansions that had been built with slave labor across the river in neighboring Mississippi, many of the 49 structures on a Fourth of July Marianna Heritage tour in recent years sponsored by the Marianna/Lee County Chamber of Commerce were still an architectural delight. A house on Poplar (the Williamson House) boasted a "curved front porch, Tuscan columns, leaded windows and second story porch."[3] Most notable was the house built in 1912 for possibly the richest man in town on West Main Street by Charles Thompson, one of the region's most prominent architects. W.S. McClintock and Sons sold plantation supplies, general merchandise, and bought cotton, lucrative businesses in Lee County. The McClintock home would be the first structure in Marianna to be honored with a place on the National Register of

Historic Homes: Nothing less than a mansion, enormous oak columns provided support for the living room, and an oak staircase led to a second floor.

Adorned by two majestic magnolias in the front yard, the three-story brick house (including a basement) that Effie and Dave eventually could afford to purchase on "Magnolia Place" was lovely but not in the McClintock class. According to Effie's most acclaimed contribution to the historical research of our patch of the Arkansas Delta came on October 26, 1926. According to the book *History of Lee County*, it was her dogged work as a historian that was the primary impetus for the L'Anguille Chapter of the DAR having a marker placed at the exact location where the 1815 Louisiana Purchase survey began. Historically, this was no small beer. The significance of such a spot is that it is the initial point of the survey of every foot of land contained in the purchase from France west of the Mississippi River. In material terms, its importance was that Congress had set aside six million acres for veterans of the War of 1812 in lieu of paying them in cash, and correct surveys were essential.

Aided by the state DAR, the dedication ceremony was attended by numerous worthies, including Arkansas U.S. Senator Thaddeus Carraway.

The phrase "a picture is worth a thousand words" had just made its appearance in America in the early twentieth century, and whether she was familiar with it or not, Effie got it and made certain she and her young son, David, whom she dressed as a French page for the occasion, were in the group photograph that appeared in the papers (Figure 3, p.113). The dedication ceremony was the biggest event in Effie's career as a historian. People in the Walls' social circle not only took history seriously but at least in Effie's case, saw themselves as part of it. One of the articles about the dedication notes that the L'Anguille Chapter also received private assistance in this endeavor from W.S. McClintock. Effie and Dave cemented their friendship and social standing a few years later with the marriage of youngest daughter Sarah Hope to one of the McClintock's sons, Oliver, who, after graduating from Washington & Lee, obtained a master's in business from New York University and became a successful manager in the South of J.C. Penney stores.

Effie was on a roll in 1926. Her published interview that year with early Lee County settler Lon Slaughter hinted at the ferocity of white supremacy during the Reconstruction Era in the late 1860s and early 1870s. Slaughter alluded to the violence committed by the Klan occurring in the Delta after the Civil War:

> "The Ku Klux was all that kept us from being ground into dust. ... Yes, I could tell you a great deal about the activities of the Ku Klux Klan. We had six Klan in Phillips County...Helena...Marianna [then a part of Phillips County]..."[4]

Unfortunately for scholars of the Arkansas Delta, "the great deal" of specifics Mr. Slaughter could have personally added apparently never made its way into print, at least as reported by Effie.

Not mentioned in this article by Mr. Slaughter or our grandmother was the fact that the Ku Klux Klan after the Civil War was for a while an effective and horrifically brutal terrorist organization that had as its goal the prevention of Republicans, Carpetbaggers, native unionists and blacks from acquiring political power. Organized by former Confederate General Nathan Bedford Forrest, the massacre of black soldiers by white troops under his command during the battle of Ft. Pillow outside of Memphis had become the gold standard for racial atrocities committed by white Southerners during the Civil War. Though not formally allied with the Democratic Party in the South, through murder and intimidation the Klan supported the Party's efforts to maintain "A WHITE MAN'S GOVERNMENT IN A WHITE MAN'S COUNTRY" as an Arkansas Democratic Party newspaper blared in 1868. Enough supporters of the Old Confederacy, however, were unlawfully disenfranchised to allow passage of a new state constitution giving black males the vote. From our point of view, the Klan in that period had been a patriotic resister of a new political order and not a terrorist group at all. In fact, the brief period of Reconstruction still meant the continuation of a "white man's government," just not one controlled by the Democratic Party.

Perhaps not coincidentally, at the time our grandmother interviewed Lon Slaughter in 1926, the Ku Klux Klan had been reborn in parts of the United States, including Arkansas, and had become a major political organization that was hostile to Jews, Catholics, foreigners and blacks. Initiates outside of Little Rock in the center of the state, according to an article in the *Arkansas Gazette* "knelt before the cross, kissed a Bible and an American flag...swore absolute fealty to the tenets of the Klan."[5]

Whether Dave, then raising his family in Marianna, was a member, we don't know (naturally we prefer to think he was not), but the Klan attracted prominent white men from doctors to lawyers as well as bank clerks in Arkansas. Unlike the earlier Klan, however, violence was only occasionally part of its methodology in the most recent incarnation in the 1920s.

As suggested, the specifics of Dave's death in 1933 at only 52 in the Arkansas State Hospital for Nervous Diseases in Little Rock are still a bit vague. According to cousin Allison, whose information came from her mother, Dave contracted an amoeba while he was serving as a physician on a troop ship in England during the First World War. His death certificate states the cause of death was arteriosclerosis and a contributing cause was psychosis. Allison says that her mother told her Dave was taking opium to control the pain caused by the amoeba. The treating physician, a Dr. Shaw, attended our grandfather from July 1 to July 9, 1933, but apparently could do little for him except watch his fellow doctor die and sign his death certificate. Whether Dave's diagnosis of "psychosis" was a consequence of opium addiction, how much of a problem it was for him, and whether anything could have been done to save him, have been lost in the ether. Even before his death, strains had already begun to appear in the Wall family. The Depression hadn't reduced the family to begging, but it hadn't helped matters any. According to his son, our uncle David, our grandfather, probably like most physicians during this time, took some of his fees in produce, but during this time Dave and Effie had been able to send their two oldest children off to college and their son to boarding school, so their situation was in no way desperate as it was for some in Lee County who lived on the edge of starvation. Seventy-four year-old Marianna resident Lucy White, a former slave, told her federal writer project interviewer in the 1930s, "I gets ten dollars and some little things to eat along. I say it do help out. I got rheumatism and big stiff j'ints (enlarged wrists and knuckles)."[6]

Whites in our social class had less pressing problems. Temple dropped out of the University of Arkansas at Fayetteville, but my sisters differ as to the reason. Sally says that she came home to help take care of Dave; Harriet thinks she was told she didn't make her grades. What is beyond doubt is that his early death emotionally devastated his family. He left a widow who would never marry again, two minor children, David, Jr., who had been sent off to military school as an adolescent, and Sarah Hope, who was only ten, as well as two grown daughters, Temple and Harriet.

After Dave's death and Temple's marriage, Effie moved next door to the "little gray house" on Magnolia Place in Marianna. Aunt Tissie and her husband, W.C. "Dubby" Oursler, a successful businessman who with his brother owned four auto parts stores and four service stations in the area, purchased Effie's interest in my grandmother's house and moved in. Sarah Hope is believed to have spent most of her time as a child next door with Uncle Dubby and Aunt Tissie instead of with her mother.

Without her husband, Effie grew increasingly insecure and emotionally dependent on her eldest daughter, who was most like her in her intellectual curiosity. Tissie didn't work outside the home and didn't work inside it either, and neither did her mother during that time. Even during the Depression, Allison recalls that her mother had "a housemaid, washwoman, and yard man on staff 24-7." The housemaid's duty also included looking after Allison, so Aunt Tissie had plenty of time for her mother.

Effie, whose intellectual interests went far beyond Marianna, encouraged her oldest daughter to follow in her footsteps, and Tissie was an avid pupil. In return Effie demanded attention and got it. Allison remembers those times when her mother occupied herself with "hooking rugs," a favorite hobby, while Effie read out loud to her. Allison, who forever has been called "Tootie," would enter the room where this activity was occurring to ask her mother a question. Effie would insist that her granddaughter wait to speak to her mother until she had come to an appropriate stopping place in her reading. Allison also recalls the day that Nannie told her that she shouldn't have been given the honor of having the Wall family name (Allison). That should have gone to our sister Sally because "she would have appreciated it." Allison says she avoided Nannie when she could, not an easy thing to do, since she lived next door and was often over at the house. Allison remembers that "Nannie was so jealous of me and Daddy." Effie's words could hurt. According to her granddaughter Hope, Effie called her own daughter Sarah Hope a "nigger," because of the way she tanned in the summer. A little of Effie went a long way, and a lot of Effie could be difficult. As her oldest grandchild, Allison was around her for 35 years and knew her on an intimate basis since her own mother was her favorite and she lived next door. What Allison saw in our grandmother all those years was "anger, impatience and laziness." Frisky as he may have been, Dave's early demise did not improve her disposition.

Jealousy and envy were not unheard of emotions among the two older Wall sisters and their mother. Temple was jealous of Effie's close relationship with Tissie, but as time went on was relieved that Tissie had assumed most of the burden of her care.

Temple was also envious of Tissie's intellect and college degree and her husband's financial success. Close in age, the two sisters were not immune to quarreling, especially after the consumption of alcohol, according to Allison. Like a number of people in Lee County, some of us in the Wall family self-medicated with alcohol. And like a number of other families in Lee County, some also celebrated with alcohol. Its consumption didn't necessarily bring out the best in us and at times exacerbated tensions that otherwise seem normal and inescapable in any family. Yet, despite everything, Temple named her younger daughter after her oldest sister and many years later would invite her sister to fly with her to Colombia to visit me while I was in the Peace Corps.

There was also rivalry between Tissie and Effie as her eldest daughter began to blossom in Marianna society. Though Effie's scrapbook documents that she meticulously researched the origins of John Patterson, "Arkansas' first native born child of Anglo-Saxon parentage," it was Tissie, then President of the L'Anguille Chapter of the DAR, whose picture was made with the Governor of Arkansas. On May 19, 1938, the Memphis *Commercial Appeal* published a photograph of Aunt Tissie (Figures 7 and 8, p.115) with Arkansas Governor Carl Bailey and the great-great granddaughter of John Patterson, the "first white child born in what is now Arkansas." The grave, unsmiling picture of my aunt shows Tissie, photographed without her glasses, to be a pretty and stylish woman just entering her thirties. A stone highway marker in memory of this first white child was soon placed at Patterson's Branch outside Marianna by the Arkansas Centennial Commission. It was again Effie's research that made the event possible. Patterson, by the way, was quite the character. Married seven times, he buried six wives, and when he finally died, his seventh wife promptly died, too.[7] It was not the only time our Aunt Tissie upstaged her mother. Tissie wrote several published historical articles that appear in the scrapbook, but to make sure she would one day get proper credit, Effie writes in the margin of each one, "All taken from my notes."[8] As a historian, I understand her concern.

Entering into this complicated family dynamic was Jake Stockley, who was from a prosperous and well-connected Old South Memphis family, a pedigree that suited Miss Effie just fine. She had more in common with Jake's ultra-conservative political beliefs than Tissie's husband Uncle Dubby, who made no secret of his support of Franklin Roosevelt's "New Deal."

"Marianna," Effie writes a bit smugly in her scrapbook, "in seventy-five years became a place of some consequence." With all the cotton and timber being shipped out of Lee County and together with her historical activities, it may have seemed that way to my maternal grandmother. Raised in a real city, Jake Stockley surely did not share his mother-in-law's beliefs about Marianna's significance, but saw no reason to challenge "Miss Effie," as he and others called her. Many years later, Jake said more than once to his only son that it was better to be a big fish in a little pond than the other way around.

How Jake and Temple met is in question—either at a Thanksgiving Day party in 1933 at the home of O.W. McClintock, or at Harrington's Drug Store where Temple had gotten a job. Marianna was where Jake would have bought supplies for Whitehall, and likely he would have been a customer of McClintock and Sons. Since he was an eligible bachelor it was inevitable that they would meet.

We can only speculate about our parents' previous romances. When-ever we asked, Temple delighted in teasing Jake about a girl (Eileen) he had apparently liked but who was quite a bit taller. Allegedly, his head only came up to her bosom where it rested comfortably when they danced. During this recital by Temple, Jake—bald, gray, and looking older than his chronological age because of decades of smoking and drinking and weathering from the sun—would shake his head innocently and smile as if in all those years as a bachelor he had never even thought of loving another woman. In time he would tell this story on himself. Twenty-nine when they married, he likely had, but not a woman who loved him as much as Temple, and this may have been what charmed him the most.

It may have been love at first sight for Jake, but perhaps not so for Temple. For decades I would think she had taken all of six weeks to meet and marry our father, but as usual they liked to tell a good story. It was more like six months, and as their wedding day got closer, Jake's beloved seemed to be having second thoughts or maybe was just feeling the heebie-jeebies of an engagement to a man who spent almost every day in an isolated area of the county that made her hometown of Marianna by comparison seem like Paris. Jake wrote Temple:

> *Please Sweetheart, never again even mention or think we are not going to be married on the 23rd [of May 1934]. Tonight I have gone through agonies of the damned. Do you love me Sweetheart as I love you? I know that you do, but how can you think of putting off our wedding for anything.*

Even the thought of it has up-set [sic] me so, that I don't know what would happen to me if any thing [sic] really did happen. Oh, Sweetheart you have to love me, love me lots, for I love you so.

The letters to Temple reveal a side of Jake I wish I had gotten to know. It might have helped me understand myself better, but I never heard him wax so passionately about anything. Though crazy in love, he was also ambitious. A 2005 doctoral dissertation on file at the Butler Center for Arkansas Studies in Little Rock describes who controlled what in the county where I lived most of my life until I went off to college. Dr. Blake Wintory states, "Since the 1870s, Lee County has been dominated by agricultural elites who strived to transfer their economic power into political power."[9] They succeeded and, along with others, made the Arkansas Delta a force to be reckoned with in state politics. A member in good standing of the "agricultural elites" for approximately two decades, first in Arkansas and then briefly in Mississippi, was precisely what Jake Stockley wanted so badly to become. Though his personality was generally marked by a characteristic mildness, a single snapshot of family history reveals a fierceness that was a part of the Stockley gene pool. Joanne Cullom Moore, my cousin by marriage, and herself a well-known "local" historian, has preserved the Stockley family lore, particularly as it relates to the Old South. While Effie took enormous pride in her ancestry, she had nothing on the men and women who made up the Stockley/Trigg/McSpadden family tree. The most telling example of Jake's side of the family's devotion to the belief in the rightness of the white South's struggle is an anecdote which appears in *Early Families of the Memphis Area*. Joanne writes about my great grandmother on my father's side:

> *For the Charles Stockleys and their extended family, the War Between the States was a time of sacrifice and of steadfast*

opposition to the Northern invaders. When the Yankees occupied Memphis, they requisitioned Lucy and Charles Stockley's house and 30 acres of land there, which had been a gift from Lucy's father. Lucy loaded her young children in a wagon to go to Corona, but before she left, she knelt down in the front yard and prayed to God that He would not allow the enemies of her country to enjoy the use of her house. When Lincoln died, the citizens of Memphis were ordered to drape their houses in black. When Lucy objected to this, the Yankees burned down the house.[10]

Lucy was a woman whose family had no intention of acknowledging defeat, and its members had already found kindred spirits. In the days before the Civil War, that side of the family tree would eventually have connections to the Memphis power structure. For example, Joanne writes in *Early Families of the Memphis Area* that Samuel A. Moore, who had risen to the rank of Lieutenant General in the Civil War and whose son married one of Jake's sisters, "came to Memphis with Nathan Bedford Forrest and was in business with him."[11] Forrest, as mentioned, inspired dread in the hearts of his enemies, not just in the war but afterwards as well.

Two of Lucy's brothers served in the Confederate Army, and Jake, born in 1904, would be named for a fallen warrior at the battle of Franklin, Tennessee. As Griffin Jasper Stockley, Jr., I am part of that legacy, whether I wish to be or not. Though at one time there were acres by the thousands owned by the Stockleys, Jake was apparently too low in the birth order to benefit directly. Of Jake's siblings, an older sister Elizabeth and her husband Horace Moore would own and farm land in Tennessee (though quirkily situated on the Arkansas side of the Mississippi thanks to a course change in the river), and his brother Charles would buy and farm land in Crittenden County, Arkansas, across the Mississippi from Memphis. Fortunately, Jake, for his future as a plantation owner, had a beautiful younger sister who married extremely well and was kindly disposed to him.

Visiting eligible and likable bachelors eager for company were most welcome in Marianna, especially those who looked to have promise, and Jake made a charming guest. Though he had never gone to college, he had joined a high school fraternity in Memphis and had made a number of friends and had stories to tell. Like many of our family yarns, some of them understandably were designed to entertain, but also to impress—like his oft-repeated account of swimming across the Mississippi River, an impressive feat at Memphis. Probably he had (he did swim beautifully), but maybe he had walked part of the way across during a drought. It was the way he told it that enhanced its credibility among his peers. Jake had a drawl that made his southern birthright unimpeachable. Words delivered from his mouth arrived in two speeds: slow and slower. As a young man, he and his life-long friend, "Buzz" Land, had managed to get hired as merchant seamen. A touristy photo of Jake and Buzz mounted on camels with the Pyramids of Egypt in the background testifies to his interest in the wider world (Figure 5, p.114). Less adventurously, for a time he worked in a bank in Memphis.

As indicated, Jake was a man not in a hurry. I never saw him run, but I never saw Temple break into a trot either. Only 5'6" and 135 pounds, Jake had almost unnaturally soft skin and was fastidious in his personal habits. I can still see him in their bedroom, pushing down his trousers, flexing his knees and tucking in his shirt ever so carefully as if he had just come through an ill-advised hernia operation the previous day. Before premature male pattern baldness and a need for bifocals overtook him, he was handsome in the way of young men looking to make their mark in the world. In short, Jake didn't fit the image of a farmer like his brother Charles and brother-in-law Horace, and, for the most part, he wouldn't be, at least not the kind who enjoyed getting his hands dirty. He would have been more comfortable in the role of an English squire, albeit a diligent one. He rented out his land to sharecroppers, an arrangement that had come into practice throughout the South after slavery was abolished. In return for advancing tools, seed, a shotgun house, supplies and the land to be worked, the plantation owner would take a percentage of the crop at harvest time (a third or a fourth) and deduct what was owed to him. Still in his twenties, family connections made it possible for him first to rent Whitehall and later buy it. His sister Carolyn had married Herbert Humphreys, an heir to the Humko lard fortune in Memphis. Herbert's father, Hugh, among other investments, had bought Whitehall, a huge plantation in Lee County that was just shy of 5,000 acres.

In 1940, Hugh's widow and her children, including Herbert and his wife Carolyn, sold Whitehall to Jake and Temple for a total of $14,000. Only $500 of that amount was required as a down payment. Despite the ravages of the floods of 1927 and 1937 and Depression-era prices for cotton, Whitehall was still a bargain considering that three of the five thousand acres were under cultivation. Today, allowing for inflation, that amount would have been more than $250,000. Jake and Temple would have had to come up with a little over $9,000 in cash in 2020 dollars to make the deal go through.

While part of the early twentieth century economic history of the rural southern United States is the saga of privileged risk-takers like Jake and Temple, witnessing how the sausage was made back in the kitchen is the rest of the story. "I have travelled over most of Europe and part of Africa, but I have never seen such terrible sights as I saw yesterday among the sharecroppers in Arkansas," wrote Naomi Michinson, an English novelist of this period.[12] She was referring to the shocking conditions in which the sharecroppers were living, which had become a national disgrace during this era. Starvation, freezing weather, inadequate housing, and sickness all took their toll. During the 1930s, destitute sharecroppers, both white and black, joined the Southern Tenant Farmers Union, an organization that was begun by two white Arkansans. Despite attracting national attention because of the violence and intimidation by planters, their agents and law enforcement, the STFU does not appear to have been active in Lee County. On the other hand, there is no evidence the conditions for the sharecroppers at Whitehall were less dire than anywhere else in Arkansas.

Indeed, had Naomi Michinson witnessed how my parents and my two sisters were then living at the time, she would have wondered about the entire system. Sally, born in 1937, writes that the plantation at Whitehall was so isolated that there was "no electricity, telephone, natural gas, or indoor plumbing" at the "little, yellow house." A new house was constructed before our sister Harriet was born in 1939, but it also lacked the amenities of electricity, natural gas, and telephone. Effie, writing about Whitehall for *The Courier Index* in 1938, referred to their house as nothing more than a "cottage," not a compliment. But what my sisters and parents lacked in creature comforts, they made up in black servants. In scenes that could have come straight out of the slave era, Sally remembers the Whitehall years as ones in which she and Harriet "were taken care of by Negroes." [Our] "Negro washerwoman [was] named Mattie Whitehall,"[13] who did her work "under the house which was built on pilings...to put it above the water should the Mississippi flood again. She was at least shaded from the summer sun and protected a bit from the cold." While the Stockley sisters lay in their beds, "Willie Chambers, Daddy's hostler [took care of the horses and mules]...also came to our house early every morning when it was cold to light the fire..." Sally remembers "snuggling down in the feather bed until the room warmed up enough for us to get up."

My sisters' first playmates, Clarice, "Bill" and "Tot," were the daughters of Estelle, the family "cook and housekeeper."[14] A photograph of Bill and Tot with then infant Harriet (see cover photo) confirms her memory. Sally writes:

> I want to think that Daddy was honest and never took advantage of the Negroes who worked for him either on Whitehall or in Lake Cormorant or in any of the businesses he ran in Marianna. I certainly never saw Daddy mistreat a Negro. He thought of them as "children," for whom he was responsible, and in my memory that is the way he treated them. It was paternalistic and condescending but not mean. Also, Daddy emphasized being honest, fair, and kind in our own dealings with others; so it is difficult for me to believe that he exploited those who worked for him; but I have no evidence or facts either to back me up or to prove otherwise.[15]

Given Estelle's working conditions alone, it would be hard to claim that the "Golden Rule" were buzz words on the Stockley plantation, capitalism/feudalism and Christianity being such incompatible bedfellows. Yet, like my sisters, I can personally vouch for the statement that our father "emphasized being honest, fair [to] others," etc. when we later moved into Marianna. I never saw him nor our mother "mistreat a Negro," meaning only that they never cheated or abused blacks in my presence. But the point is that they would have had no motive to mistreat their help. Blacks were paid so little in the South during this era that the adage, "You can't get blood out of a turnip," applied.

But before I wax too self-righteously from my vantage point in the twenty-first century, I remind myself that I need to stop at Dollar Tree later, but prefer not to dwell on the living conditions of the overseas workers who made my two-for-one Christmas cards.

Exploiting sharecroppers financially was an easy proposition if Jake wanted to do it. As mentioned, present-day historians have documented the rampant cheating by planters of their black tenant farmers in Arkansas as well as the South after the Civil War and well into the twentieth century. Sally remembers that Estelle (we do not know her last name) and Willie Chambers made the move to Lake Cormorant in 1942, a fact that might be interpreted to suggest that as during slavery, we treated blacks who labored in closer proximity to us somewhat better than those who did not. Whether their move accompanying the Stockleys was proof that these two individuals felt they were being treated fairly, or merely evidence that they preferred not having to guess where their children's next meal would come from, I know of no facts to support either conclusion.

Temple took the plunge and married Jake at the Wall home on Magnolia Place in Marianna on May 17, 1934. Oddly, the wedding was performed by an Episcopal priest. Jake was Presbyterian; Temple was raised Baptist by Effie but began to attend the Presbyterian Church with Jake after their marriage. Jake had sweetened the pot with a honeymoon trip to Monterrey, Mexico, a luxury obviously denied to his sharecroppers, but then he had to take his bride back to live at Whitehall. Under any scenario, Temple surely would have had doubts about the life he was asking her to lead in the 1930s. In no way was she cut out to enjoy a rural country setting even if she had black servants to cook and clean and follow around her children. She hated the outdoors, heat, humidity and bugs. For reasons never made clear to their children (the isolation alone, floods, and lack of decent roads may have prompted the move) Jake and Temple sold Whitehall in 1942 and moved across the river to Lake Cormorant, Mississippi, in Desoto County, approximately 30 miles south of Memphis. By entering into a complex land swap with an individual named E.L. Shields and his wife, Temple and Jake acquired 637 acres of land which they would sell four years later for $50,000 (equivalent to $660,000 in 2020) to a John and Helen Stout. Why they sold so quickly (perhaps the lack of decent schools in the area at the time) we don't know. I have wondered if Jake had realized what a risky proposition farming was always going to be. Mechanization was on the horizon, and huge capital outlays were going to be required.

In 2013, according to the Internet, the asking price for Whitehall was $11,200,000. It was described on Landflip.com as follows: "Farm lease income averaging approx. $375,000 annually plus hunting lease income." In the meantime (1944), though I was born in the First Baptist Hospital in Memphis as had been my sisters, Mississippi was my first home for less than two years. It is not clear whether Jake contracted with sharecroppers as he had done at Whitehall or whether he hired labor and tried to farm himself. It is hard to imagine him personally coping with all the physical challenges that farm life entailed. If he ever developed calluses from working with his hands, I never saw them. But then neither has his son.

William Alexander Percy's best selling *Lanterns on the Levee: Recollections of a Planter's Son,* brought out in 1941 by New York's premier publisher Alfred J. Knopf, would serve years later as a treasured walk down nostalgia lane for Jake's and Temple's rural experiences. In 2014, though uncertain when our parents first read it, our sister Harriet remembers how much they said they had loved this book, and no wonder: It reinforced every feeling they might have had about race and white privilege during their years in rural Arkansas and Mississippi. Still in print today, the book binds together, in undeniably sumptuous prose, the themes of race and class that ran in tandem on both sides of the Mississippi in this once teeming (mostly black) hothouse area of the South.

During a book signing for one of my earlier Gideon Page novels in the 1990s in Jackson, Mississippi, an aging but prosperous-looking customer spontaneously declared his love for *Lanterns on the Levee* just at the moment I was hoping he was going to praise my most recent book. I shouldn't have been at all surprised. More than fifty years after its publication, Percy's memoir was still everywhere in bookstores in Mississippi and Tennessee during my book tour. I had my girlfriend Lynn Pence take a photograph of me (Figure 1, see front matter) reading a library copy of *Lanterns on the Levee* for the book jacket of *Blind Judgment*, my fifth and last Gideon Page novel. As he does on more than one occasion, Percy, a native of Greenville, Mississippi, describes in his book the view I had at that moment: I am sitting on the levee at Greenville sipping a plastic cup filled with Cold Duck looking across the river into Arkansas. Behind me is the Mississippi Delta.

Even today one can go on the Internet and read admiring customer reviews of *Lanterns on the Levee* and understand why Jake and Temple would have accepted Percy's account of his life as a rousing defense of white supremacy and the measures needed to implement it. A gifted stylist and a well-published poet in his day, Will Percy cast all the blame for the Delta's historic racial outrages after the Civil War ended and into the twentieth century at the feet of poor whites who migrated into the Delta. "At their door must be laid the disgraceful riots and lynchings gloated over and exaggerated by Negrophiles the world over."[16] From the first chapter forward, Percy constructs an elaborate fantasy of the past that relieves him, his family and our planter class, generally of responsibility for the violence and exploitation that characterized the economic and social systems before and after the Civil War in these similar areas of Arkansas and Mississippi.

Along the way, like other whites of his station who have written about race, Percy insisted he loved and understood the black sharecroppers on Trail Lake, his 3,000 acre cotton plantation, an inheritance from his father. Even as his black tenants sorely tried his patience, he proclaimed his fondness for them. He wrote, "His manners offset his inefficiency, his vices have the charm of amiable weaknesses, he is a pain and grief to live with, a solace and a delight." He opined, "the American Negro is interested neither in the past nor in the future, this side of heaven. He neither remembers nor plans. The white man does little else: to him the present is the great unreality." And certain ones he did love until they got uppity. Percy describes a scene in which his loyal black retainer "Fode" finds him naked in the shower and observes, "You ain't nothing but a little old fat man."[17] Having crossed a line, the black man is temporarily banished from his presence.

Alongside Percy's chapters about his broadening travels, his love of the classics and beauty, his Harvard legal education, poetry, brave service in World War I, family background, adoption of three nephews, and paternalism, is an unapologetic account of the ruthlessness of his grandfather and father (the white Arkansas plantation manager his father hired to run Trail Lake established his authority by shooting a tenant his first day on the job). Will Percy's justification of his father's actions he deems simple necessity. Whatever was needed to insure the degree of white supremacy required to keep the Percy properties profitable in an up-and-down cotton market was done. Impossible to capture in any brief description is Percy's emotional complexity and worldly sophistication. Only someone to the white Southern "manner born" and "manor born," as Will Percy was, could convince himself that this sow's ear of an agricultural economic system—sharecropping—could be made into a silk purse.

Nowhere is it written that parents have to tell their children their innermost thoughts. But I'm convinced Jake and Temple would have been more forthcoming if we had only asked. As with Nannie, I regret enormously not having asked them more questions and not just the easy ones that they could turn into a humorous story. What surely attracted Jake and Temple about *Lanterns on the Levee* was Percy's fierce defense of the planter class and white supremacy in general. Simply by birth, their class entitled them to the opportunities they had been given. Percy's wealth had been acquired the old-fashioned way: he had been given it, but not for an instant did he think he was undeserving of all the privilege he had been handed. Noting his lack of spatial intelligence while an officer in World War I, he wrote that a sergeant "icy with contempt, put together my machine-gun when its *disjecta membra* unassembled [and] would have returned me in disgrace to America…" He wrote of his inability to "drive a car or fix a puncture or sharpen a pencil or swim or skate…my incompetency is almost all-inclusive…."[18] He would attribute to his own "good manners" the fact that people helped him as he bumbled through the everyday chores of life that most take for granted.

Jake, as Sally notes, thought of blacks as children. Whether he thought of himself as his black tenants' protector, friend and benefactor to the same degree as Will Percy, I have my doubts. Though not one given to pontificating on the subject of race in front of his children, nevertheless, Jake (and Temple) shared Percy's view of appropriate racial behavior. Palatable to the adults in our family and others in our class was Percy's often expressed view in *Lanterns* that nothing was more important to peaceful relationships between blacks and whites than the requirement that both sides of the racial equation exhibit "good manners" toward each other. "The Negro," wrote Percy, "has the most beautiful manners in the world followed by the white man, and the Southern white, learning from him, I suspect, is a close second."[19] Percy's frequent discourse on both races displaying "good manners" toward each other presupposes that blacks must acknowledge their inferiority or "place" by acting in a subordinate manner in encounters with whites. The deference demanded by whites of Southern blacks was non-negotiable. Blacks knew it as well. Thus, blacks observing "good manners" meant that they knew their place, called whites "Mr. and Miss" and cheerfully followed whatever the customs and laws of white supremacy required in a given situation. In fact, it was not a matter of "good manners" for blacks, but rather survival. In return, whites who considered themselves of a certain breeding (Temple and Jake and their peers) made a consistent effort from their vantage point to overtly avoid demeaning blacks. In fact, the entire system of white supremacy demeaned blacks, however much whites protested this was not the case.

While they would have readily acknowledged that they weren't remotely as wealthy or as educated as Percy, Jake and Temple may well have seen him as an exemplar of a way of life they had hoped for themselves. Indeed, Temple, in particular, had an ability to play the role of a cultured Southern white woman when she wanted to try to impress people as she did in Pittsburgh, Pennsylvania, during the pre-wedding festivities involving me and my first wife. Though Temple's circumstances were reduced by 1969, seven years after Jake's death, you would have thought she owned ten plantations and was merely volunteering as a housemother at Ole Miss as a favor to the University of Mississippi. I had alerted Temple and my sister Sally to the fact that Susan's family was quite accomplished. Herb Minter, my father-in-law to-be, was a chemical engineer for Westinghouse in Pittsburgh with several patents to his name, including the development of the insulation of the nose cone that went to the moon. A lovely, sweet man who was stricken with Multiple Sclerosis and in a wheelchair, Herb and I had nothing in common except we were born on the same planet, and I was marrying his daughter. The first night I was in Pittsburgh, and before my family had arrived, I was left alone with Herb for a couple of hours. Since my aptitude for science had peaked in the ninth grade in Marianna, I was immediately faced with the prospect of trying to convince the man that his daughter was not marrying a character out of *Tobacco Road*. Thinking, maybe hoping, that I was minimally literate, Herb tried desperately to explain some of his patented inventions but very little penetrated. Poor man! He couldn't have been kinder. I had never been so glad to see my family. I felt like the cavalry had arrived just in time. Sally sounded so Southern that I could not resist calling her "Sister Woman" after the character in the film version of Tennessee Williams's *Cat on A Hot Tin Roof*.

CHAPTER 3

The "White" American Century

"I think whites are carefully taught not to recognize white privilege, as males are taught not to recognize male privilege. I have come to see white privilege as an invisible package of unearned assets which I can count on cashing in each day, but about which I was meant to remain oblivious."[1]

—Peggy McIntosh

TIME MAGAZINE kept Jake company in a way we did not. One of my consistent pop-up memories in the 1950s until his death in 1962 is of Jake sitting in a chair in the living room of our house or at the kitchen table at 358 Pearl Street in Marianna reading long after we had finished eating and had let the room. Jake had an uneven bite which caused him to eat at the pace of a glacier before Global Warming. A member of the Marianna Rotary Club, he complained to his family that he was never allowed to finish eating at the meetings before his plate was whisked away. At home he could read and eat in peace, and he liked what he read in *Time*.

Acutely aware of his influence and with characteristic hubris, *Time*, *Life*, and *Fortune* magazine publisher Henry Luce had announced in a pre-Pearl Harbor 1941 editorial in *Life*, that this was the "American Century," and that its citizens must recognize it and act accordingly. A son of Christian missionaries to China,

Luce insisted that the country was, for all practical purposes, already in World War II, and isolationism was not an option. This war was first and last about democracy, and America must use all its formidable resources, human and otherwise, to preserve it. This grandiose notion of an "American Century" was widely hailed and would be fondly remembered by commentators (except perhaps by those who wished they had thought of it first), notwithstanding the fact that a sizable portion of America did not practice democracy. Not for nothing was Dixie called the "Solid South." Since the end of Reconstruction, in exchange for aligning with the national Democratic Party in elections, we white Southerners were allowed to go our own way, which meant implementing white supremacy without interference from the federal government. In Arkansas, we never had any doubt about what this meant. In 1933, John Gould Fletcher, then the state's most acclaimed writer and a contributor to the literature of the Southern writers' group known as the "Agrarians," wrote a letter to the editor of the *Nation* in which he warned the country, "But we are determined, whether rightly or wrongly, to treat him [the Negro] as a race largely dependent upon us, and inferior to ours."[2] As the saying goes, Fletcher, who won the Pulitzer Prize for poetry in 1939, wasn't just "wolfing." Forewarned by federal judicial decisions suggesting a broader interpretation of the Fourteenth Amendment *vis-à-vis* one's right to vote, Arkansas governor Ben Laney put his signature to two acts passed unanimously by the legislature in 1945 that prohibited blacks from voting in the state's Democratic Primary. John Moore, a state senator from Phillips County in the heart of the Arkansas Delta where the Elaine Race Massacre had occurred, announced that the intention of the legislature was "to secure what he terms 'white supremacy' in Arkansas' Democratic primary."[3]

When Jake and Temple moved to Arkansas from Mississippi

in 1946, our father had no problems with Henry Luce's prognosis to cure the world's ills except with one important proviso: continue to leave us alone in the White South to deal with racial issues as we saw fit. There was nothing unusual at all about this proposition in Lee County when we moved to what would be our parents' final destination. In 1947, *The Courier Index* listed county births for the year as either "white" or "non-white."

Thus, it was a worrisome harbinger of things to come when, after Roosevelt's death in 1945, Vice President Harry Truman took the presidential oath and soon began to make noises about civil rights for blacks, even going so far in 1948 as issuing an executive order forbidding discrimination in the Armed Forces. Legislation had also been proposed, which had it not been filibustered to death by Southern Congressmen, would have created a permanent national Fair Employment Practices Commission. This particular nightmare, had it passed and been enforced, would have begun to undermine much of what white Southerners so prized in our "way of life"—a coolie-cheap labor force. Northerners also sought to abolish the poll tax and lynching, efforts again blocked by Southerners in Congress. These attempted reforms and what they signaled for the future were unacceptable to Jake and Temple and many other whites in Lee County. Our parents' champion became South Carolina's governor Strom Thurmond, who, in 1948, bolted the national Democratic Party to start the "States Rights Democratic Party," which became known informally as the "Dixiecrats." Purely an Old South phenomenon, "States Rights" was code for white supremacy, and most of the official party platform of the Dixiecrats was devoted to it. Labeling the platforms of the Democratic and Republican Conventions "totalitarian," which, if implemented, would lead to "a police nation," we Dixiecrats stood "for the segregation of the races and the racial integrity of each race."[4] Dixiecrats pointedly opposed the repeal of miscegenation laws. Though still racist and hypocritical, the rest of the country had a broader vision of itself. Even most white Arkansans could not be stampeded into a view of itself so fearful. Thurmond won only 2.4 percent of the popular vote nationally, and in Arkansas, out of 75 counties, only Lee gave the majority of its votes to Thurmond. Two of those votes were from Jake and Temple Stockley.

Temple's politics followed Jake's at this stage of her life. In his bid for president, Thurmond, who would live to be a hundred, made a campaign appearance in Marianna on August 26, 1948, telling his Lee County supporters that President Truman's civil rights initiatives were the product of "agitators and socially maladjusted persons."[5] The Fair Employment Practices Commission would "turn America into some kind of a socialist, or fascist or Communist state." My sister Harriet remembers attending the campaign rally with Temple and Jake.

Upon taking up residence in Marianna, our father participated in local politics. According to my cousin Allison, in 1948, Jake, who by then had two children in the Marianna schools, was likely to have been recruited to run for the School Board by his longtime friend, W. H. "Buddie" Daggett, who was Sally's godfather. In turn, Temple was godmother to a daughter of the Daggetts. "Mr. Buddie" is said by my cousin Allison to have shared Jake's views on race. Jake remained on the School Board through 1957. To avoid a conflict of interest, he was no longer a candidate after my sister Sally was hired as a teacher in the Marianna public schools. The importance of school board elections in Arkansas was profound because of the routine practice of local all-white boards "diverting" state education funds intended for black schools to white schools. In 1948 alone, it was revealed in the *Arkansas Gazette* that, according to Ed Mccuiston, the white director of Negro Education for racial moderate Governor Sid

McMath, diversion amounted throughout the state to $4,250,000, which was the equivalent of over forty million dollars in 2012.[6]

Given the stinging defeat of our champion, the elites of Lee County returned to our old strategy of keeping a lower profile nationally and working behind the scenes. We were just as determined to maintain white supremacy, but there was nothing to gain by making an uproar about it. Keeping our powder dry had worked well in the past.

In the Marianna school system, the disparities were obvious, and despite pleas from Sid McMath's administration to stop the practice, stealing educational funds intended for blacks continued. Diversion involved much more than giving black students our old textbooks and paying their teachers lower salaries. A *Lee County History* photograph of Jake, Buddie Daggett, and other school board members, shows them at the ground-breaking ceremony in 1949 for a new white school (Nunnally Elementary).[7]

While Governor Sid McMath and members of his administration wished to end the disparities in funding, it was not going to happen any time soon, given the political power exercised in the Delta by the agricultural elites. While I was in high school in Marianna in the early 1960s, my Spanish class (taught by my sister Sally) was equipped with a modern language lab complete with individual microphones and recording devices. Our school had tennis courts[8] and a state-of-the-art gymnasium that was the site of the Class "A" girls state basketball tournament. In 1962, T.A. Futrall High School hosted the state Student Council Convention. Robert R. Moton High School had none of these amenities, with the exception of a new gymnasium constructed in 1950.[9] It had taken litigation in federal court by black teachers in the 1940s in Little Rock to achieve salary parity there, and whites found loopholes around it.[10] One didn't have to imagine the differences between white and black schools in the Delta. The disparities were a national scandal. An article in *Life* on March 21, 1949, accompanied by embarrassing photographs of black schools in the town of West Memphis in Crittenden County, disclosed that in 1948, the local School Board had spent an average of $19.51 for each black student and $144.51 for each white student.[11]

In February 1946, Marianna became my home until I left for college 16 years later. Jake and Temple bought an unpretentious house on the corner of Pearl and Locust Streets, so modest that my bed was in their bedroom. Harriet and Sally shared a bedroom, as well as they would later in a new house. What our parents' day-to-day precise financial situation was then (or at any time) is only a guess. With his family's connections, Jake had gotten interested in the New York stock market and the Memphis futures market in cotton long before they moved to Marianna. Our memories are too vague and contradictory to nail down any figures, but at various times Jake made and surely lost money in the markets. Judson McKellar, his favorite nephew, was involved in the cotton market on Front Street in downtown Memphis, the *de facto* capital of eastern Arkansas and northern Mississippi. Handsome and likable, "Jud" was Bamboo's son and was active in Memphis social circles, so much so that his daughter made her debut during the Christmas holidays at the Memphis Country Club while I was a senior at Southwestern. Following tradition, Martha, whom I remember meeting only once before then, asked me to be one of her escorts for the evening. No more sophisticated than I had been in high school, the evening was lost on me. For all I know, the governor of Tennessee was standing next to me the whole time trying to get my attention, but I doubt it. Nevertheless, Temple loved hearing about it, including what family gossip I picked up (even though it was Jake's family), so in her mind my peek at Memphis society was a success.

Though the details, in probably the early 1960s, of a trip with

Jake to Front Street across the Mississippi River Bridge from Arkansas and meeting Jud and watching clerks scribble cotton prices in chalk on a big board behind them elude me, Jake's interest in the markets was keenly apparent. *The Commercial Appeal* was delivered each morning to our house from Memphis in eastern Arkansas, and Jake followed the markets with as much interest as I read Major League baseball box scores. Not too long before he died, he told me wistfully that he could have made a lot of money on a particular transaction, but what market it was I have no memory. According to Harriet, it was after a successful investment in the stock market that Jake told Temple we could proceed with the construction of a new house on North Pearl.

For various reasons, routine trips to Memphis from Marianna were deemed necessary for all who could afford it. The few blacks who had the money shopped in Memphis just as whites. Donna Grady Creer, whose father was a busy brick mason, remembers her family shopped for clothes in downtown Memphis at Goldsmiths as my mother and sisters did and were treated better by the clerks than they were in Marianna.[12] When a medical specialist was needed, we went to Memphis. At one time you could take the train, which I did with Temple at least once as a child. After the highway was paved, it was only an hour's drive to the bridge, and downtown was right across the river. Jake drove to Memphis to see a doctor for his sinuses. Memphis was where you would go for operations. My tonsils were removed in Memphis and two of the cysts on my neck were removed in Memphis. A Dr. Smith fitted me for orthodontia. I hated him because the fitting and tightening of the appliances were painful. You waited and waited for your turn in a room full of kids who had the same terrified expressions on their faces. Some were crying or trying not to cry like I was. We knew he was going to hurt us and were never disappointed, judging from the tears from those returning from his torture chamber. For one visit I carved out of wood something that resembled a knife and put it up my sleeve. I told myself I would stab him if he hurt me. I was humiliated when it fell out of my shirt. He saw it and laughed. Over about two years, he reduced the gap between my front teeth but there was no mania for whitening them in those days. No matter how much Jake and Temple spent on my teeth, they were never like "Bucky Beaver's" in the Ipana commercial.

Jake put most of their available cash from the proceeds of the sale of the farm at Lake Cormorant into businesses he started in Marianna. Over the years he owned a "Jim Brown" hardware store and the building that housed it; he bought equipment to start a plant that manufactured concrete blocks; he started a dairy but ended up only as a distributor of Sealtest milk that was trucked in from Memphis. These ventures ended in failure, or in the case of the milk distributorship, at most had only very limited success. It was not until Jake obtained a business partner in the 1950s that the Stockley financial situation in Marianna gained a firmer footing. He needed someone who knew how to sell merchandise and, more importantly, didn't think it was beneath him. Owens & Stockley carried quality goods such as Motorola televisions, Carrier air conditioners, Frigidaire household appliances and B.F. Goodrich tires. Francis Owens, "Mr. Pee Wee," was short, quite round, and an excellent salesman. Jake's primary role consisted of doing the paperwork which included keeping the store stocked with goods and parts and sending out the repairmen who installed and fixed the products sold by Owens and Stockley.

For a few weeks one summer, I helped Owens and Stockley employees install appliances, television antennas and air conditioners, but totally inept with tools and instructions requiring even a smattering of spatial intelligence, understandably I was not the preferred assistant. The Owens' oldest son, Bill, was my age and a brilliant student who would go on to get a degree in chemical engineering from Oklahoma State. In our high school physics class, Bill would occasionally have to help our teacher with the math. Bill was handy with tools, could follow directions and was the helper of choice. We were friends throughout our years in Marianna. We played on the same Little League team where "Mr. Pee Wee" was one of the coaches.

If Jake and Temple were shaken by his business failures, they didn't discuss it with their children. They didn't sit around wringing their hands over the contradictions in capitalism, the Bible, or the meaning of life. Like Effie and everyone in our social class, their choices and behavior defined them more than anything they said about themselves in public.

By the time Jake and Temple moved from Lake Cormorant to Marianna in 1946, it was readily apparent to some in the State Department that the United States had a new enemy. It was the beginning of the "Cold War," and my first conscious memory of it was in 1953 with the report of Joseph Stalin's death on March 5 crackling over the little radio by their bed. At the age of eight, I didn't know who Stalin was or what he had done, but I knew he was important because of my parents' excitement over the announcement of his demise.

The execution of spies Julius and Ethel Rosenberg followed in June, and I would remember that news, too, because the charges against them were related to passing atomic bomb secrets to the Soviet Union. Before long we white school children in Marianna were practicing hiding under our desks. During this era, a film was screened at our church in Marianna purporting to explain that Communism was spreading throughout the world as well as the United States. In the movie, a map covered the screen with parts of the country tinged in red (Washington, D.C. in particular) and becoming more red all the time. A published short story of mine in 2012 in Volume 6 of *Best of Tales from the South* records my memory of our mindset during that era. As a 13 year-old narrator, I ask my best friend's father, "Why would they drop a bomb on Marianna?...Seems like it would make more sense to drop one on Little Rock or Memphis. They're a lot bigger and would kill more people. Marianna's only got 4,500 people, and half of them are nigras."[13]

For years even as an adult when I couldn't fall asleep I would pretend that Communists were outside my window trying to find our house, but if I lay perfectly still and emptied my mind of all thoughts, they wouldn't be able to kill me. The phrase "better dead than red" was bandied about in Marianna during the 1950s. It was a mark of patriotism to say that you would rather die than live under Communism. Instinctively, however, I said I would rather be red than dead, but I didn't say it very loud or often.

Even in the face of the "threat" of international Communism, in a farewell speech to the nation in 1961, President Dwight D. Eisenhower, who had been commanding general of the Allied Command in Europe during World War II, warned his fellow citizens of the insidious dangers of "the military-industrial complex" in the United States. Though loved almost like a father figure, Eisenhower's words fell on deaf ears as the United States engaged in an unending global arms race through its successful effort to become the most fearsome nation on the planet. Communism was equated with atheism, and people who were atheists were regarded with amazement, pity, and perhaps even horror in Marianna. Christianity still equated with fundamentalism and had already been given in the white South a twist as far back as the Civil War to accommodate slavery. As the *Encyclopedia of Religion in the South*, under its entry on "Segregation," notes in almost a humorously understated way, "[t]he adaption of religious values to racial needs had a long history in the region."[14] The Stockley family was scrupulously regular in our church attendance in Marianna. My sisters and I went to Sunday School as well. Made to attend a Sunday evening group called the "Pioneers" as a teenager, I got more than my fill of church life. Temple occasionally taught Sunday School and shepherded the Pioneers, and Jake was a deacon in the church, but there is no agreement on what they actually believed. The 11 a.m. service at the Presbyterian Church in Marianna in the mid-1950s and early 1960s was an hour-long study in tedium. Jake would inevitably fall asleep, and it was my job to nudge him in the ribs when it was time to get up and sing a hymn or repeat in unison the Apostles' Creed. When he opened his eyes he would have the sweetest smile on his face as if he had never intended for a moment to nod off. The big donors, and there were very few, wanted a minister who would not rock the boat. As a segregationist, Mr. Sessions passed the only real litmus test that was required. The minister before him, Alan Anderson, was said to have been too liberal in this regard, but what that actually meant I don't know. There would be the incident of an African gentleman who had been converted by Presbyterian missionaries and came to spend some time at the Agricultural Experiment Station outside Marianna. Obviously thinking he would be welcomed as a Presbyterian convert, the man let it be known that he wished to come to a worship service at our church. This caused much discussion, but after a meeting of the governing body, it was determined that he would be allowed to do so, but my friend Lee Brown believes he remembers that it was agreed that no one would speak to him afterwards so as not to encourage him. Lee recalls his family did greet our visitor but also recalls how red the neck of Mr. Paul Benham, Sr. became upon seeing a black person in the First Presbyterian Church of Marianna.

Church was serious business in both the white and black communities. Though the First Baptist Church of Marianna was the largest by far, we Presbyterians thought of ourselves as superior to Baptists and evangelical churches with their emotional altar calls to be "saved." Our theology was more sophisticated; certainly, it was more esoteric with its doctrine of the Trinity (God the Father; God the Son; and God the Holy Ghost). Plus, our ministers had to be seminary educated. Which church you attended was important because it designated your class status, whether it was acknowledged or not. We knew such things without being told. People who attended evangelical churches surely wasted no time worrying about what we in the "mainline churches" thought of their worship services and beliefs. Still, Presbyterians, Episcopalians, and Methodists were, in my mind, high status; Baptists, because they were so numerous, could only be disparaged in the privacy of one's home and the rest low status. Black churches in Lee County were outside any hierarchy and were not taken seriously by us. In *Ruled by Race* I would quote an academic paper that summed up the attitude whites generally had toward black worship in the early 1900s. "[W]hites sneered openly at the practice of blacks in their churches 'as a joke, a cheap and flawed imitation of white worship.'" That this writer was referencing a newspaper article in the daily *Helena World* written in 1895 didn't make this dismissive attitude toward black worship any less prevalent more than a half century later.[15] On the other hand, this contempt and condescension would not be expressed so crudely for a number of reasons. By mid-twentieth century, despite the poverty of most blacks, African-Americans made up a crucial segment of consumers in towns like Marianna. Regardless of your class, a merchant risked losing a customer if he or she went over a line. In the *Helena World* article, two local black preachers were identified by name as "a couple of common negro broilers, neither of whom know anything about Christianity, nor are they governed by any consideration except the desire to work their gullible fools in the congregation for all the money they can get."[16]

At a certain point, children who are taken to church regularly are encouraged to take religion seriously, and I was no different. Somewhere along the way I took to heart the standard Biblical doctrine that if you didn't accept Jesus as the Son of God you were going to hell. The obvious injustice of this was that a person who lived before Jesus was out of luck. The utter unfairness of this proposition never resolved itself in my mind.

Little did I know that my concerns as a child had years earlier been raised by a former president of Southwestern at Memphis, my future *alma mater*. Charles Diehl's influence would still be evident when I attended Southwestern in the early sixties when I began to struggle in earnest with the whole business of religion. In high school the ordeal of all this church attendance was ameliorated by the fact that Diane Palmer, the prettiest girl in my class and one of the nicest, was a Presbyterian who was made to go as much as I did. She dated older guys but was a good friend through high school.

The question of what Jake and Temple thought about all those years we sat in church has always intrigued me. Harriet believes that they had a "personal faith." Sally labels Jake "a Deist because the God he believed in was totally distant and too busy to be concerned about what was happening on earth." From an early age, Sally was convinced that she has experienced "God's presence" and is today a retired ordained Presbyterian minister. I don't know about Temple, who once in my presence said she envied Catholics because of their strong "faith." The implication was that her faith was not so strong. Whatever their beliefs, they were regular attendees and participated in the activities of the church.

Christianity could have been routinely challenged by science when I was in high school, but no one seemed overly concerned with the contradictions in the Bible and the natural world. In the tenth grade, our biology teacher, Mr. Lowery, told my class that we could believe we came from monkeys if we wanted to, but he didn't believe it. That ended our class discussion on evolution, but in Arkansas it has never ended no matter how much proof is offered.

While Jake had *Time*, Temple was a reader, too. My mother's magazines over the years included *Ladies' Home Journal*, *McCall's* and *Redbook*. Jake and Temple both read, *The Saturday Evening Post*, and *Readers Digest* condensed novels, *The Commercial Appeal* and the *The Courier Index*. On Saturday nights he, Temple and I watched Lawrence Welk, *Gunsmoke* and *Paladin*. Jake and Temple went to few movies. His movie of choice starred John Wayne and Maureen O'Hara. For their own recreation they socialized with a circle of friends their ages in each others' homes where alcohol was a regular lubricant.

Jake taught me to ride a bicycle, roller skate, threw a football with me, but it was hunting on Sunday afternoons that he enjoyed most. "Hunting" was what we said we did, but it was primarily an excuse to walk in the woods and cotton fields with Buttons and Bows, our beagles. After a nap after dinner (we had gone to church, of course), Jake was ready to get outside. In all those years from about 12 to 17, he and I spent many Sunday afternoons together. He took the Remington .20 gauge shotgun, and I carried our .22 rifle. I can only remember killing a couple of rabbits in all of those years. After every "hunt," he cleaned and oiled both weapons and insisted I learn how before he let me take one of them out hunting by myself. Adamant about gun safety, he never knew that I missed by a couple of inches shooting my foot off with the shotgun one afternoon after school when I had gone out by myself in the cotton fields behind our house. The shotgun somehow "went off" twice in the space of a minute. I would have bled to death. That was my last time to go hunting alone. Jake was methodical and careful. I can't imagine him accidentally shooting himself or anyone else. But one Fourth of July weekend he made an error in judgment that could have cost us our lives. He and I went to shoot turtles and gar from the St. Francis River bridge on the way to Memphis. You could steady the muzzle of the rifle on the side of the bridge and see the gar right below the surface. In a short while we had killed everything we could see. I may have been about 12. Jake said that we could walk out on the railroad trestle beside the bridge and see if we could spot anything else. After we got out to about the middle, we could hear a whistle blowing. He told me to follow him, but I wasn't walking quickly enough to get off the bridge. The train was going too fast to stop. He told me to take two steps over the trestle cross-ties instead of one. I thought about jumping into the water below but was too scared. He said I had to walk faster. He couldn't hold my hand since it was too narrow. We barely made it to safety. Watching the train roar by reinforced how lucky we had been. I gulped down the water we had brought. I couldn't get enough of it so frightened I had been. Naturally, I couldn't wait to tell Temple, who was not happy to hear about such stupidity. Had not her sister Sarah Hope been visiting us at the time, we would have seen more sparks than occurred. Why we took satisfaction killing defenseless creatures I don't know. Even now, I flinch at the memory.

Jake was not a competitive individual, but he wanted his children to do well. One of his proudest moments was Sally's induction into Phi Beta Kappa at Southwestern her senior year, a national honorary society limited to students with outstanding grades.

Because of the importance he attached to it, I have a vivid recollection of the ceremony. He took off work early, and we drove over to Memphis to hear the poet Randall Jarrell give the keynote address. We were the only family members to attend.

Not as smart as either sister (Sally was co-valedictorian in high school; Harriet was fifth honor student; I was a measly tenth in high school), I was terrible in math. When I brought home C minuses in Geometry and Algebra II, Jake would say, "Son, do your best. That's all we ask." I would feel miserable, knowing I had disappointed him. I didn't torture myself or him by taking Trigonometry.

Despite his forbearance (I can remember only one spanking from him when I was about six), Jake had his blind spots when it came to discipline. Somehow, he got it in his head that my acne was purely a matter of not washing my face and not normal adolescence. He could not restrain himself and would march me into the bathroom and lean me against the wall. Under a bright light he would grit his teeth and conduct search and destroy missions on blackheads and pimples that were ripe for popping.

Temple could do nothing to spare me this humiliation and pain. My sisters were fortunately omitted from this torture.

My normal shyness as a child exasperated him beyond all reckoning as it does many fathers. "Hold your head up, Son!" he would hiss when we came upon adults I was supposed to know and be able to greet. "Look them in the eye and shake hands and talk so they can hear you." I couldn't do it. I would be able to do it at some point, just not as early in my development as he would have liked. Not charged with the responsibility of making me behave like a man was supposed to act, Temple seemed to accept the fact more readily that I was still a child and was far more sympathetic. In other words, she didn't take it personally. I finally understood this when I had a daughter and could simply enjoy her without needing to make her into an idealized version of myself.

Likewise, my first year of Little League baseball when I was ten was a trial to him. I struck out early and often, and once back home after a game he mocked my stance at the plate which I had been taught by my coaches. It was frustrating to both of us, and I went upstairs and cried. The next two years were better as I improved. Harriet has reminded me that when it was my day to pitch, Temple would cut the yard for me (my one scheduled chore along with taking out the garbage).

I hated conflict and as my refuge of choice would flee upstairs at the earliest possible moment and get in the tub and run it full of warm water. Standing up for myself has always come much harder than defending others, as would become apparent after I became a lawyer. When it came, and it wasn't often but often enough, Jake's anger, and it was only expressed verbally, was intimidating. My most vivid memory was his response to an acknowledgment by Sally when she was home from college that she had gone to a church function in Tennessee and had square-danced with a black male student. Unwilling to accept she had taken the first step toward a life of shame, she argued back, not a good idea in our house. Their fight ended with Sally in tears. Only 12 or 13 at the time, I began crying, too, as I hit the stairs for the safety of the tub.

Temple was more competitive than Jake, and I surely inherited my competitiveness from her. When we got a ping pong table, it was Temple who would make me laugh by saying she was going to play me "like I had some sense," whatever that meant. She said she had played basketball in high school, but it is difficult to imagine her being particularly athletic. What she really enjoyed was playing bridge with her friends. She taught us to play. Temple had card sense and liked to win. Again for Jake it didn't seem to matter whether he won or lost. Both of them wanted us to be good sports in victory or defeat. Wanting me to experience a taste of the kind of life he had lived, Jake arranged with his sister Elizabeth for me to spend the summer on Corona (Figure 15, p.118) which was then farmed by her two sons, Sam and Horace Moore. I was 14. I learned that summer how hard farmers worked. I stayed with Sam, who was still a bachelor, and my aunt whom my sisters and I called "Ditty." Every morning six days a week we got up at five where Sam fixed breakfast and then we went to their commissary to sell food to their hands, both black and white. Afterward, we went to the fields with their employees and, depending on the need, a busload of blacks who came over from Memphis. My primary job that summer was to carry water to the cotton choppers. They started at seven in the morning and knocked off at noon for an hour. Sam would pick me up and we drove back to the house for a dinner of meat, tomatoes, corn-on-the-cob, rolls and a desert that was served by their black maid. We had to get back to the fields by one to make sure the cotton choppers were back at it. They worked until six, all for three dollars a day. Then we went back to the commissary for an hour to sell food to their own hands before we went home to supper. Besides cotton, corn, and hay, Sam and Horace had pigs and cattle the summer I was there. One weekend there was an anthrax scare, and the cattle had to be rounded up to be vaccinated. They let me ride their best, most experienced horse. All I had to do was hold on. We worked straight through that weekend and got up Monday morning and started all over again. On Thursday night every two weeks, I would ride in to Osceola with Horace and his wife "Sister Moore" so that she could play bridge. Horace and I would go to a movie and both of us would fall asleep almost as soon as it started. Though I genuinely liked my cousins and aunt and they treated me well, I knew I didn't want to be a farmer. They had to work too hard.

 Whether Jake was disappointed that I didn't want to follow in his footsteps as a farmer, he never said. I would have summer jobs after that, the most legitimate at Wonder State Dairy, Jake's dairy business. The 1950s were still the days that some people liked to have their milk delivered to their door. Mr. Hilyard, Jake's one regular Wonder State Dairy employee by then, would pick me up at 4:30, and I would run from house to house delivering milk, and then we would stock the grocery stores in town. By eleven we were done. In order to sell the oldest milk first, I was supposed to move the crates of milk stacked on top of each other from the back to the front of the refrigerated vault, but they were too heavy for me. Though he was getting on in age and somewhat heavy, he had to do it himself. Undoubtedly, he much preferred as a helper someone stronger, but since I was the boss's son he was not about to complain. I slept down in the basement that summer so I wouldn't disturb anyone getting up. I read, played tennis and Babe Ruth League baseball.

Despite denials, class was an issue that continually asserted itself. In the ninth grade I was attracted to a slightly chubby seventh grader who had coal black hair, dark eyes, and the reddest lips I had ever seen. Cora (not her real name) was being raised by her grandmother who lived behind the city jail and took in sewing. Though only 14, I was allowed to drive over to Cora's house and take her to the Dairy Queen. One night a carload of my friends came to spy on me as Cora and I sat out on her grandmother's front porch. I interpreted their presence as an indication that they found it titillating that I liked a girl who was so clearly outside our social circle. I would prefer to think their reaction didn't bother me, but it must have or I wouldn't remember it.

Every job I had when I was growing up was because of family connections. One summer I worked at Oursler Parts for Bob Blankenship, who was married to my cousin Allison. It was basically make-work, sweeping, putting up some parts and delivering orders. I did the same busy work at Mixon Bros. & Webb which sold farm implements and parts the summer before I went to college. I knew nothing about farming or cars.

Mainly I just stood around in the back waiting for something to do. While in high school, Sally and Harriet got legitimate jobs in Big Star Department Store in Marianna. It didn't hurt that when we first moved to Marianna we had lived next door to the Dooley's, and Jake had been on the school board with Mr. Dooley. The Dooley's daughter Anne was a family friend as well.

Class privilege opened different doors. At times I was the boss's son. Family members Sally and Voris (my brother-in-law) were my teachers in high school, and because they were liked and respected, I was a beneficiary of this reflected esteem. To Voris's credit, I didn't make the basketball team (he was the boys' senior high coach), though he didn't give me the D in geometry I deserved, but it was probably the longest C minus in the history of education. Temple would have been livid had he given me lower than a C.

Simply because Marianna was a safe place for me to grow up in didn't mean I didn't do stupid things. The dumbest was letting my friend Oliver Humphreys shoot at me with a bow and arrow. Bored out of our minds one summer afternoon, we walked over to McCullough's Hill five minutes from his house (Marianna is located on Crowley's Ridge, part of a geological fault line that extends to Missouri). He counted to twenty while I sprinted down the hill, zigzagging as I ran. An arrow landed a few feet away. It was another story that I didn't tell Jake and Temple though it did make it into the short story in *Tales of the South*.

I prefer to think that sheer tedium more than stupidity explained some behavior, but in my case I'm not so sure. In these days before women entered the workplace in large numbers, I think Temple was at times bored with the role of housewife. Jake eventually gave Effie and then later Temple some bookkeeping chores for Wonder State Dairy, but Temple wanted more to do. Still feeling inferior to her older sister and mother, Temple took a Dale Carnegie course in public speaking to boost her self-confidence. She got a job taking the 1960 census in Lee County. She liked talking to people. Temple's reaction in dealing with dissatisfied customers was always predictable. When someone would call and complain that Wonder State Dairy had gotten the order wrong, Temple would take offense but only once she got off the phone. She wasn't used to being talked to that way, especially by people whom she considered inferior. She would huff and puff but would hold her tongue while on the phone. One of her complainers was a Chinese woman which really scorched her. But she also was infuriated by calls from whites whom she considered not in her social class. She would have preferred that customers at least be apologetic for bothering her.

Throughout high school, class and ethnicity remained issues in our family. In her memoir, Sally recalls that Effie was fond of saying that we were descended from William the Conqueror, which prompted Temple to say, "Yes, and he was a bastard." Despite this rather backhanded gesture to social equality, neither Temple nor Jake were ones to break any barriers, and our parents never socialized with the Chinese adults in town or any of the Jewish families, though Temple claimed to like one of the wives. Unlike Mississippi, Arkansas had no law prohibiting Chinese from going to school with whites. Coming from an entrepreneurial part of China (the Canton region), Chinese families in the Arkansas Delta owned and operated "mom and pop" stores that sold a variety of inexpensive goods on the edge of black areas. Open early and late and on Sundays and holidays, their stores filled a niche for both the black and white communities. Their children always seemed to be working. A number of their children were excellent students and athletes and also popular. Jerry Fong, who was a year behind me in school, was elected president of the student body at T.A. Futrall. A warm and talented kid, Jerry, in those days, I don't recall, ever had a date while he was in high school. At school dances he was always taking pictures, clearly a way for him to be involved without putting himself or others in an awkward social situation.

Jerry and I became good friends in school (he was friendly to everyone and teachers liked him, too). My senior year he was the quarterback and I was the center on the football team. In *Blind Judgment*, I set the story in an eastern Arkansas town which is easily recognizable as Marianna. The murder victim is Chinese. It had once been thought that they would work for whites in the cotton fields, but soon they were setting up their grocery stores. There was a line socially most didn't cross and apparently didn't want crossed in that era.

In the summer in our neighborhood we played games outside at night like "kick the can" and other games that involved chasing each other. I could ride my bike to the Marianna library adjoining the "Community House" where I checked out books like *Lad, A Dog* by Albert Payson Terhune, once a famous children's author who died in 1942. "A collie down is not a collie beaten." I checked out books about boys in high school playing baseball and basketball. Though there was no law against it, blacks were not allowed to use the public library in Marianna.

Unquestionably, there was an innocence to my childhood that would find its way into my fiction. My best friend before I was ten was Sally Mixon, a year older. Louise and "Hal" Mixon, who lived two doors down from us, were the best friends of Temple and Jake. Their two other children, Kay and Lee, were comparable in age to Sally and Harriet. I call them the Carltons in *Blind Judgment*, and Sally was no tomboy, but she was a delightful companion. We made pipes out of acorns and matchsticks and pretended to smoke like our parents; we played with their snapping turtles in the vat in their backyard; Jake took us in the back of his truck to Wonder State Dairy for chocolate milk; on rainy days we played games in the attic of her house. I describe how one day in her bathroom we pulled down our pants and showed each other our microscopic genitalia and went back to playing. It was a friendship that has lasted all our lives.[17]

In 2013, my friend Lee remembered Marianna as "idyllic." But there is a catch to that memory. Lee forwarded a response he had made to a friend's granddaughter in New Mexico who was doing a school project on the South during Jim Crow. He says, "I had many personal encounters with segregation while growing up in Marianna, all of which are very embarrassing to me in retrospect."

As a nationally known water economist and professor, now retired from the University of New Mexico, Lee e-mailed me that while he "would occasionally ask questions, it never occurred to me to challenge the status quo." In his answers, he gives the standard litany of white privilege in that era: he was instructed by his parents to refrain from calling black adults "Mr. or Mrs." but to call them by their first names. In a summer job at the Lee County tax collector's office he made the mistake of asking a black man if he wanted to pay his poll tax (a routine question for whites), and was "told afterward that I was never to ask that question of black people."

In her memoir Sally writes while she was in high school that while riding around with a group of teenagers on "Locust Street" where "Lula Mae our ironing woman" lived, the boys "threw water balloons at the people who were sitting on their porches." Sally writes that while she didn't throw anything she "didn't stop them from doing it or say anything against it either." She writes that "she is very ashamed," and "I didn't like what they did, but I was a moral coward." Harriet recalls a similar experience. She recalls that she "didn't want to be there."

Though by the early 1960s I didn't throw water balloons or ride through black neighborhoods with anyone who did, I recall as an adolescent calling at least one black person on the telephone and asking if her refrigerator was running and that she should go catch it. Our actions were all about conformity and wanting to be accepted as part of whatever group we were in. However much our participation in such activities embarrassed us at the time or later, our actions signaled our commitment to white supremacy. When our class sponsor Mary Alva Burke in 1962 told us that our senior class play would be an old-fashioned minstrel complete with some students in blackface, no one objected, including me. This was five years after Central High School in Little Rock had become a national embarrassment and two years after the Student Non-Violent Coordinating Committee (SNCC) had begun its efforts to desegregate public facilities in the South, including Little Rock. For many years I thought that everyone in the senior class was required to take part in the minstrel, therefore making my participation less embarrassing. But there in the 1962 "Quill" yearbook is a photograph and listing of the 19 cast members out of our class of over 70. It was only then I began to realize how much I repressed my memories of my behavior regarding race.

White supremacy, among other things, meant in Marianna an ever-present two-tiered justice system. Two incidents in particular stand out in my memory. Both involved law enforcement: One day I was walking home from T.A. Futrall with Lee and Oliver, who both were two years ahead of me in school and obviously had more sense. We were playing "follow the leader," and when it was my turn, to try to impress them, I stepped out into Pearl Street and slapped the back fender of a passing car. Naturally, it turned out to be a state police patrol car driven by an officer named Otha Pace. Terrified I was going to jail, I told him who my father was and burst into tears. I ran home and still crying called Jake at work, telling him what I had done. Apparently, he never even received a call from patrolman Pace.[18]

Another incident involved my family. We were driving home at night from somewhere in Marianna when a car pulled up right behind us. Angrily thinking it was a car full of my sisters' friends, Jake wouldn't let the vehicle pass by swerving back and forth in front of it. In fact, it was a policeman trying to pull us over. I remember crying that night, too, because Jake had been so angry and the cop was furious as well. My memory is that one phone call to Hal Mixon, who was municipal judge, took care of the problem. Social class and a white skin could make these kinds of issues vanish instantly. White supremacy guaranteed that the status quo would remain in place for as long as we could control it.

Shortly before his death, I interviewed Arkansas State University historian Calvin Smith, who in 1970 had become the first African-American professor to be hired by that institution. Calvin and I never met while we were both growing up, though he lived only blocks from me in Marianna. He was a year ahead of me at the black high school. Though he had once been interviewed for the Butler Center for Arkansas Studies Oral History project, I asked him specific questions about his memory of white supremacy in Marianna. In an e-mail in 2008 he recounted that he witnessed the savage beating by a white policeman of an inebriated neighbor:

> *I was about twelve or thirteen...and knew he often got drunk on the weekends. He never bothered anyone, he just stumbled home and went to sleep. He was in front of his home when he was stopped by the police. He tried to explain he was at his home, pointing to his house, but the cop demanded that he get into the patrol car and when he refused he was brutally beaten with a blackjack. We, several kids in the neighborhood, could see the blood running down his head. He was forced into the patrol car and taken to jail. I felt sick throughout my body and have had little use for cops since that day and I have not witnessed any behavior on their part to change my mind/feelings. Adults were aware of the incident but said and did nothing.*[19]

Calvin also remembered an incident involving an encounter with a white girl about his age.

My mother was in [McCutcheon's Hardware] store to make a payment on a Crosley T.V. she had purchased. While I waited for her to finish her business, a white girl behind the counter where I was standing noticed my new class ring and asked if I was going to college. I said I did not know. She said she was going to Ole Miss or to Arkansas but had not made up her mind. At that point I felt the pressure of my mother's hand on my arm as she pulled me toward the door. Outside I pulled free and asked what was wrong. Protesting I had done nothing. When we got home I was told how in the past black men had been killed for being too friendly toward white women. A number of my friends told me that they had been told the same thing; subsequently I kept my distance from white women. I was a senior in high school...[20]

Calvin went onto say that his parents "were quite protective" but there was nothing passive about either of them. "They were well aware of segregation and burned under its burden and when they got the chance to fight the system they did with everything they had." At the same time he said that he had no complaints about his treatment by some of the whites he worked for in Marianna.

Somehow I did and didn't think of myself as "privileged" while growing up in Marianna, but there was little doubt of it even though Jake and Temple began to worry about money as time went on. We never lived like we were "poor," but vacations to Washington D.C. and Gulf Shores ended before I was ten. Before then Jake and Temple had built a new, spacious two-story house complete with basement, attic, and garage further north on Pearl Street, and it probably gave the impression that we were better off financially than we were. Though it didn't have the charm of some of the homes built before and after the turn of the century, with the new homes that would be constructed at that end of Pearl Street it was a good investment. Jake drove an Owens & Stockley truck to and from work, and the family cars in Marianna were Chevrolet and Ford until after Jake's death when Uncle David, a salesman for Balch Oldsmobile in Little Rock, talked his sister into buying an Oldsmobile—a Cutlass Supreme at that. It was more car than Temple needed, but Uncle David probably needed the money.

The combination of being spoiled and being a recipient of white male privilege made for a comfortable existence for me, whatever our resources. The summers before I had my mostly make-work jobs were some of my most vivid memories. By the time I would get up (Jake, always an early riser, was at work by seven) and come downstairs, Temple would have laid out for me the sports pages of *The Commercial Appeal*, and like a prince-in-waiting I would sit in Jake's seat while she served me a breakfast of hot tea, toast and bacon. For a reason still a complete mystery I had become a fan of the Cleveland Indians baseball team, and the summer I was ten I would turn to the box scores to follow that magical year when they beat the hated Yankees for the American League pennant by winning a record 111 games. After breakfast I went outside to play with Buttons and Bows, where I was greeted by the two black men working in Temple's flower beds. They called me "Mr. Grif," and I called them by their first names, "Newt" and "Andrew." Though employees of Jake's "concrete block plant," they served in any capacity we wanted.

Around noon I would take out their "dinner" to the back steps of the garage where they were permitted to eat. My squeamishness was a part of my make-up in ways that seem unbelievable. Temple and my sisters, who washed the dishes, claimed I avoided even drinking after myself. What this fear was about I don't know, but it carried over to race. It was with distaste that

I carried their dishes back into the house, fearful that I might touch their forks where their mouths had been. I may not have been the only child in our neighborhood to have these feelings. I don't remember which of my friends proposed this hypothetical, but someone did: "If you had to choose, would you rather suck snot from a dead nigger's nose or have sex with a woman?" At that age (around ten), these alternatives were somehow equivalent to a hideous death. The disgust and fear these "choices" engendered were part of some mythology that I was in the process of absorbing about race and sex. How they came together I don't know.

Growing up in Marianna in the Stockley household as one of two "pleasers," it would have been hard to avoid a sense of entitlement and I certainly didn't try. I loved both Temple and Jake and wanted to make them proud of me, and in that cocoon-like existence there wasn't a rebellious bone in my body. I was allowed to express physical affection for them in ways that were silly. As a child, I delighted in coming behind Jake while he was seated at the kitchen table and smelling his hair or what little he had left of it. He would shake his head in consternation and ask, "Does it smell good, son?" But he never stopped me from doing it. Both Sally and Harriet would throw a baseball and football with me. I remember wrestling with both Sally and Temple as I would later do with my daughter and step-son while they were about ten. When I leg-wrestled with Temple on their bed, she would call out to my father who was invariably in the kitchen trying to finish his breakfast, "Jakie, Jakie, he's killing me." He would answer mildly, "Don't kill your mother, son."

Sally writes that as a child she "absorbed racial prejudice in the same way that I breathed the air. In my early years, it never occurred to me that Negroes were human beings just like us or that they were oppressed and discriminated against."

My answer to how and why we privileged white Southerners

didn't believe "Negroes were human beings" just like us or that they were "oppressed and discriminated against" would eventually be that we rationalized our treatment of black people to justify our exploitation of them. It would take most of a lifetime to put in writing and occupies a modest place in the unending debate between some academic historians and much of the rest of humanity about how to read and not read the nation's racial history.[21]

It has only been writing this memoir that I learned that our Aunt Tissie had a very different attitude about race. Our cousin Allison recalls as a child going with her mother to visit Mrs. Anna Strong, principal at Robert R. Moton, at her home and hearing the noted black leader Mary Cloud Bethune when she visited Moton at Mrs. Strong's invitation. Anna Strong was admired for her intelligence, character and leadership in both communities. Aunt Tissie's feelings were not shared by her mother.

In Sally's journal, she writes that she had been told by our grandmother and aunt "never to call [Mrs. Strong] "Ma'am" or "Mrs." but simply to use her first name," if she came to the front door instead of the back, which, being Anna Strong, she did. When told this, Allison says that her mother never would have told a child to call Mrs. Strong by her first name. Sally has since agreed that Tissie was very sympathetic to blacks on the issue of civil rights and acknowledged she was mistaken. The Ourslers were exceptions, though for business purposes they were quiet about it. Allison says that her mother wrote a book about Marianna but was told by her husband, [Uncle Dubby] that if it was published they would have to move. Allison says her father, as a member of the school board, would not have voted to divert funds from the black schools.

Despite his status as a white businessman in Marianna, as noted, my memory of Jake is that he took no pleasure in commerce.

I recall a painful incident as a teenager which drove that point home to me. As mentioned, one of his businesses was distributing Sealtest milk to retail grocery stores. It was Christmas time, and he had hired me to give out samples of eggnog in a grocery store that sold his brand. I had thought I had pleased him when at the end of the day I had actually sold around 20 quarts of eggnog. He was furious, suspecting correctly that I had pestered the store customers, many of whom were poor and black, into buying a product they wouldn't have ordinarily purchased. I interpret this memory of his anger as an indication that he knew only too well how easy it was to intimidate black people and how poor many of them were.

Sally remembers a day in Marianna coming home from school for lunch and quoting one of her classmates, Charles Flowers, as saying, "My daddy says he will never let me go to school with niggers." In her unpublished memoir she wrote:

> *My mother and daddy, as prejudiced as they were, were not unkind or mean to Negroes. We had a Negro maid/cook at the time named Emma, and both my parents said, "Shh! Emma can hear you." For the first time in my life it dawned on me that Negroes had feelings that could be hurt, just as I had. I remember bursting into tears and running to Emma who was on the back porch, throwing my arms around her and telling her I was sorry. Like the kind-hearted woman she was, she soothed me and told me it was all right.*[22]

Whatever Emma thought, she didn't have a choice about displaying her real feelings if she wanted to keep her job. As a child I never doubted that blacks were human beings, but I never thought about their families or what their lives were like. I merely assumed their primary function in life was to do jobs for whites, and my family in particular. In this I was undoubtedly correct. Later when I was allowed to drive at 14, each week I took a basket of clothes to be ironed to "Lula Mae," who lived in a shack on a gravel street four blocks from our house. I could hear asthmatic wheezing inside before I opened her screen door. Where blacks lived then in Marianna formed more or less an outer semi-circle around homes owned by whites. You knew immediately you were in a black area because of the gravel streets, the lack of street lights, and the condition of the houses.

I asked Calvin Smith if "segregation was enforced by white violence or the threat of white violence or the knowledge that white violence would be the consequence [of] a serious violation of the customs of segregation in Lee County."

Perhaps thinking of his own experiences, he replied, "A combination of both." His parents had never told him, for example, about what had happened in 1919 just miles south from us in Phillips County. "If they were aware of the Elaine Massacre it was never talked about. I only became aware of the incident while in college doing research for a term paper and then it was only a casual reference."

In a book written about Marianna published in 1995, Calvin had told his interviewer, "The books that we got from Futrall [the white high school] had nothing on black history. To read them was to reinforce your nonexistence."[23]

There was, of course, a reason for that. As mentioned, white historians still did not write about Arkansas black history in a way that recognized what social scientists term "agency" or self-directed behavior. Nor did they seriously interview black Arkansans. If we couldn't have slavery, we demanded the next best thing to it—a black servant class and docile laborers who had learned that if they were going to stay in Arkansas and the South they had few other opportunities than to work for a pittance and accept white supremacy and all that it entailed. If I had begun to ask why we treated blacks as we did, I would have risked feeling anxiety, fear, shame and my popularity. I wasn't about to do that.

CHAPTER 4

"The All-Pervading Doctrine"

> "The all-pervading doctrine, then and now, has been white supremacy, whether achieved through slavery or segregation, rationalized by a professed adherence to state rights and bolstered by religious fundamentalism."[1]
>
> — James W. Silver, *Mississippi: The Closed Society*

"WAR IS PEACE," "Ignorance is Strength," "Freedom is Slavery," read the tortured litany of slogans in *1984*, George Orwell's world-wide bestseller published in 1949 and still in print today (65 languages and counting). First reading his dystopian masterpiece for a high school class, I was intrigued, like most people, by Orwell's description of a society in which history was constantly being revised to conform to the needs of those in power. My friend Larry Shurlds and I walked around school parroting Big Brother's slogans. That anyone would subscribe to the premises of such ridiculous sounding propaganda seemed outrageously funny to us, and yet Orwell's portrayal of a totalitarian world was too creepily real to do more than snicker. There are many obvious reasons why Orwell's book does not function as even a rough template for the South of that era, but there would come a time when I could imagine that Orwell had done research for his book in the Arkansas Delta. The racial "double-think" we practiced in Marianna and the rest of the South was stitched into every part of the culture so intricately it became part of our professed innocence. Over and over, we whites told ourselves, blacks, and the outside world that race relations were "just fine." The spying, informing, intimidation, torture, lies and numbing conformity presided over and enforced by the mysterious "Big Brother" seemed so over the top that no author could have imagined it all. We were told that Orwell had, in part, modeled *1984* on events in Nazi Germany and the Soviet Union. It didn't occur to any of us at the time that what Orwell was writing about applied to us.

Eighty-three and still practicing law at the prestigious Little Rock firm of Wright, Lindsey and Jennings at the time I interviewed him in 2013, Ron May, 23 years earlier, had written an unpublished memoir about his experience of working and living in Marianna for five years during the 1950s. Some years ago he had asked me to read it after I had spoken at the Butler Center for Arkansas Studies. Now writing my own memoir, I prepared for the interview by asking him to send me a copy to replace the one I had lost.[2]

Quite a bit younger than my parents, Ron did not remember Jake or Temple. Raised in Waterloo, Iowa, he had been hired by the Daggett law firm right out of law school. He had proved his enjoyment of things in the South by attending Vanderbilt in Nashville where he had been an editor of its law review. With his strong academic credentials one might be tempted to wonder why he would accept a position in a small town firm in the Arkansas Delta. Had he been more sophisticated about the interview process, he would have found more lucrative employment in an urban environment, but in fact, the Daggett firm represented clients far beyond the borders of Lee County and by the 1950s already had an outstanding reputation. When May was hired, the principals in the firm were Jimason Daggett, W.H. "Buddie" Daggett and John Daggett. They took most civil cases that walked in the door but soon developed an expertise in certain fields of law. The firm handled the affairs of Missouri Pacific in eight counties.

Labor law was another specialty after the National Labor Relations Act was passed. After he was hired by the firm, May would come to regard Jimason Daggett as "the single most versatile lawyer I've ever known." His cousin Buddie was widely regarded as an expert in "land, farming, estates and riparian rights."

What interested me most was what Ron had said about race relations in Marianna. Writing about some of his contemporaries in his social class, he explains:

> I think these decent white people in Marianna truly believed that "colored people" were happy with their "separate but equal" position in society and that decent "colored people" didn't really want to attend white schools and churches and parties. I suppose I should have taken offense at these delusions, but my own Midwestern upbringing wasn't really all that alien to such thinking.[3]

And besides that, Ron was trying to make a living and support a wife and child (later two) at a time when he "had very limited financial resources." Yet, he records in that time the presence of two different maids (Mattie followed by Betty) who walked several blocks to and from his house each day. Though he saw them five days a week, he didn't know anything about their personal lives, nor was he certain if he ever knew their last names. Ron writes that "every white household had black domestic help on a regular, if not daily basis," probably an exaggeration but many whites employed maids as he describes.

Succeeding as a lawyer at Daggett and Daggett meant following the rules of racial etiquette. After his first jury trial, Jimason Daggett told him he had done well, but "noted my calling our client a 'colored lady' when the expression 'colored woman' would have been more appropriate." Juries were all-white. He writes, "I never saw a black juror in eastern Arkansas while I lived there."[4] There were no black lawyers in Marianna at the time. May also noted the disparity in jury verdicts depending upon whether the plaintiff was black or white. He represented a black man who had been "hit by a truck while walking on a county road. He was badly bruised, his ear was cut off and he had a broken leg. His all-white jury awarded him a little over $900 for his injurie [sic]...a white man would have received five or ten times that amount."[5]

He writes that:

> [M]ost of my friends and associates (and all of the Daggetts) were significantly generous in a social sense. These were people like Clyde Andrews who served for many years as Mayor, and Mr. Jesse and Buddie Daggett who had both served on the school board. There were not professional do-gooders, and all of them were political conservatives. But they did feel a strong sense of social responsibility.

Though not naming names, he distinguishes his friends and colleagues from "The Bad People." "[T]hese immoral people I knew in Marianna couldn't have cared less about the lower social orders in our community. They voted against tax increases. They brutalized their own black servants and employees..."[6]

In my interview with him, I suggested that one of the reasons for the socially elite's involvement in civic affairs was that his friends and associates (as Jake had) were making certain that white supremacy would continue as it always had. He agreed with me and consented for me to state this in any book I would write.

May writes that he found Marianna "quite attractive" and he and his family were welcomed by his professional associates and others in his class. Hunting and fishing were the primary social activities for the men. He and his wife Naomi (nicknamed "Nonnie") became involved with St. Andrews Episcopal Church.

Playing bridge and visiting in each other's homes were standard entertainment for couples. At parties "drinking went on for hours. Even a simple dinner for a few friends was preceded by many rounds of drinks and followed up by many more."[7]

Despite his friendships, Ron missed intellectual companionship. Writing about Charles West who had obtained a doctorate in Philosophy from Columbia University but had returned home to Marianna to live the life of a planter, he writes, "In more sober moments Charles and I did sometimes carry on intellectual conversations, which was gratifying to me. I read a lot but had no one, other than Naomi, to discuss books with. Education wasn't highly valued in Marianna except to the extent that it prepared one for a profitable profession."[8]

It was only when I visited Ron in a rehabilitation center in Little Rock in October of 2014 that I saw his books on mathematics and philosophy (Wittgenstein) on a shelf beside his bed. About the least pretentious person I've ever met, he would have had difficulty finding that level of intellectual companionship in most small towns in Arkansas.

To get along in a small town in the South, you had to be careful about whom you offended, and the time Ron wasn't, he got into trouble. Naively, during the Little Rock school desegregation crisis he wrote a letter to Governor Orval Faubus criticizing him for defying a federal judge's court order to admit a handful of black children to Central High School in Little Rock. "To my surprise, people began turning away from me when I spoke bitterly about Faubus." His letter brought a visit to his office by John Daggett, one of the senior partners, who "said he was sorry I'd written it and that my outspoken opposition to Faubus could hurt me and the firm."

While it seemed to Ron that he was almost a minority of one in opposition to Faubus, there were a few other whites in

Marianna who disagreed with the Governor's action in calling out the National Guard to prevent black children from entering Central. Two of them were Jake and Temple, along with some of their friends. It must have been a matter of continuing discussion in our household, for I wrote a brief letter that was published in the *Arkansas Gazette* criticizing the governor for defending his actions during a speech he gave to a student council convention that I attended in 1961 (Figure 12, p.117). I complained that "he used the convention to make a campaign speech."[9]

Since there is no evidence that Jake and Temple approved of ending or even modifying segregation, their disagreement with the majority of whites in Marianna seems largely tactical, but there were other reasons for their disdain. Faubus reveled in his reputation as someone whom his enemies couldn't corner, couldn't pin down. Jake and Temple saw themselves as above all the sleazy deals politicians make, no matter how successful. More importantly, demagoguery was abhorrent to them. In 1952 they had supported Francis Cherry, a terrible politician who got nothing done in the Legislature but was perceived to be an honest man and someone who did not routinely pander to the lowest common denominator in the electorate. That Cherry did so in his run-off election loss to Faubus they seemed to overlook.

One way of measuring the impact of race in the Delta was by the absence of its discussion. African-American professor James A. Banks, a native of Lee County, who is credited with being the originator of "multiculturalism," writes, "Marianna and Lee County, Arkansas epitomized the institutionalized discrimination and racism that existed throughout the Deep South in the mid-1950s." Banks was in the eleventh grade in a segregated Lee County school when the Supreme Court handed down *Brown v. Board of Education* on May 17, 1954. He writes, "My most powerful memory of the Brown decision is that I have no memory of it being rendered or mentioned by my parents, teachers or preachers. In my rural southern Black community, there was a conspiracy of silence about Brown. It was completely invisible." He adds, "That system was never publicly challenged or questioned by Whites or Blacks. Black resistance to racism was deep but covert. Blacks wore a mask as they feigned contentment around Whites as their anger seethed below the surface—ready to explode."[10]

Implicit in his comments is that blacks felt they were powerless, and with that powerlessness and dependency came fear. There were no black judges, no black policemen, no blacks on the city council, no black legislators. James Banks' observations would prove correct, but it would be more than a decade before that explosion occurred. In the meantime, blacks coped as they had in the past. In a published essay on Marianna, sociologist Gordon Morgan, who would become the first tenured African-American professor at the University of Arkansas, noted the following:

> Colorism permeated southern life to such an extent that very many citizens thought and acted in terms of a hierarchy ranging from low status dark to high status white ... In Marianna the color leaders more or less accepted the facts of mass black poverty and did not try very hard to function against or undermine the official discrimination of the period.[11]

As mentioned, it was Ms. Anna Strong who functioned as the leader of the black community in Marianna and was recognized as such by both races. Morgan explains that working within the system of segregation she prepared black students to leave Marianna in order to get work. She was very much a force during my 15 years in Marianna though I would not be aware of her influence on black students until much later.

We carried on as if white supremacy would continue unchanged forever. Ron writes, "The people in Marianna didn't really regard these events [lynching and the Elaine race massacres] as relevant to them. When we heard or read of atrocities like the Emmett Till affair only a few miles away in Mississippi, it seemed to us as if Mississippi was a foreign country."[12]

Ron was, of course, speaking for whites. In effect, he acknowledges that our commitment in that era was to remain in denial about our actions and rationalize them. As mentioned, black residents in Marianna had no illusions about some whites' penchant for going off on them. But it would not be until the 21st century before a handful of native Arkansas whites began to acknowledge publicly and in detail the physical and emotional violence inflicted on blacks in everyday life in the state during the era of white supremacy. The publication in 2006 of *Crisis of Conscience: Arkansas Methodists and the Civil Rights Struggle* by the Butler Center for Arkansas Studies while I worked there was a little noticed watershed event in the civil rights history of the state. Though also containing essays by black members of the Methodist Church from all parts of Arkansas, it is the first-time published accounts of whites which resonate for me the strongest, for they detail not only the routine acts of viciousness perpetrated against blacks in the small towns of Arkansas but the often lifelong consequences to themselves and their families as a result of their efforts to bring even modest changes to race relations in the state. In a blurb for *Crisis of Conscience*, I wrote in part:

> *Until this book, white Arkansas Christians have been largely silent about their roles in the civil rights era during the tumultuous years of the 1950s and 1960s. In unforgettable vignettes, Methodists, black and white, confront the painful legacy of racism and white supremacy in their personal lives, churches and communities.*[13]

I would learn in *Crisis of Conscience* that not every white teenager in a leadership role in Arkansas had remained silent in this era. As a 15 year-old president of the student council in Van Buren in western Arkansas in 1958, Angie Evans had shamed the School Board during its integration crisis at a meeting in which she said, "We think it is only fair that the Negroes be permitted to attend the high school... If we don't object, why should anyone else? ... Have you thought what you make those Negro children feel like, running them out of school?"

Evans and others had taken a poll that showed most students didn't object to having a handful of black students desegregate the white high school at Van Buren in the western part of the state. In fact, desegregation had begun the year before, but the actions of Governor Faubus in 1957 in defying the federal government had prompted a strike by segregationists. Denying she had been "coached," by adults, she said, "I just don't think segregation is a Christian thing."[14]

Since reading *Crisis of Conscience*, I have tried to understand my failure to at least object to the minstrel performed at T.A. Futrall when I was a senior, in contrast to Angie Evans's vocal support of desegregation. She had acted without the support of her parents, and there would be a cost to her family financially and emotionally. Because of the on-going media attention given to integration in the state, her actions attracted national media attention and she received hundreds of letters from all over the country, most in support of what she had done. She has written she had taken seriously the words of two Methodist ministers who believed Christianity required a different response than silence. Obviously, there were differences in Van Buren and Marianna, namely the paucity of blacks in that part of the state, but speaking "truth to power" took courage and integrity. During those years I had no desire other than to conform. During a discussion with some older boys on the school grounds at T.A. Futrall about what was going on at Central High in Little Rock I was asked for my opinion. I responded, "They [blacks] just don't smell right," provoking the laughter and approval I desired.

I was involved in a far different quest. Probably my junior or senior year in high school, I read *The Fountainhead* and *Atlas Shrugged*, both novels by Ayn Rand, and, like many Americans, became immediately convinced that I had found the key to life. Government accomplished nothing but sucked the life blood out of any endeavor. The only thing that counted was rugged individualism. Selfishness was not only justified; it was absolutely necessary to live an honorable, moral life. The hero was a lonely but proud individual struggling against collectivism of any kind. Money was good; a great deal of money was even better and richly deserved. That was how progress occurred. If you were an Ayn Rand male hero, you got to fall in love and have great sex with a beautiful, equally heroic woman.

The philosophy of "Objectivism" contains much more gloss than the above, and its defenders, who have included personages as august as economist William Greenspan, would howl at such a description. Its emotional appeal was irresistible. Who wouldn't want to emulate lonely but brave geniuses who not only understood what was wrong with the world but did something about it?

Of course, I was hardly the prototype of an Ayn Rand hero. My entire life I'd had help from everybody and given advantage after advantage. Thanks to my parents, I expected to go to college. I wasn't a misunderstood genius. I was moderately successful in whatever I tried and was learning what not to try like math and science, music, art, or basketball or track. I was in no way a rebel with or without a cause. I hadn't had sex. I didn't smoke, drink or do drugs. In spurts, I tried to imagine my own path out of Marianna, but not because I disliked it or was unhappy. I couldn't imagine how I would make a living. I had no desire to follow Jake in farming or business nor did he encourage me. My sisters had become teachers. Maybe I would, too, but teach in college somewhere. Now, as a result of two books, I was being challenged to become some kind of creative outcast who would make the world safe for free enterprise and creativity.

In the meantime I had to finish school. Grades 7 through 12 were all in one building, and initially I lived in the shadows of my sisters. Sally was already in college, but teachers remembered her since she had been co-valedictorian. Harriet was a senior when I entered the seventh grade. In "Who's Who" at T.A. Futrall, Harriet had been voted "best figure" and "cutest." She was first-chair clarinet in the band and in competitive try-outs made first band at the state competition. By far a better athlete and the most talented of us, she made all-district in basketball and also played the piano. Sally had married at 20 and came back to Marianna to teach high school by the time I was in the ninth grade.

My junior year we learned that Jake had lung cancer. He had surgery in Memphis. He was told it had been successful but that he would need cobalt treatments. In fact, the doctor had opened his chest cavity and seen how far it had spread and closed him back up. Just as we pretended that nothing had occurred in Little Rock in 1957 that would affect us, now we colluded in the fiction that Jake wasn't dying. It was a year of ignoring the elephant in the room. Lee Brown remembers playing bridge in our house with me, Temple and Jake, and admiring Jake's stoic suffering. Looking back on this period I realize how much I have repressed those memories. There were days he couldn't go to work, and there were times that I had to help him get into the bathtub. On Thanksgiving Day in 1961, for the last time, we went out to one of the farms owned by Nannie and walked around with "Bertha," one of Button's and Bow's puppies. To say that we were hunting that day would be to totally mischaracterize what we were doing. It was the last time we went out together in the woods, and it was only for a short time.

T.A. Futrall had our annual Thanksgiving Day game with the white school in Helena that afternoon, and I had to be at the school by ten.

On Christmas Day, Temple routinely fixed a big breakfast that included something as exotic then as winter grapefruit. Sally and Voris were there. When Jake tried to recite grace or the "blessing," as we called it, "Lord, make us thankful for these and all Thy blessings," his voice broke and he couldn't finish it. In my memory Voris said the rest of it, and we got through breakfast. Jake was only 57.

On Valentine's Day 1962, he sent Temple to the store and called "Mr. Pee Wee" to come to the house immediately. He left a note in the kitchen that explained his decision to take his life. A recent visit to his doctor in Memphis had finally made it clear he was going to die from lung cancer. He acknowledged that somehow he had convinced himself that he was going to beat it. He said he loved us all and to take care of our mother. The note was stained from his own tears. Jake took his .22 pistol and shot himself. It was Voris who called me out of a student assembly that morning and told me. I never have once questioned his decision to take his life. He had begun to suffer in earnest, and it would only get worse with the time he had left. My reaction was typically male. I didn't cry and wouldn't for decades until I was reading aloud with my second wife *The Floatplane Notebooks*, a novel by Clyde Egerton. It involved a father who was taking care of his son who had come home from Vietnam a hopeless cripple and whose wife had left him. I burst into tears, and realized at that moment I was finally crying for my father.

Temple grieved terribly for Jake. Upstairs in my room the rest of the winter and into the spring and summer I could hear her sobbing night after night. They had truly loved each other during their 29 year marriage. Nelda Mitchell, a neighbor, recalled years later seeing them outside in the backyard at 358 Pearl hugging and kissing each other. My sisters and I remember very few arguments between Jake and Temple or even tension. If they fought, it wasn't in front of us. Like any relationship, it had its problems whether they fought or not. Truly a Wall in this regard, alcohol and Temple didn't mix. Temple couldn't hold her liquor while Jake could. Two shots of bourbon made a perceptible difference in her, and they drank most nights.

My uncle David had a major problem with alcohol, and at times it affected our lives as well. I was a junior in high school when I answered the phone late one afternoon and learned it was Uncle David who had made it to Forrest City on the bus from Little Rock and wanted to come for an uninvited visit. It was clear that he was drunk and had no money. Always eager to get behind the wheel, I volunteered to drive the 17 miles to pick him up. Temple put him to bed upstairs to let him sleep it off. He had promised to get up and leave the next morning because she was driving Jake to Memphis for one of his treatments. She must have given him some money, but instead of leaving he walked to Moye's Liquor Store and came back to the house and passed out in my parents' bed. Worse, he defecated on Temple's exquisite white bedspread.

Horrified, I called Sally who came over immediately. We took the bedspread to the cleaners and were asked if a dog had gotten on the bed. Enraged at Uncle David, we said, yes.

David eventually quit drinking and joined AA. It was impossible not to like him, because the older he got, the funnier he became, and perhaps because of his wretched experience with alcohol for so many years there was no pretense about him. After he sobered up and was working as a salesman for Balch Oldsmobile in Little Rock, he would come by and pick me up for lunch. All the while talking, he drove his car like a battering ram, bumping parked cars, signs, and curbs, seemingly at will. Whether his stories were true I didn't know and didn't want to know. Was he married five or six times? We would drive past some wooded area, and he would tell me that he bedded down some woman "right over there." One wedding may not have counted. Did he really man an anti-aircraft gun in his underwear while drunk in the Aleutian Islands in the Second World War during an attack by the Japanese? David and I had come a long way from the day he called me a communist. I've forgotten the reason. He meant that I was a socialist or something.

Despite his pledge, confidentiality was not his long suit, and in the course of a visit he would divulge the names of AA member after member, many of whom were among the elite of Little Rock. For a number of years at Christmas, my daughter Erin (Figure 17, p.119) and I drove out to his home in Saline County. Jean, his last wife, number five or six, had also been his second. Jean, quite a talented artist, was wonderfully kind and would give Erin a present, and we would take homemade cookies. They had one son, David, Jr., who was gay and an only child. When he died of AIDS, Jean, who was also a recovering alcoholic, was so distraught that she began drinking again after she had been sober for years. Uncle David did not, but my cousin's death was something neither got over.

Had I been a better athlete, I might not have ever started writing. Not making the basketball team meant I had nothing to do after school except eat ice cream and watch the *Mickey Mouse Show*. I and millions of other adolescent boys all across America drooled over Annette Funicello. I had played football since the seventh grade in junior high. After the season was over my junior year I went down to *The Courier Index* and asked Marvin Caldwell if I could cover high school sports. Since at that time *The Courier Index* carried no news about black people except for criminal activity, we both understood, of course, that I would write about sports at T.A. Futrall. There would be no pay, but he gave me a press pass which became my most valued possession for the next two years.

From the beginning, my by-line was on the front page almost every week during the school year, and nothing fed my ego like seeing my name in print. Midway through my senior year I asked Mr. Caldwell if I could write a sports column as well, which he ran on the inside pages. It was thin stuff, because I didn't have any idea what to write about. In those days sportswriters were complete "homers" anyway, and I had no intention of upsetting my brother-in-law and my friends on the team. I didn't get paid for the sports column either, but it was all good practice in getting my copy in on time which was appreciated by the publisher.

Since I was a pleaser all through high school, Betty Sue Kell, the wife of our head football coach, chose me without a tryout to play the role of Sheridan Whiteside in the Speech Class play, *The Man Who Came to Dinner*, because she said she knew that I would learn my lines and not wait until the last minute. There were others in the class who had much more acting ability, but she didn't trust them not to make her a nervous wreck. A couple of days before the performance I got visibly frightened during rehearsals and started forgetting my lines. She stopped practice and took me aside and calmed me down, telling me I was going to do fine. I was so grateful that I've never forgotten it.

Though I had little to offer in the way of actual leadership abilities, I was elected class president time after time and eventually president of the student council. It wasn't that I was the most popular kid in school. In fact, I wasn't at all. I never won anything in the annual "Who's Who" contest. At T.A. Futrall, once you won something though, you kept on being elected unless you were gracious enough to refuse the nomination and let someone else have a turn. There was precedent for that kind of behavior. In the class ahead of me, I was told, Gene and Jerry Elphingstone, twins, bowed out of races for that very reason. I wasn't that generous or didn't feel that secure with myself, obviously. As a senior, I was even elected co-captain of the football team with Chester Key (Figure 11, p.117), one of our best players, who was genuinely a nice guy and who was voted Mr. Marianna High School with Diane Palmer as Miss Marianna High School. I was not even mediocre as a football player and should have declined to run. Once I bragged that I never got hurt, and Voris, who also was the line coach for the football team, pointed out that I never hit anybody hard enough to get hurt. That hurt my feelings, but he was right.

My decision to run for student council president caused a rare backlash, and I was nearly beaten by David Ward who had never run for anything. David had been encouraged to run by a group of seniors who understandably resented the fact that the same people won election after election. It was the closest thing to a student revolt that ever occurred while I was in high school. Bill Owens also ran, but being the smartest boy in our class probably worked against him.

As mentioned, my family's disapproval of Faubus didn't prevent me from participating in a minstrel while I was serving as student body president in 1962. And it would be misremembering the conditions of my participation that has helped to convince me how much denial and other defense mechanisms have played a part in my own development. At least I didn't appear in "blackface," but was that anything my fellow classmates who did should be embarrassed about? Was ridiculing the dialect and speech of African-Americans an innocent activity for white Southerners in that era? It, of course, depends on how one defines "innocent." So long as we didn't allow ourselves to think about what was going on around us, we can claim to be innocent. The difficulty is that this was in the spring of 1962 and the Civil Rights Movement was in full swing in the South, including central Arkansas. Certainly, our senior class sponsor, Ms. Mary Alva Burke, who taught senior English and Latin and chose the play, would have said there was no harm intended, that on the contrary, it was just "good clean fun." As far as my own participation in the play, I prefer to think that I was glad I was only in the chorus, but in light of my memory's convenient rearranging of the facts, it would be quite a stretch to make that claim some forty-odd years later.

Photographs

Figure 2: "All Woman Wedding," (L-R) Harriet "Tissie" Wall (Oursler), Temple Wall (Stockley), Martha Turner (Hopkins), Jane Turner (Schrieber), Marianna, Arkansas, c.1917.

Figure 3: Effie and young David (left, in white costume), October, 1926.

Figure 4: Sally and Harriet at Whitehall, circa 1940.

Figure 5: Griffin Jasper "Jake" Stockley (left) and his life-long friend "Buzz" Land on camels in Egypt, c. 1930s.

Figure 6: Harriet and Sally at Whitehall, summer 1942.

Figure 7: Tissie with Governor Carl Bailey and the great-great granddaughter of John Patterson, *The Commercial Appeal*, Memphis, May 19, 1938.

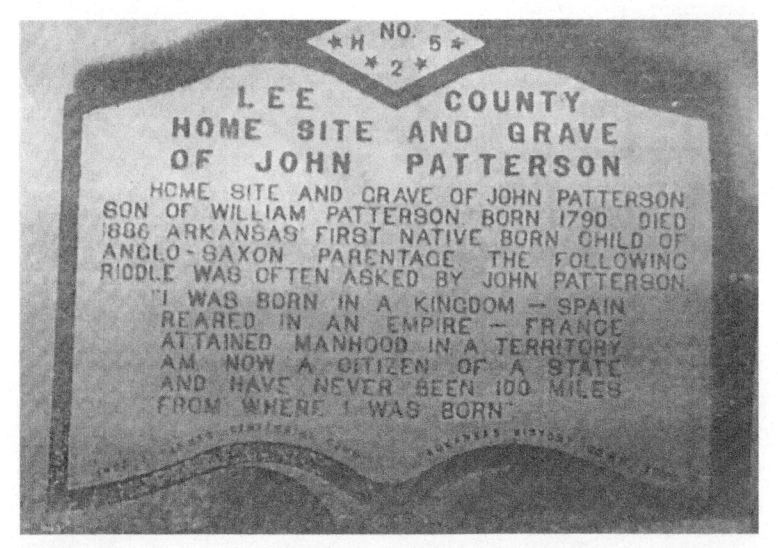

Figure 8: Arkansas Centennial Commission marker in memory of John Patterson at Patterson's Branch outside Marianna, *The Commercial Appeal*, Memphis, May 19, 1938.

Figure 9: Whitehall cotton plantation, Lee County, Arkansas, early 1940s.

Figure 10: "Jake" Stockley (right) with older brother Charles Stockley, early 1940s.

Figure 11: Grif (kneeling) with Chester Key, fall 1961.

Figure 12: Grif (left) with other state Student Council officers, 1961.

Figure 13: Return to Peace Corps job site in Colombia, January 1981.

Figure 14: Grif after Arkansas Supreme Court ruling overturning *Ex Parle King*, *Arkansas Gazette*, Jan. 21, 1987. Photo by Steve Keesee.

Figure 15: Grif with Horace Moore, Cousin Sally B. and Sam Moore at "The Island" (Corona, Tennessee), where young Grif had worked as waterboy to cotton choppers. Date unknown.

Figure 16: Harriet "Boo," Grif and Sally, c. 1990s.

Figure 17: Grif with daughter Erin and granddaughters, 2017.

CHAPTER 5

College—Let Me Out of There!

> Mr. Stockley, you can't write. You should change majors. Is there anything else you might choose that does not involve so much writing?
>
> — Advisor Dr. John Hemphill

WITH AN ADVERTISED annual price tag of more than $47,000 in 2013 and not quite 2,000 students, Rhodes College in Memphis, my alma mater, was fighting as a feisty middleweight in a no-holds-barred nationwide heavyweight Liberal Arts and Sciences competition for money, students, prestige and relevance. Despite a strong academic reputation and rating, Rhodes has traditionally had a difficult time establishing a national identity and turning out famous alumnae. On a prior website it claimed Abe Fortas, a United States Supreme Court Justice, and the actress Dixie Carter (both deceased) who became best known for her role as Julia Sugarbaker in the television series, *Designing Women*. Unfortunately, Justice Fortas resigned from the Court as a result of ethics scandals, and Ms. Carter ultimately graduated from the University of Memphis. In 1984, though it is said officially that the school changed its name to "Rhodes College" from "Southwestern at Memphis" to honor a former president, Peyton Rhodes, the more urgent motive was for branding purposes. Its trustees' hope was to attract wealthier and brighter students, some preferably from the east coast who would have fond memories of the school when they sat down with their tax lawyers to do estate planning.

During my time there in the early 1960s, Southwestern still strongly identified itself as a church-affiliated institution (Presbyterian) and received substantial financial support and students mainly from a conservative base of local and regional Southern churchgoers. Today, as the saying goes, when they tell you it's not about the money, it's about the money. But long before then it was also about religion, too, that old-time religion of the Bible Belt versus the modern world.

Sally writes in her memoir that Jake had probably planned for her to attend Southwestern the day she was born. It was Jake's beloved three-quarters sister Martha who personified the old-style Presbyterian believer and to whom Southwestern by reputation functioned as a godly institution where Biblical faith and education were merely opposite sides of the same coin. "Bomboo," as she was known by one and all in the family, was cherished by everyone who knew her. Twenty-two years older than Jake, she had an oldest sister's influence. When Bomboo, a strict teetotaler, came to visit, Jake and Temple didn't drink that weekend. She had married the brother of Kenneth McKellar, a powerhouse U.S. Senator from Tennessee whose political partnership with Memphis political boss Ed Crump was the stuff of legend. With his brother dead, it was probably Senator McKellar who helped Bomboo, who had two children to raise, one of whom with mental disabilities, get a job with the Juvenile Court in Memphis.

The difficulty for people like Bomboo was that Biblical scholarship and science, even in the South, as time went on, were not headed down the same path. As far back as the 1920s, Southwestern President Charles Diehl repeatedly ran into trouble with local Memphis Presbyterian ministers. According to

Rhodes Professor Stephen R. Haynes' *The Last Segregated Hour: The Memphis Kneel-ins and the Campaign for Southern Church Desegregation*, published by the Oxford University Press in 2012,[1] Dr. Diehl, with degrees from Princeton University and Princeton Theological Seminary, "had expressed doubts about the historical and scientific value of the early chapters of Genesis."[2] Besides the contradictions and inconsistencies of the creation narratives, all kinds of dicey issues presented themselves the more President Diehl thought about it. For example, he couldn't conceive of a philosopher as high-minded as Plato, who through no fault of his own was born before Christ, roasting in "undying hell." Exactly my sentiments as a member of the Marianna First Presbyterian Church, though I wouldn't have told you much about Mr. Plato. The unfairness of it all was a problem, to put it mildly. Any child with siblings recognizes injustice, even if *he* is spoiled rotten. *Rotten!*

With his concerns over Biblical inerrancy, President Diehl wasn't breaking any new ground, of course. The Scopes "Monkey Trial" in Tennessee in 1925, over the teaching of evolution in public schools, has remained famous because its heavyweight lineup of Clarence Darrow and William Jennings Bryan was so spectacular. Diehl, however, survived an effort to fire him because of the support of his trustees, not because they agreed with him so much as they wanted to avoid what they termed "sectarian" disputes. By the time I got to Southwestern, the fight over Christian fundamentalism was finished in the liberal academic community, not only to the dismay of Bomboo but also to many wealthy Southern Presbyterians in Memphis who had the means to support Southwestern financially. The question of what to replace it with and how to interpret the Bible in a modern world was a sticky question for theologians and ultimately religion professors who taught at Southwestern. By the time I enrolled in the fall of 1962, woven into the curriculum at Southwestern was relevant information, which, if followed to its conclusion, sorely challenged the meaningfulness in an increasingly scientific world of the Biblical description of a physical universe with a God "up or out there" and humans "down here" and a three-tiered cosmology of heaven, earth, and hell. In fact, this theological assault on Christian fundamentalism was well under way long before the 1963 publication of English Bishop John Robinson's controversial, run-away bestseller *Honest to God*, which popularized the views of theologians such as Rudolph Bultmann, Dietrich Bonhoeffer and Paul Tillich. We also read Karl Barth, Soren Kierkegaard, Reinhold Niebuhr and Martin Buber. Almost from the first day of class we could not avoid learning that throughout history, humankind, in a variety of settings and cultures, had traditionally explained cause and effect by the construction of creation myths which were remarkably similar to accounts in Genesis.

The "Man In Light of History and Religion" freshman course at Southwestern inspired by President Diehl probably seemed innocent enough with its sexist title in 1945, but it was a ticking bomb and would only ramp up as science and Biblical scholarship forced Christian theologians to come up with new thinking about how to believe in God in a world where science reigns and bears little resemblance to how humanity explained events 2,000 years earlier.

Though the sixties are regularly and profitably denigrated and/or praised by pundits as primarily a cornucopia of freedom, sex, drugs, and rock and roll, it bears remembering, as time passes, that a handful of theologians, including those already mentioned, were being taken almost as seriously as the Beatles in cautiously theologically liberal church-affiliated colleges throughout the country, including, of all places, the Bible-Belt South. Their influence was profound not only among elbow-patched, pipe-smoking professors and wool-gathering campus intellectuals but also among painfully earnest small-town boys and girls who were now wondering if we had been sold a bill of goods by our parents, preachers, and Sunday School teachers.

The continuing effort to package Christianity in terms of a God "up or out there," who, depending largely on your upbringing, is a "God in Three Persons" and/or who arranges for his son to be born of a virgin and performs miracles before dying and rising from the dead, was harder and harder to swallow. And we hadn't even gotten to the utter randomness of natural events. But if God wasn't "up or out there," where was He or She or It, and what on earth was our relationship?

Whimpering in the wilderness in the 1980s, I would write my own 163 page never published and unpublishable manuscript, a layman's lament against creedal orthodoxy, I titled, *The Half Believers*. By then I had begun to reread snippets of the books on theology I had read in college and others as I occasionally wandered in and mostly out of churches. But there was more to Southwestern than theology.

With its Memphis old-South, old money orientation in 1962, there was still a cocoon-like, genteel feel to Southwestern despite the creep toward theological modernity.

Located across the street from exquisite Overton Park, the school was, within my time there, occasionally known by the following ditty: "Southwestern by the zoo, where the girls are girls, and the boys are, too." This strong whiff of homophobia was stereotypical at the time and arguably sprang from jealousy of the school's deliberately snobbish and gentlemanly and lady-like image. The school's beauty alone would have made any student at Memphis State (now the University of Memphis) green with envy. Spiting the doubters of a resurrection narrative and rebirth, the campus every spring was a glistening emerald with matching

Gothic buildings, its majestic Halliburton Tower named after the once-famous explorer Richard Halliburton, and the glorious Fisher Gardens where graduation was held. Coats and ties were required for dinner.

Well out North Parkway in those days in Memphis we were insulated from the reality of urban life and black poverty as much as we wanted to be, or were, until the advent of the Civil Rights Movement. If you wanted to show off your skepticism, you could argue this theological thrust toward modernity was simply an intellectual exercise on the part of our professors. A skeptic might even imagine all this rigorous handwringing was an effort merely to achieve intellectual respectability in a region of the country better known for its football teams than theological trendsetting. Whatever the motives of our professors, only a few students had the will, confidence of their convictions and fortitude to convert intellectual theory into some kind of action, and I wasn't one of them.

Professor Haynes traces the involvement of a handful of Southwestern students, then all-white, to help Movement blacks in Memphis desegregate a few handpicked, lily-white Presbyterian churches. One church where efforts were made repeatedly was Second Presbyterian Church (SPC) in Memphis, one of the richest, and before the advent of mega Evangelical churches, one of the largest congregations anywhere in the South.

Its church fathers did not take kindly to the sight of young black activists seeking entry, especially if they were paired with Southwestern students. "Second Pres" ratcheted up the pressure by threatening to withhold its generous financial support of Southwestern. At a tense meeting in 1964, President Peyton Rhodes responded bravely to the trustees by famously saying, "The College is not for sale."[3] While the President's unequivocal statement for all practical purposes ended this particular conversation, it was not a conversion moment for Rhodes, who as Haynes generously understates, "was not generally viewed as an advocate of social change."[4]

Nor, three months out of high school, was I at this point in my life. Ready or not, in my first weeks on campus in the fall of 1962, the South was beginning to implode. Civil rights pioneer James Meredith was insisting on desegregating Ole Miss, and President John F. Kennedy called in federal marshals (instead of regular U. S. Army troops as his predecessor Dwight D. Eisenhower had done at Little Rock) to make it happen. On campus, Temple had just unpacked her bags and would tell the story that a man had been killed outside her window at the Alpha Delta Pi sorority house during the turmoil.

Notwithstanding Temple's penchant for making even a good story better, two people did die in this latest effort to enforce the equal protection clause of the Fourteenth Amendment. At Southwestern there were few minorities of any kind then, and those who wound up on our campus seemed to be from European countries, meaning they looked just like us but had more charming accents.

At Southwestern I was a non-entity. Accustomed to being recognized as a leader, I wasn't even in the follower category. Short (I had quit growing in the tenth grade), I was a terrible dresser and haven't improved. My sister Harriet had tried unsuccessfully to get me to buy some clothes that would keep me from looking like a refugee from deep inside the Soviet Union. When at the beginning I nerved myself to approach the prettiest girls at mixers, I could see the panic in their eyes. God, please don't let him come over here. Nice Southern girls, a couple were too polite to lie and agreed to go out with me one time. The kindest was a lovely girl from Pine Bluff, Arkansas, named Kay Willis, who would marry Bill Allen, the president of our freshman class. From Brinkley,

32 miles from Marianna, Bill, smart, likable, with a good sense of humor, would go on to represent the state of Arkansas and Governor Bill Clinton in a long-running school desegregation case featuring the Little Rock School District.

I took refuge in sarcasm that was intended to be humorous but invariably wound up hurting girls' feelings. I distinctly remember two girls (I won't embarrass them by mentioning their names) in college who lightly slapped me out of exasperation and another who burst into tears during my efforts to impress her. I can remember calling a girl on the phone for a date and being given the hardly original excuse she was planning to wash her hair that night. It took most of a lifetime to realize that my sarcasm was a form of passive-aggressive behavior instead of humor.

Social life revolved around the fraternities and sororities. My friend Lee was a Sigma Nu, and it was due to his influence that I got an invitation to join the "Snakes." Liked and respected because of his fundamental integrity and decency, not to mention his world class brains, Lee pointed out my high school accomplishments to his "brothers" and that was enough. It was my only "bid," and I gratefully took it.

Fraternities and I were not a marriage made in heaven. Very soon I seriously considered "de-pledging," having been turned off by the total rejection by all the Greek fraternities of my roommate. I hadn't known Mike (not his real name) before we were assigned to room together but soon found him to be a gentle, sweet and thoughtful soul whose effeminate manner was a neon sign. Mike was bright, studious and made good grades and would have worked himself night and day for any group that would have taken him. He was clearly crushed and humiliated when he didn't receive a single bid. Not used to seeing this kind of emotion in a male, I found it painful to be around him, and it made me dislike even more the ridiculous exclusivity of the system. He eventually joined the "Independents" which I wish I'd had the guts to do or not join anything at all. I was told by my sisters that if I "de-pledged," it would hurt Temple since she was a housemother of a sorority, so I didn't, since she was paying for it. The truth was that I was too insecure to quit. After our freshman year I would occasionally see Mike on campus. He seemed to be doing fine. Then, when I was in the Peace Corps, I would learn that he had committed suicide while in graduate school at the University of Texas. Today I still believe it had to do with the way we treated gays in that era.

Whether he was actually gay, I would never know. Though Southwestern was supposed to be an institution where people were above this sort of thing, harassment of guys who were suspected of being "sissies" occurred. Since nobody was out in those days, all it took was for somebody to act in the least bit effeminate to arouse suspicion. One night in my dorm guys somehow flooded the room of a boy who was assumed to be homosexual. I still remember the panicked expression on his face. Intimidated, I don't recall doing anything to stop the harassment.

Nice guys finish first, at least once in a while. Lee would marry Ann Autry, whom he had met his freshman year. The daughter of a successful Little Rock heart doctor (for many years chief of staff at St. Vincent's Hospital). Ann, who has a dry sense of humor and is kind and bright, would prove the perfect wife for Lee and he the perfect husband for her. At last count they had been happily married half a century. I later became the godfather of Dana, their eldest daughter.

Parents got their money's worth in those comparatively low tuition days. Southwestern was a serious environment. It was a jumping off place for the mostly white upper-middle class students who were going into the ministry, med school, law school and graduate school. People studied hard, and so did I, but usually with only modest results. After taking placement tests, I was consigned to what we would call the "dumb" English class my freshman year. It was taught by the Dean of Men and seemed to be full of football players, which at 150 pounds of soft dough I had no intention of trying to be. Dean Diehl's father had been Charles Diehl, the president of the college, but if his son had ever wanted to follow in his footsteps, he didn't seem disappointed or bitter by the time he taught me. A paper of mine he seemed to enjoy was my description of having a blind date gotten for me by the fraternity to go to a dance on top of the Peabody Hotel. These dates for people like me were perfectly nice pledges who had been passed over by the more popular guys. It was humid and hot as only Memphis can be in September. My date was as chubby as I was short. On the dance floor our combined sweat was like an unending lava flow, but gamely we kept at it, for we knew we would have to make more conversation if we stopped, and we had exhausted our quota well before we arrived. The pressure to pretend to enjoy blind dates was immense. No one had to tell us that we were the left-overs or that we should be grateful for having been "fixed up." Finally, the night ended. Though I expected to see her almost every day afterwards, we became invisible to each other until I was about to graduate two years later, having gone to two summer sessions at Memphis State. But she smiled and we greeted each other warmly as if we had survived the Bataan death march together.

The second semester of my senior year I actually had a girlfriend for the first time since high school. It was hard to believe. Lynn McDow was sweet, smart, pretty, popular (vice-president of the Tri-Delts) and for some reason responded to my sense of humor at the library where we often studied. She got over it, but while it lasted, it did wonders for my self-esteem, for the intervening years for me at Southwestern had been at times embarrassing, even humiliating. A meeting my sophomore year with my academic advisor, Dr. John Hemphill, had vanquished what little confidence I had. He taught the American history course that was required of all international relations majors. He told me bluntly, "Mr. Stockley, you can't write. You should change majors. Is there anything else you might choose that does not involve so much writing? What about Spanish? I see you made a B. Maybe you should major in it." In other words, get the hell out of here.

Obviously, I had made a terrible mistake in following Sally to Southwestern. Near tears (maybe I cried), I called her and told her Dr. Hemphill's opinion of my writing. Since she had taught me ninth grade English and had me in a course called English Composition my junior year where we had read novels like *Franny and Zooey* and *1984* and wrote papers, Sally didn't think I was a terrible writer, but, after all, I was her brother.

A sick puppy with his head and tail dragging the ground, I trudged over to see the head of the Spanish department. Understandably, he was not eager to encourage a reject from another professor. Despite my B in his class, I had a terrible Spanish accent (a marvelous Southern accent though—every syllable that came out of my mouth was drenched in corn pone). There wasn't anything I could do except finish out the semester. Determined to graduate in three years, I was taking 18 hours both semesters that year. As it turned out, the only C I made that semester was from Dr. Hemphill. Uncharacteristically, I had made two A's, one in English and one in political science, and the rest B's. When I told Lee my grades, he predicted that once Dr. Hemphill saw how well I had done in my other courses, he would give me a B the next semester, and he was right. I showed him my grades and told him I was sticking with international relations. Whatever respect I had for professors took a hit that semester. There would come a time when I would appreciate how subjective the experience of grading students was, but there would also come a time when I dearly wished the man were still alive to eat his words.

I had convinced Temple that I could save her a whole year of tuition and room and board if I went to Memphis State for two summers since it was much cheaper than Southwestern. I had no desire to get a job and stay in Marianna during the summer.

Fortunately for me, then at Southwestern you could take Latin or Greek and avoid taking math. I'd had two years of Latin in high school and knew I could pass it. I couldn't avoid a science credit, so I took zoology and botany at Memphis State during the summers, along with other courses that would give me enough hours to graduate in three years. Zoology was a disaster. Looking through a microscope with contact lenses was seemingly impossible for me. My contact lens would invariably roll out on the floor. With gritted teeth, the professor said, "Mr. Stockley, if I have to come back and adjust your microscope one more time..." He didn't finish the sentence. We were supposed to be making drawings of what we saw in the microscope for our notes for the final exam. Mine looked like a bunch of squiggles sketched by a two-year-old no matter what I saw through the microscope. Another assignment was to dissect a fish. When the professor came around to check mine, he shook his head in disgust at the mess I had made and told me to go partner with the black girl behind me. Her fish was perfectly dissected, and she was very kind to me. After I made a D (maybe it was an F) on the first exam, Harriet asked her high school and life-long friend Rita Dickey, who was living in Memphis, to tutor me. Were it not for Rita, I would still be in that 7:30 a.m. classroom choking on the smell of formaldehyde. I got out with a C. My poor partner behind me flunked the classroom portion of the exam. Had she been given my advantages, she would have passed.

The rest of my intellectual experiences at college, whether at

Southwestern or Memphis State, were generally enjoyable. Among the highlights, I took philosophy and a Spanish literature course at Memphis State. Dr. Charles Biggers had taught philosophy at Southwestern. My Spanish professor, a Mr. Brewer, was also an excellent teacher, proving to me that I could have gotten a perfectly good education at Memphis State where Harriet graduated. Being the favored male, I got to go where I wanted.

Since she had made better grades in high school, Harriet would rightfully feel slighted that she wasn't given the chance to go to Southwestern.

The reason I majored in international relations was part of a fantasy that had to do with the kind of unwarranted arrogance that comes with a spoiled, privileged existence. I thought I could become a Foreign Service Officer until I flunked the written exam given by the government my senior year. Though I could have taken it again, I never would have passed it. And even if I had, I wouldn't have gotten past the oral interview. I had flunked every part of the written test. I was too embarrassed to admit that I had taken it and failed so miserably until I found that other people much brighter than I hadn't passed it either.[5] I knew a couple of people from Southwestern who did, but intellectually I wasn't in their league. Early on, it had become obvious that I was not going to set the world on fire socially, politically or academically at Southwestern. It was all a badly needed reality check, but there were still niches that white male upper-middle class privilege made available to students like me who occupied a distinctly second tier status. One of the benefits of growing up in white-ruled Marianna had been, as mentioned, the construction of two tennis courts that A.L. Whitten, the superintendent, an outstanding athlete in his day, had placed in T.A. Futrall's budget, obviously hoping his sons would become proficient. In the land of the blind, the one-eyed man is king, and it was a sport I played early and often with Bruce, his son, and a few other kids like Lee and Jerry Fong. I attribute my own mediocrity after so many years to never having been taught correctly as a child, but that is the excuse of the ungifted. Still, by the time I got to Southwestern, Lee and I both made the tail end of Southwestern's tennis team.

Competing at a NCAA Division Three school that gave no athletic scholarships, my freshman year Lee and I played on a team that went zero and fifteen. Some members quit as the season progressed and we got to play in a few matches. I would play the next two years, never higher than five or six. Derrick Barton, our coach, told me never to follow my serve into the net to hit a volley or the ball would hit me in the back of the head. It was a joke, but I got it. Soon realizing my skills were limited to trying to become a human backboard, Coach Barton gave up trying to teach me and told me just to try to get the ball back any way I could. Tennis generally gave me what little identity I had at Southwestern, plus something to do other than study. Some of the students (including Sally seven years earlier) had jobs on campus, but that was not seen as necessary for the boy king. The hoity-toity nature of the sport was evidenced by the fact that my first two years we practiced and played our home matches at the exclusive University Club in Memphis where Derrick Barton served as the tennis professional.

International relations would have been a totally fascinating major at Southwestern during my time there had there been more professors like Dr. David Amaker, an old-school Mississippi gentleman in his sixties who had been educated at Princeton and was a Rhodes Scholar at Oxford. Even more impressive was the fact that he had been a translator at the Versailles Peace Conference in 1919 and had never stopped dreaming of what might have been had not Woodrow Wilson collapsed with a stroke and the United States not retreated into isolationism. Dr. Amaker's course began with the Pax Romana and was interspersed with balance of power theories that made perfect sense. He was a southern Henry Kissinger with his stories of realpolitik, and yet Dr. Amaker, like no one else I've ever heard before or since, made world peace sound plausible and led you to believe that with the right people in leadership positions a world government was perhaps not right around the corner but definitely an achievable and logical dream of rational human beings. It was in his class that I heard of Esperanto, an invented universal language that, if taken seriously, would connect us all. But that seems too easy a solution and puts too many people out of business.

Of course, today the idealistic strain that was a part of Dr. Amaker's course about global politics would be a howler in the hands of the right comedian, but this man, so buttoned up and formal and correct in class (he seemed as serious as God), would have had the last laugh had he been inclined to cynicism. Global warming hadn't occurred; nuclear weapons weren't lying around for the taking after the Soviet Union collapsed; conflicts over scarce global resources were not even nightmares; and technology with its "Big Brother" surveillance was still on the funny pages with Dick Tracy's two-way, Skype-like wrist watch.

The Department of International Relations, then in its infancy, was then chaired by Dr. David Likes, a former colonel in the Air Force. In time, the Department would grow and become a major sell to prospective students, but in my day we met in the same building that housed the gym. It seemed to me that Dr. Likes saw his main role as getting his students into graduate school with good fellowships. There was nothing wrong with that. It made Southwestern look good to be able to demonstrate that it was sending its charges on to graduate schools and who knows, maybe lives as future secretaries of state or CIA operatives. For our senior seminar, Dr. Likes had us read *New York Times* articles about southeast Asia and the United States' growing involvement there. As someone who was hot and cold about the Vietnam War, I began to realize that in the vernacular of the day that compared to Dr. Likes, I was a "dove" and he was a "hawk." I perceived correctly that I was being steered onto the B list of graduate schools in international relations. Still feeling entitled, I wondered if I received just a B in an all-important senior seminar because I was somewhat "wobbly" on the Vietnam War, as England's Margaret Thatcher would one day famously warn George Bush over Iraq. The reality was that I just wasn't as good a student. Still, Dr. Likes would come through for me with a $2,000 fellowship in international relations to the University of South Carolina graduate school, which was reputed to be notoriously conservative.

Though I would have gone on to South Carolina, it would have been a disaster. By my senior year I had begun to have a different understanding of the world. Until then, still smitten with the philosophy of Ayn Rand, I had joined the Young Republicans, but quit going to meetings in 1964 when I found I was the only person voting in a mock election in favor of the Public Accommodations Section of the 1964 Civil Rights Act, which required whites to serve blacks in restaurants. I hadn't realized it, but I was becoming a liberal Democrat. John F. Kennedy had inspired me with his call for Americans to ask what we could do for our country and not what we could do for ourselves. It was hard to explain why Kennedy's enthusiasm was so infectious to some Southerners, but it was. In fact, it may not have been all that complicated. Probably, like a number of people, I was starved for a politician who seemed to care about making the world a better place for everybody. Orval Faubus had embarrassed the state, and most everything that was coming out of the white South had shamed the nation and some Southerners as well. I wasn't so naive that I didn't know that Anti-Communism was the beginning and end of American foreign policy, but surely there was more to it than the out-of-control military industrial complex that Eisenhower had warned about and an endless obsession with an ideology and empire that offered its people so little. Even more important in changing my ideas was Lyndon Johnson's commitment to civil rights after Kennedy's assassination. As he amply demonstrated on more than one occasion, Johnson's crudeness could make a hog wince, but his willingness as a Southerner to make civil rights legislation a reality was unprecedented, and only he had the political skills to accomplish it. In the summer of 1964 I watched on television as Johnson told the country:

> *The reasons for racial discrimination...are deeply embedded in history, tradition, and the nature of man.... But it cannot continue. The Constitution, the principles of freedom and morality all forbid such unequal treatment.*[6]

This was a Southerner talking to other Southerners, and in a commencement address at Howard University in June, he had said that poverty in the black community was caused by "the devastating heritage of long years of slavery; and a century of oppression, hatred and injustice." This unending poverty reminded African-Americans "of their oppression. For the white they are a constant reminder of guilt."[7]

Lyndon Johnson's words about race relations delivered directly to the American people were as unprecedented as they were unwelcome to a sizable minority of his audience. No president had talked so movingly and candidly about racial guilt, nor has one since. While an overwhelming majority of white Southerners wanted no part of Johnson's message, I became convinced he was right. It was certainly not his delivery or his personal charm that made the difference. Indeed, his lugubrious, mournful tone and his hangdog look stood in such contrast to his handsome and eloquent predecessor it was almost laughable. Civil rights was a moral issue not because the president had said it was, but because he was right. I didn't have the courage or inclination to do anything but silently agree that summer. Meanwhile, white and black college students were coming South to join "Mississippi Freedom Summer" to help register blacks to vote. One of the major regrets of my life is that I wasn't part of the civil rights movement. Lee and I have corresponded by e-mail about the impact of the civil rights movement on our lives. Lee worked with other student leaders to have James Meredith invited to speak on campus in 1963, a decision that was reversed after Kennedy's assassination. He and others allowed three black musicians to use their rooms at the Sigma Nu house when the Lorraine Motel in Memphis had no vacancies and they needed a place to stay. Had the fraternity or administration found out, there well could have been repercussions, but he "concluded it was the right thing to do and didn't worry about it further." Of course, these were small gestures, but they were necessary steps. He writes, "I began reaching out more in graduate school, and we marched with Jesse Jackson in Indianapolis, but it was the Vietnam War that really made me active. At the same time, I'm convinced that the civil rights movement changed my life by demonstrating the reality of injustice and the possibility of change."

Those years were genuinely a time of hope. I had been a sophomore when Kennedy was assassinated, and like almost every American over a certain age, remember exactly where I was when I heard he was dead. Mr. Lowery (he did not have a doctorate) was a beloved political science teacher at Southwestern. His conservative philosophy fit me perfectly at the time, and yet I think everyone loved him whatever their political orientation because he took our government so seriously and conscientiously. Someone came in the classroom and told him in the middle of his lecture. He passed the information to us and stopped for a long moment and looked down at his desk. I don't know whether he was praying or what. Then he resumed his lecture as if nothing had happened, which seemed exactly the right thing to do. There was not the rabid hostility and condescension between liberals and conservatives then. When my political philosophy shifted decisively in 1964 I didn't look back on Mr. Lowery's class with disdain or contempt. I had learned a great deal in his class and valued my time there.

As it turned out, Lyndon Johnson was only beginning. He pushed through Medicare and Medicaid. He said he wanted to create the "Great Society" by declaring a "War on Poverty," and use some of the resources of the United States to create equal opportunities for the poor. The result was a plethora of programs and legislation, including, but not limited to, Head Start, the Job Corps, Community Action Programs, and Legal Services for the Poor, where I would work for 32 years. But first I had to go save the world.

CHAPTER 6

Me Not Talk Pretty, EVER

As people walked by I think they were so shocked that I was doing some of the actual labor instead of standing around like a boss that the word got around fast, and eventually the men showed up to work.

I HAD BEEN in the Peace Corps in Colombia a few months and was going through the motions, I suppose, to be able to say that I had been in the Peace Corps.[1] Had I been an actor (and I was acting at that point), I would have been rightly accused of "phoning in my performance." It hadn't been until the flight to South America with 70 of my fellow trainees who were assigned to do rural community development that I began to face the prospect of spending 21 months in a Third World country where I didn't really speak or understand the language.[2] We landed in Bogotá and that morning a few of us got out to look around and went inside a shop near the hotel. I started speaking English, and one of my friends had to yell at me, "Grif, get a grip! He can't understand you." Was I already experiencing culture shock? Decades later when David Sedaris came out with his book about his adventures in speaking French, *Me Talk Pretty One Day*, I laughed until I cried. But as bad as my Spanish sounded to Colombians—even after I had become relatively fluent I could see them trying not to sigh when I spoke in public—at first it was *understanding* Spanish that flummoxed me. I could pick up nouns, but consonants and verbs on the northern coast where I worked sometimes disappeared into the ether before making contact. Some people had an ear for languages, and then there were the rest of us. I not only had no ear, I didn't have much of a tongue either. I used my eastern Arkansas Southern accent as an excuse until I met one of our architects from Jonesboro, who should have sounded as awful as I did if my theory was correct, which it obviously wasn't. Bill Booth sounded like a native speaker. I could translate written Spanish into English because I did well in grammar; writing it was more difficult. A fall-back excuse is my life-long lisp of certain letters that emerge totally mangled, especially over the telephone. "Yes, Chris." "No, no, my name is Grif." "Oh, right, Chris." *Whatever!*

Nor did I have any meaningful survival skills. I had never cooked; I didn't know how to do simple household repairs. I never had cleaned anything in my life except Jake's shotgun and had nearly amputated my own foot with it. Cleaning was what Temple or my sisters or maids did. There were definitely some moments in Colombia that tested my legendary squeamishness. I opened my suitcase one day to discover that a mama rat had chosen it as a maternity ward. Attempting to escape was half a dozen or so of her decidedly unattractive offspring, none of which, I'm not sorry to say, were destined for a long life. Later, trying to sleep in a hammock in a different job site, I would lie awake nights hoping the rats scurrying across the rafters wouldn't choose to dive-bomb me. Crossing a ditch once near my house in the town of Plato, I nearly stepped on the biggest snake I would ever see outside a zoo. The fact that it was dead has never closed that memory bank.

How did I cope? Like any good Southern boy and the volunteers before me, I had a cleaning and laundry lady. Out of my hundred dollars a month "pay," I gave Ernestina a few pesos a week to do my laundry and clean the house. She wasn't always very thorough, but she wasn't working for the most demanding or fastidious employer. If she got the "big pieces," that was enough for me. The exchange rate was 16 to one, so $100 a month went a long way. Peace Corps volunteers were supposed to live like people in the host country. Since I've always been pathologically cheap, living as a poor person was no problem. Was I exploiting Ernestina, who, by the way, was very dark-skinned? Had I been even remotely sensitive to the situation, I would have appreciated the irony. Truthfully, labor relations seemed the least of my worries. On paper I probably looked normal. But who on earth would think I was capable of helping anybody in "real life"? I had fooled the trainers at Albuquerque, but it looked like in Colombia the jig was up.

Howard, my Peace Corps "leader," had gotten me settled in. By training an architect, for some reason Spanish rolled off his tongue. A tall, good-looking guy who radiated competence and confidence, he had made me feel better by admitting he, too, had flunked the Foreign Service exam. There were so many volunteers in Colombia (over 500 at that point) that the best were assigned to supervise the rest of us—get us moved in, help us open a bank account, and walk us through the activities of daily living in our job site that were complicated by language and perhaps culture as well. Because volunteers cycled in and out every two years, these leaders would change over time. They were provided a Jeep and traveled to our job sites to check up on those of us assigned to rural areas. I was always glad to see them, even when I melodramatically imagined they were coming to see if I was turning into Kurtz in Conrad's *Heart of Darkness*. There was status attached to these positions, but over time I began to feel that perhaps volunteers were being asked to give up the kind of day-to-day experiences they had joined the Peace Corps to have. Still, they performed a valuable function in a mid-level management sort of way.

Perched at the top of the supervisory structure over rural

community development volunteers in Colombia for most of my 21 months was the international aid agency CARE, which had the contract administering our program. Equipped with Master's degrees in international business from the highly respected Thunderbird School of Global Management, the CARE administrators were trained professionals in community development. As important, they were enthusiastic about what we were doing and spoke fluent Spanish. My supervisor, Ron Burkard, personified CARE's philosophy: if you want to help somebody, don't give him a fish, teach him how to fish. At home in a foreign culture, he made it all look easy without an ounce of condescension, a true role model for me and others. Decades later, I would visit him in Oklahoma City where he had become head of World Neighbors, which has the same philosophy as CARE.

Being spoiled rotten and a privileged white heterosexual male had finally caught up with me. I was about to turn 21 but might as well have been seven. But "fake it 'til you make it" was the one course in which I had excelled. Before I left Marianna, I had agreed to send articles back to *The Courier Index* about my training and experiences in the Peace Corps. Temple, my cheerleader as long as she lived, saved the copies, and like Effie before me, I made sure that I sounded like I knew what I was doing. Reading over the articles and the report of a speech I gave when I returned from Colombia, I wince at how superior and judgmental I sounded. It would be nice to believe that we rural community development volunteers had no egos and were somehow a unique breed of selfless creatures come to save the world's poor or at a minimum serve as interchangeable human parts in the battle against world poverty. But I wasn't Mother Teresa; probably there were moments when Mother Teresa wasn't either. What that said about me personally may not have been particularly flattering, but from my perspective of a rotten spoiled American, ambition, whatever form it takes, comes with the territory of being human. In my heart of hearts, I wanted to accomplish something while I was in the country, and I surely wasn't all that different from anybody else.

Was I scared the day Howard pulled out of Plato in a Peace Corps Jeep leaving me to cope all by myself? Was the Pope Catholic? In time, I decided I might starve, but I probably wouldn't be murdered, having arrived at a time when the United States was still enjoying the good will originally spawned by John F. Kennedy's Alliance for Progress in South America, an economic aid program that was intended to help grow Colombia's economy.

I didn't starve, but I can recommend Colombia's weight loss program for Americans. An unending daily diet of white rice, yucca and *plátano* did the trick for me. And if you like the nude look, the northern coast was perfect. Something, perhaps my diet, made my hair start falling out. For a while it was like harvesting wheat every time I combed it. Already destined for male pattern baldness, my diet probably kick-started the process. Since I was careful about not drinking the water, my teeth began to look like I was brushing them with battery acid. Six or seven soft drinks a day was not on anyone's food pyramid, but the choice seemed between dying of thirst, dysentery, cirrhosis of the liver, or cavities the size of craters on the moon.

I was going to survive, just not in poster boy fashion. *La Violencia*—the civil war that took 200,000 lives over almost two decades—had ended in 1958, and the country was enjoying a relative degree of peace. Though Colombian Gold marijuana was said to be a cash crop around Santa Marta, the capital of the *departamento* or state of Magdalena where I was living, the drug cartels had not yet gotten cranked up. Nor had the revolutionary group FARC begun on a large scale the guerrilla violence that would later terrorize parts of the country. On the other hand, imprinted on my memory is the chilling newspaper photograph of the body of Camilo Torres who was killed on February 15, 1966. A Catholic Priest turned revolutionary, Torres was a hero to the same people we volunteers were there to help. Liberation theology had already begun to make the academic rounds in those days, but understandably it was more appealing to discuss it in a college classroom in the United States than to see it played out in the daily newspaper.

The typical Peace Corps scenario for those of us involved in rural community development was that the volunteer or volunteers lived in a town and hiked to poor neighborhoods or took a bus to organize "community action groups" in smaller surrounding towns. Interestingly, Plato, probably about 15,000 people, had its own Lions and Rotary Club, but their service projects didn't necessarily involve rural community development. Arguing the obvious—that I would learn Spanish quicker if I were the only American around—I had requested to be the only volunteer placed in my job site. Many of us were sent out in pairs and had no problems with it. But the real reason for my request was that after going to all the trouble of coming to Colombia, I wanted to do things my way instead of negotiating everything out with another volunteer. Though I didn't say so, I felt two volunteers in the same site were redundant, a further rationalization on my part. Whenever I had worked with others in the past, it seemed like I was always the one to "give in," an insecurity that has lasted a lifetime. Initially, the plan was to place me in a site where there had never been a volunteer before, which was fine with me. According to the articles I wrote for *The Courier Index*, I was to be the first volunteer in the town of Cerro, but that changed when it was decided that a volunteer needed to be sent to Plato, Magdalena, because of an ongoing project that had not been completed.

In reviewing my articles in the *The Courier Index*, a case can be made that the rural community development volunteers who had worked together in Plato over the past 30 months before I got there were models for the whole country. After I had been there a month and a half, I wrote a piece listing their achievements:

> "With a substantial gift from CARE, a school has been built in a slum district of Plato... Out of the 10 community development organizations that were formed by the former [three] volunteers in the neighboring communities, a federation has been formed..."

The biggest project in my area was a joint venture by the Peace Corps and AID (Agency for International Development) involving an electric light plant for the town of Apure, 30 minutes by bus from Plato; however, by the time my predecessors left, it had not been installed by the *municipio*, a jurisdiction analogous to county government in the U.S. As was often the case, there was some problem with the bureaucracy which had delayed the installation. Initially, my job was somehow to make sure the project was completed. Since my ability to communicate in a meaningful way was limited, my presence in Plato seemed merely symbolic, but at least signaled that the American government was not going to forget its investment. I recall only one meeting with the municipal *electrificadora* in Plato responsible for the installation. He eventually got around to it, but not because I was making eloquent arguments in Spanish for him to honor his commitment.

Rural community development was nothing new to the Colombian government, but however well or badly the process was working, it could only be a drop in the bucket because of the massive poverty throughout the country. Too, there was often corruption in public works projects on the coast—I would read about highways abruptly ending in the middle of nowhere because the money was gone. I would learn personally the second year that if volunteers were involved in a local project, there was a better chance it would get funds from somewhere, because we had no political axes to grind and were trusted not to run off with the money or take kickbacks.

Despite real successes and the best of intentions, it was clear that community development was often a hit-or-miss proposition. We had been taught to identify a "natural leader" in a community, but timing was everything. The "natural leader" might be having personal or financial problems; local politics within the community could be a stumbling block. Two cooperatives—one involving savings and credit and the other a consumer program to lower prices for goods—had already been abandoned when the members failed to pay back loans or for lack of participation. The "federation" had fallen apart. Some projects were begun and abandoned before I got there. The reasons weren't always apparent to an American who was only taking in about a third of the conversation. It wasn't that Colombians weren't trying to help me. Whatever one's opinion about the Catholic Church, many of its priests cared about social justice, and there were several times that Padre Paez was permitted by his superior to accompany me on short trips to meet with community members. Another Colombian, whose name was Álvaro Ospina, was occasionally given time off from his job to help me, but generally that first year my efforts to keep some of these groups going were over my head.

I remember the day in Plato that first year when I realized I was just checking off the boxes and the calendar. It was an epiphany of sorts. I needed to quit and go home or start trying harder. I made up my mind to try harder no matter what excuses I had. As hokey as it sounds, it was that day I decided to take responsibility for my life and became an adult. Despite my sense that I had been just marking time, there were upsides to that first year. The primary one was that, as a rule, I liked the people from the northern coast of Colombia, whatever their economic status or skin color, which ranged from very dark to white. In a way it was like the South in the United States, but more so. Though a stereotype, people did move at a slower pace, so much so that *mañana* time took some real getting used to. We had been taught this, but it was easier said than done to realize that no meeting would ever start on time. Cartagena had been the port of entry for slaves brought from Africa, and the result of decades of racial intermingling with Hispanics and the native Indian population was everywhere on the coast. Though Colombians themselves acknowledged that racism and discrimination existed throughout the country (white skin was preferable), on the northern coast there had been so much mixing that skin color seemed to make no difference to an outsider. For someone who had witnessed no racial equality in the South, the northern coast of Colombia was liberating, regardless of how naive I was about the actual situation involving class and race.

The second year was better, but one night I didn't think I was going to live to tell about it. Saturday night in the town of El Difícil, I woke up with a pain in my stomach so awful that all I could do was roll around on the floor. Finally, I managed to crawl to my landlady's apartment. The weekend in small town Colombia isn't the best time for a medical meltdown. It had to be my appendix bursting. I could see the headlines in *The Volunteer*, the Peace Corps magazine we were sent monthly: "Agonizing Death on the Coast." But not a front page story. It wasn't like I had been eaten by a crocodile. Since I had been told her husband ran contraband in and out of Venezuela, my landlady was probably not eager to have a Peace Corps volunteer die on her doorstep. She brought back both the town doctor and a pharmacist. One or both had been drinking, and I would have been happy to have joined them if I hadn't been in such agony. It was the pharmacist who gave me a shot of... *something*. Finally, the pain subsided. When morning came, I was on the first bus to see the Peace Corps doctor in Barranquilla, hoping I would make it. "Just a kidney stone," was ultimately the diagnosis. Easy for him to say. I finally passed it.

Because of the excellent reputation of my predecessors and the friends they had made, I had been genuinely welcomed by a number of people in Plato. As advised, I started an English class as a way of meeting people and learning Spanish, and soon I had a class of around eight to ten who met with me once a week. These were middle-class, young educated people who liked Americans. I liked them, but they were not the poor that I had come to work with.

I made a good Colombian friend almost immediately. Álvaro Arrazola (my spelling is only approximate) had a good job with American-owned Antex Oil Company and spoke English about as well as I spoke Spanish at the time, and we hit it off. He had been good friends with my predecessors. Probably in his late twenties, Álvaro was married to a lovely woman some years younger. They had kids. They had me over to their house several times, and he invited me one weekend to travel to Cartagena four hours away to visit his parents and family, who were very hospitable to me and allowed me to use their telephone to call Temple.

One cultural difference, however, was troubling. *Machismo* was alive and well in Colombia and could be painful to watch. Even though it was clear he loved her and she loved him, Álvaro ordered his wife around in ways that would have been demeaning in the United States. Once she burst into tears during one of my visits. *Machismo* apparently was catching. When I came back to the United States and lived in Sally's basement for three months, she remarked that I sounded sexist, and she was right. I had to unlearn the habits I had acquired.

Álvaro teased me unmercifully when I admitted I had not yet

had sex. What was I waiting for? He took me to the local whorehouse in Plato, which turned out to be a place where you could run into the mayor and have a drink and go home or not go home. Sometimes men just went for a meal or to drink, and that was all we did, but like a big brother, Álvaro wanted me to know where it was. Prostitution was carefully controlled in Colombia. Doctors regularly checked prostitutes for disease, and women kept their record of inspections by their beds in case you wanted to check on them (as if this was going to be adequate protection).

In my Gideon Page lawyer novels, the hero is a widower raising a teenaged daughter, the product of his marriage to a nurse whom he met while a Peace Corps volunteer in Colombia. I used my life in Colombia as background material for the series, but most of that material came from the second year. Life outside cities was like living in a time warp when it came to middle-class Colombians. Even though it was the middle of the '60s, "good girls" expected to be chaperoned and not to find themselves alone with a man. In Plato that first year I was attracted to a couple of young women my age, and it was easy to imagine they were interested in an American (we were all supposed to be rich and, of course, we were in comparison). One was a teller at a bank who slipped me a lock of her hair in the course of a transaction. Another was a pretty, sweet girl in my English class who told me once that she could not imagine going a day without eating rice. That was all I needed to convince myself that I didn't need to be involved with any young woman in Plato. In the rural areas and small towns, middle-class culture was still following traditional patterns. There were virgins and there were whores, and, at least in theory, nothing in between. Sometimes you saw prostitutes walking down the main street of Plato dressed to the nines. People looked past them as if they didn't exist. You could tell it made them furious.

Temple and Tissie came to visit me after I had been in Colombia a year. They flew into Barranquilla on the coast where I met them at the airport. I concluded I shouldn't put them first thing on a regular Colombian bus. Its routine pleasures, sweaty bodies, chickens, sick children getting sicker and throwing up, and all manner of pungent odors, took a period of acclimation they didn't have. However hearty travelers Temple and Tissie thought themselves to be, they wouldn't have appreciated that kind of bus ride to Cartagena even though the road was paved, a rarity on the coast. We took a taxi. We did the usual tourist gigs in Cartagena where Tissie, who had a bad hip, got stuck for a few minutes in the famous castle of San Felipe. Tissie, it must be said, was quite the trooper. She remembered some college Spanish and impressed the tour guide at the port where the slaves were docked and brought into the country. I put them up in the Hotel Caribe, then the nicest hotel in the city. One night at dinner in the hotel we saw the exquisite actress Jean Seaberg who had played Joan of Arc and was in Cartagena to make a movie. She didn't invite us to join her entourage. After a couple of days we flew to Bogotá for the rest of the trip and took in a bull fight and some museums. If they had given the bull a sword, I might have enjoyed it. Hard to believe it is called a sport. Tissie's knowledge of history and Spanish made her sister jealous just as she had been for much of her life. It was like being back in Marianna. The trip almost ended in disaster because two days before they left I hired a taxi which took us down to the bottom of the mile-high mountain chain on which Bogotá is situated. The taxi broke down, and we had to hitchhike back into Bogotá. A Colombian couple who had graduated from L.S.U. knew instantly we were helpless Americans and stopped and gave us a ride back up the mountain. It was dark by the time we got back to their hotel, and Tissie, who had gotten the runs, told us she was going to skip dinner and "get a snootful" and go to bed. She meant liquor, not cocaine. Once she was out of sight, Temple and I got tickled at that remark and the determined way she had said it. Temple wasn't sorry that it had been her sister and not she who had contracted diarrhea. It was a small victory but one she relished. Using her Spanish to enter places to find bathroom after bathroom had brought Tissie down to earth.

Despite my admiration for her sister and Temple's jealousy, it was a wonderful visit, and I was proud of the way I had gotten us around. Temple was her usual warm, funny, engaging self, and I realized how much I had missed her. I felt depressed as soon as they got on the plane. In Barranquilla the night after they left, I asked a cab driver to take me to a place where the world's oldest profession was being practiced. It was a rite of passage I could have done without, but I didn't.

One of the most unnerving moments I had in Colombia involved a prostitute. One night in the town of El Difícil I was having a beer with a guy from Ecuador when the door burst open and a prostitute came running down the stairs followed by an angry customer. He caught her and began hitting her, and nobody did anything. Without thinking I jumped in between them. Men weren't supposed to hit women. The guy popped me once in the chest and would have hit me again had not soldiers (not police) appeared out of nowhere and locked the place down in seconds. The woman I had attempted to protect was twice as big as I was. In gratitude, she offered to buy me a free drink and possibly a discount on her services, which I turned down.

Soldiers were not an uncommon phenomenon in Colombia. Several times they stopped buses I was riding and checked identification. I carried my passport with me and an identification card the entire time I was in Colombia. In my mind, the presence of so many Colombian soldiers was an indication of the fragility of the government. There was then a power sharing agreement in Colombia.

Liberals and conservatives rotated the presidency, an arrangement that continued while I was there. Colombia, we were told, was an oligarchy. It might call itself a democracy but power was in very few hands.

Despite my ongoing battle with the language, I was growing more confident as time went on. The second year I received my only compliment, and that from a child who asked me what part of Colombia I was from. The dialect I was speaking obviously wasn't anything he had ever heard, but at least he recognized it as Spanish!

I don't recall the circumstances of my first visit to Alejandría, a town of about 500, but it was clear from the day I met him that Horacio Viaña would have stood out in any group as a natural leader. At the age of 60, he was assertive and talkative. He was taller and whiter than the typical Colombian from the coast, and I would learn that Sr. Viaña was originally from the interior. In my memory, there were initially two factions in the town, but it was soon apparent people trusted him and his friends more than the other group. I don't remember who went with me door-to-door inviting people to come to a town meeting where we explained the benefits of forming a *junta de acción comunal* (a community action group) to work on projects to better Alejandría, but about 30 people showed up, not a bad turnout. Clearly, the town needed all the help it could get. It had no electricity, no sewage system, and no paved road. A single spigot served the town's need for water. According to the gossip, a pipe had been run from Antex Oil Company miles away for the benefit of its American boss who was rumored to have a 14-year-old Colombian mistress in Alejandría. I had no information whether the story was true, but I would occasionally see the Antex truck parked in front of the child's house. It was none of my business, but I thought more than once it could have been a plot line straight out of the *The Ugly American*, a bestseller from the 1950s.

Sr. Viaña wasn't shy about speaking up and was a strong advocate for working on community projects. Forty years older than I was, I never called him by his first name the entire year I knew him. Like other men in the community he tended a tobacco plot outside of town which he went out to on his burro. He sold a few things, mainly soft drinks and dry goods from his house, which doubled as a store. He was raising a second family, but his wife (assuming they were married) who was only in her twenties, looked quite a bit older. Like I hoped, he was elected president of the group.

Just as my trainers had taught, our first project was one in which the so-called "felt needs" of the community were addressed. In theory, it might seem ridiculous to build a cemetery wall, especially one that did not completely enclose the burial site, but it worked perfectly as a tangible and visible example of what the people of Alejandría could accomplish by working together. We raised money for the bricks by having dances. A latrine project was next. Central to its success was education—a well-dug outhouse would result in fewer people getting sick and a healthier community. Lee Paquette, my volunteer leader at the time, brought a film on sanitation and a battery-operated projector. These efforts resulted in a few latrines being dug. The county government provided the outhouses, but it was problematic how much use they had. The old habit of simply going a few feet behind one's house into the dense underbrush was all-too-convenient. They seemed more like status symbols, something to show a visitor.

Of much more interest than latrines was the prospect of building a public school and hiring qualified teachers. Alejandría had a single private teacher who was not certified. How much parents paid him or how they could even afford to, I never understood. He taught in a barn-like structure, and occasionally I could hear him drilling the class. What made him special was his willingness to teach in a place like Alejandría at all. He had to be as poor as the average parent.

At one point building schools in rural areas in Colombia was a priority, and one of the ways to obtain funds was through the School-to-School program in the United States. The bar, of course, was not high for qualifying for funds. Though the community had to agree to provide all the labor, etc., this could be accomplished by a stroke of the pen. The hard part was going to be actually doing it. The Peace Corps volunteer was the key middle man in all of this and had to have six months remaining in the country at the time the funds were approved. It was an easy decision to forget temporarily the cemetery wall and the latrine project.

On an administrative and practical level the Peace Corps was fulfilling its part of the bargain. A Peace Corps architect provided the plans for a three-room school, and Ron Burkard loaned us the CINVA Ram press that we used to make the concrete blocks for the school. The father of a local priest in the area who owned a cement factory in Barranquilla generously donated the cement. The public works office in the *Departamento* of Magdalena loaned us a truck, and we transported the cement to Alejandría. As we were unloading the cement (I had on sandals) some of it worked into my feet which were already inflected with athlete's foot. As a precautionary measure, the Peace Corps doctor admitted me to a hospital in Barranquilla for a few days between Christmas and New Year's. It wasn't serious, and I spent the time flirting with my day nurse who was a delightful, attractive and intelligent young woman my age by the name of Marbel Ruiz. She took pity on me and invited me to a New Year's Eve party at her house (she lived at home with her mother), and I went.

To my surprise, Marbel's mother operated a mini-factory in

her house. One day when I was visiting, her mother opened the door to a room, and there were around nine or so women working behind sewing machines. I felt more comfortable with these uneducated women than I did with her mother, largely because I was so conscious that the Spanish that was coming out of my mouth was not close to sounding like that of an educated person. In short, it was as if there was an obvious class difference between us, and I was used to being around people like her employees. I identified with them more than her.

Fortunately, Marbel did not seem to care if I butchered the Spanish language. She spoke a good bit of English, and her more laid-back personality suited me fine. When the international ship *Hope* docked at Cartagena, Marbel was selected to live on the ship for a few months and learn some advanced nursing procedures. *Hope* traveled the world's seas providing free medical care and training to local medical personnel. Cartagena was only four hours travel by bus from Plato, and several times I went to visit her there. When she had time off, we had some wonderful times walking the beaches behind the big hotels. Almost thirty years later my relationship with her became background material for the Gideon Page series. I hasten to add that Marbel was a devout Catholic, and our relationship was quite chaste despite the freedom she was given. She told me she wanted to have a big family and not work outside the home. Unlike what occurred in my fiction, we did not get married and have a child, and I lost contact with her.

Meanwhile, I had agreed to oversee the construction of a school when I couldn't saw a block of wood into two pieces. Sr. Viaña conveniently claimed to have experience as a builder which satisfied the School-to-School program, but after all this time, I have my doubts. At least it wasn't going to be two stories in height. Since I have pictures of the school, I have proof it was built, but I can't claim any responsibility for the manual labor involved, except the day I showed up at the construction site and nobody was there but me. I was getting worried that the school would never be more than a collection of rusting building materials, and I took one of the sledge hammers and furiously began to pound rocks into smaller pieces for the foundation. I was mad and worried at the same time. As people walked by, I think they were so shocked that I was doing some of the actual labor instead of standing around like a boss that the word got around fast, and eventually the men showed up to work.

There was an argument during the construction of the school I didn't win, and later I was glad I didn't. Fortunately, we had an experienced bricklayer in town who was doing a good job with the bricks that were being made from the CINVA Ram press, but Sr. Viaña was adamant that the school have some kind of ornamentation. Without telling me, he bought with our precious pesos some relatively fancy bricks for the top of the walls. I was furious with him, but it was their school, not mine. In fact, the prefab bricks added to the building and didn't send us into bankruptcy.

During the construction of the school, we asked Antex Oil Company to donate a partially constructed building it had abandoned for use as a health clinic. Once it was completed, one day a week a nurse came from El Difícil to provide some care.

The dedication of the school and health center in the spring of 1967 was a sublime moment. The junta's women's committee cooked food for the town and guests. Ron Burkard came from Barranquilla. Dignitaries, including the mayor and a priest, came from El Difícil to take part. We had music. I didn't try to dance the *cumbia*—I never got the hang of it, but it was truly a proud day for all of us.

The only flies in the ointment, and they were big ones, were our teachers—the lack of them. In order to get funding from the school-to-school program, an official for the *Departamento* of Magdalena had to sign an agreement that two teachers would be sent to Alejandría. But they hadn't arrived by the dedication, and the word was that they had not been hired. This was a breach of our agreement with the School-to-School program, and it was *déjà vu* all over again. Like volunteers before me, I was about to return to the United States without finishing the project. I could have extended a couple of months, but by early June I had been diagnosed with the recurrence of a cyst on my thyroid and was due to be operated on at Johns Hopkins in Baltimore. Before I left Colombia, Marbel, her sister and I took a bus to Santa Marta to talk with the head of the Magdalena Department of Education. I understood what the problem was. Just as in the United States, teachers were reluctant to come to such an impoverished and rural area; however, somewhat magically, two teachers were hired and sent to our school before I came home. Of course, we had a three-room school, but perhaps in the future there would be three teachers. How long they stayed and what they accomplished I don't know. I had hoped the one male teacher who had been there could get certified and would remain. He told me he hadn't been able to, and I wondered if I had done more harm than good. He was the type of man who would have stayed there; the two young women I couldn't imagine being there for more than a year. By the time I left Colombia, my political views were more to the left than they would ever be again in my life. The Colombians I knew on the coast in the rural areas weren't lazy or dumb. Capitalism wasn't working, or not working very well. Each day I spent in Alejandría I saw kids with the distended bellies that signaled malnutrition. I saw children with holes all the way through their teeth. Most seemed doomed to eke out a marginal existence. I had assumed that extreme poverty equated with wholesale misery, but in fact, the more time I spent around Colombians in Alejandría it was obvious from their expressions and actions that even the poorest found some pleasure in being alive and performing their daily routines. However hot it was going to be that day, I was handed a small cup of *tinto*, the Colombian coffee that jump-started each morning. The "best" coffee was reserved for the export market, but Colombians insisted on their *tinto*. It tasted bitter to me, but I got used to it. Alejandríans smiled and laughed; their children played games; they kicked a soccer ball; sometimes they kicked their dogs. A canine lover, I never got used to the way people treated their dogs.

What I learned in Colombia about myself had a profound effect on the way I saw the world and still does. It wasn't just that I genuinely liked almost all the people I met on the northern coast of Colombia. Because I had fewer practical skills and abilities than the people I had come to try to help, I could hardly think of myself as superior. For weeks at a time and occasionally months, I had no contact with Americans other than the mail I received. This was before e-mail or cell-phones, so basically it was just "me" and "them." In all that time nothing catastrophic happened to me. I wasn't mugged or assaulted. I did have a radio stolen on a beach in Cartagena. I was lonely, naturally, but that was mostly the result of not speaking the language better.

But for the language, these were people who might as well have been from Marianna. They were people of color who had been brought from Africa and had melded with Europeans and native people from South America. In retrospect, my time in Colombia was spent appreciating the obvious: as much violence and poverty as a country like Colombia has seen, the overwhelming majority of people live out their lives not engaged in war or drug trafficking, but rather follow a daily routine like most anybody else, rich or poor, anywhere in the world. This was hardly news to anyone, nor should it have been news to me, but in college I had always been more interested in politics and wars and the intrigues of nation states as they jockeyed for power, prestige and wealth rather than how people coped with their day-to-day situations. In other words, people of color were not the "other." They were like myself except they had the misfortune to be born in a country whose political system was unable to create conditions where the majority of its citizens could prosper and educate their children.

If I had wanted to think about it at the time, I would have internalized how different my life was for those 21 months. Except for Peace Corps training, I had rarely been out of the South my entire life, and culture shock could have been a real problem. I recall vividly a moment during a trip to St. Louis as a teenager with Temple, my sisters, and brother-in-law, and entering a crowded diner where the only available seats were at the counter. Temple took a seat next to a black person, and I remember being astonished that she had done so with such aplomb. I had never seen a black person eating in a white restaurant. Black people weren't allowed in restaurants to eat in the South, only to cook, wash the dishes and mop the floor. My state of mind at that moment in St. Louis seems absurd now, but I had spent 20 years in an environment in which blacks were outrageously subordinate to people like myself, and despite their superior number, might as well have been non-existent as far as I was concerned.

Looking back on my experience in Colombia, what made the transition smooth from the perspective of race was the fact that skin color did not seem to be a determinant in the activities in which I was involved as a Peace Corps volunteer or any of my daily routine. It was a much different environment from the United States where almost every encounter or transaction was being placed under a racial microscope now that the country was coming to grips with its history. Simply negotiating the ordinary events of one's life put me in contact on a daily basis with people who looked different—their skin was generally darker—and looking back on it now, I realize how quickly that became the "new normal."

I didn't pretend to myself that anything I had done in those 21 months was going to make a substantial difference in the lives of a few Colombians on the northern coast. The irony was that the poverty in Lee County, especially in the black community, was in some ways similar to the rural areas in Colombia.

Despite the presence of physicians in Lee County, the medical needs were enormous. Yet I had gone off to "save the world" and would be soon called a "hero" in Marianna. I knew better.

Living and working in northern Colombia with a population that was identical in skin color to African-Americans had helped me realize (though few, if any, whites in Marianna would have agreed) how much I had in common with black people. Leaving the South and living in a region of a foreign country that was so clearly a mixed-blood society, it had been impossible for me to explain to Colombians on the northern coast why we whites in Marianna insisted on a system that treated blacks so wretchedly. We had justified our behavior because of the alleged inferiority of African-Americans, but so far as I was concerned, after having been around the people in this region for 21 months, they weren't inferior at all. Certainly, I had much more education than the average *campesino*, but all the books I had read had little relevance to my job there, which mostly required communication skills that I never came close to perfecting. When the subject of the American South came up in conversations with educated Colombians like Álvaro Arrazola and Marbel Ruiz, all I could do was agree that our treatment of African-Americans was indefensible and feebly argue that the federal government and black people themselves were forcing the South to change. Having to answer questions about this subject was an important step for me. I had benefited from white supremacy, just as I benefit today from economic and political systems in underdeveloped countries that allow me to pay a pittance for products manufactured overseas by people who are trying to raise families on little more than pennies a day.

Admittedly, because of the language barrier I missed certain nuances on a daily basis that would have made me a more sophisticated observer of class, racial and ethnic differences in Colombia, but conversely even that deficiency made me more aware of our commonalities. Had I been smarter and more competent than the Colombians I was living and working with, perhaps I would have felt superior to them. But I wasn't and I didn't. Some class distinctions between us were obliterated by my mangling of their language and my immersion in a culture that wasn't my own. It was the United States government that gave me status and access to resources, not my own innate abilities, which, it became clearer every day, were not particularly evident—to me or anyone else. What was clear from about the second year forward was my commitment to give my best effort every day I was there. Woody Allen's comment about "showing up" being 90% of one's success has always seemed spot-on.

The longer I had been in Colombia the easier it was to imagine that except for the accident of birth I could have lived out my life as a *campesino* with children who had holes in their teeth and distended bellies. Living in Colombia that long had made it impossible for me to feel comfortable in an "Us versus Them" society. No matter how one sliced it, on the northern coast of Colombia skin color just didn't have the same importance that it did in the United States. I could add race to this equation, but what race were Colombians on the northern coast, other than overwhelmingly mixed? Decades later, the academic community would conclude that race is an "artificial construct"—that it has no scientific meaning, which is not to say it doesn't still have complete applicability in American life. That first night back in Washington had taught me that lesson.

CHAPTER 7

No Strings to Pull

So many cheated for me that I ended up firing "expert," which was good for a cynical laugh when it was announced in our barracks at the end of our training.

THE IRONIES of living in the United States after Colombia were apparent in the first 24 hours. My first stop was Washington. I was required to fill out paperwork at Peace Corps headquarters for the operation to remove my cyst. To celebrate my return to the United States that night I took a bus to a Washington Senators baseball game.

Afterwards, I took the wrong bus back to my hotel and got off in a poor area where I was the only white. Some of the crowd at the bus stop didn't seem particularly happy to see me in their neighborhood. I don't remember the specifics of those very uncomfortable moments trying to find the right bus back to my hotel, but it didn't take but a few seconds then to understand that everything I had been hearing and reading about race relations in the last 21 months in the United States had not been exaggerated. I had spent all that time in Colombia rarely being afraid for my physical safety, but suddenly America seemed a far more dangerous place with the race riots having begun in Watts in Los Angeles in August of 1965 while I was still in Peace Corps training in Albuquerque. By 1967 it seemed like open warfare in cities like Detroit, Newark and Milwaukee. A year later the commission appointed by President Johnson to investigate the race riots sweeping the urban landscape concluded in the so-called "Kerner Report," that "[o]ur nation is moving toward two societies, one black and one white—separate and unequal."[1] Of course, that journey had already begun centuries earlier and not just in the South. The massive report documenting racial inequality and its violent consequences in many of our cities was a brutal eye-opener for the nation.

When I opened my eyes two days later, after the successful surgery at Johns Hopkins Hospital, there was Temple beaming down at me. She was on her way to Europe via New York with one of her friends from the University of Mississippi and had arranged to fly into Baltimore to see her son. I was told later that the bed I was recuperating in had just been occupied by one of our soldiers from the Vietnam War who had not survived his wounds. I had gotten a "freebie," because the cyst, which was not malignant, had developed while I was in the Peace Corps. It was an unsettling feeling to know that the hospital was filled with men my age who were suffering horribly, and in some cases dying, from wounds in a war I had so far avoided.

I had thought to spend the rest of the summer hanging out in Memphis. Not certain what I wanted to do or was qualified to do, I had decided to go on to graduate school in international relations at South Carolina. Derrick Barton, my tennis coach at Southwestern, promised me a janitorial job at the ritzy University Club where we had practiced and played our matches my freshman year. My sisters rightly discouraged the idea, saying I needed to spend the two months closer to our family after having been out of the country 21 months. I had missed quite a bit. Sally had been in an automobile accident in Marianna that had nearly killed her two oldest children, Charlie and Julie, prompting Harriet to fly back from Puerto Rico. Nor had I been around to help them move to Hot Springs where Voris had been hired as the basketball coach and math teacher at the white high school. When I returned from the Peace Corps, Harriet was living in Hot Springs, too. Her husband J. D. had come back from a year in Vietnam and told her their marriage was over. The rest of the summer I lived in the unfinished basement of Sally's new house and got a job on the grounds crew for roughly $50 a week at the Aloha Lodge, one of the many motels in the resort town, which had been made famous by mobsters such as Owney Madden.

Naively, little did I know that the Lee County Draft Board was trying to find me. While I had been in the Peace Corps, the Vietnam War was tearing apart the country. One volunteer I knew who had successfully completed training and had been in Colombia for only a few weeks got on a plane and was flown straight to his induction center after his appeal was denied. A drawback of privilege is that you expect everything will work out the way you want it, no matter what. Since I had not heard from my draft board, I stupidly thought I would be permitted to go straight on to graduate school. I had gotten two deferments, why not three? In 1968 there were over 536,000 American troops in Vietnam.

At a "Grif Stockley Appreciation Dinner" in Marianna, held the last week of August in 1967, the honoree failed to mention in his remarks that it seemed strange to him that there were no black people in attendance in light of the fact that the school in Alejandría overwhelmingly served people of color. The headline of the article in the *Memphis Press Scimitar* on August 29, 1967, read, "Marianna Pays Tribute To Its Returning Hero." The story about the dinner of "two hundred townspeople at Whitten School to honor one of Marianna's native sons" omitted the fact that the attendees were representative of only approximately half the population of the town. I told myself that it would be rude and the behavior of an ingrate to raise the issue of race at an event in my honor. After all, a number of people went to a good deal of trouble to pull off a dinner involving 200 people. But what better time and place would there have been to raise the subject? I was a coward. Certainly, I was still a pleaser. I didn't want to make anyone mad.

My friend Bruce was in Marianna during this time. Bruce's father was still superintendent of the Marianna schools. A year ahead of me, Bruce had gone to Hendrix College in Conway, Arkansas, where he was elected president of the student body and graduated near the top of his class. Gifted in many ways, Bruce was put on the program honoring me and sang, "Let There Be Peace On Earth and Let It Begin With Me." I would have numerous occasions in the future to remember Bruce's singing that song.

In fact, the purpose of the dinner was not so much to honor a native son as it was to raise funds for the construction of a school in an underdeveloped country through the School-to-School program, which my articles back home had inspired. Looking back now, it would have been an ideal project to co-partner with Marianna's black high school. But that kind of gesture would have suggested that blacks were equal to us. As long as the subject was paternalism, we were comfortable with it, racial equality not at all. White people helping out black people in a foreign country was something we could embrace. There was at least one black person from Lee County (Sterling King, Jr.) who had already served in the Philippines in the Peace Corps, but he didn't qualify as Lee County's hero. It seems unlikely that any of Marianna's black citizens even knew of such an event. As I have implied, few read the *The Courier Index*. And we knew next to nothing about what those black citizens were accomplishing, and what we did know we discounted as insignificant or as rare as a sighting of the Ivory-billed Woodpecker.

White male upper-middle class privilege had kept me out of the Army, but those days were over. I was asked by someone who will remain anonymous if I wanted someone to "try to pull some strings." I said I did, but apparently there were no strings any longer to be pulled. Jake was dead. Temple hadn't lived in Marianna except during the summers since 1962. Or, if there were strings (and there always were or are), I didn't want to know how it was done—I just wanted it done. More than 50 years later, I can claim to be ashamed, but because I have taken advantage so often of having been a Southern, white, upper middle-class heterosexual male, it doesn't pass the smell test.

I wasn't a pacifist; I did not oppose killing on religious grounds. I had no justification for seeking conscientious objector status. Much, much later in life I would be in a book club in Little Rock with Michael Vogler, a legendary Arkansas peace activist against the war in Vietnam. Mike had the courage to serve time in a federal prison for his refusal to allow himself to be drafted. He was the type who made the authorities literally carry him into jail. They didn't make it easy for him either, but he survived the bumps and bruises with his integrity intact.

Though it seemed I had spent a good portion of my 22 years reading about freedom and the loss of it, it took less than 12 hours in the Army to begin to understand what it was going to mean on a personal level. In my typically overheated way, I imagined my loss of it put me in touch with what it felt like to be a slave, as absurd a notion as I would ever hold. And yet that feeling of the loss of my liberty was as intense an emotion as I have ever experienced. I suppose I could have reacted by thinking it was a privilege to serve in the Army, but the idea of dying in the Vietnam War seemed as meaningless a death to me as dying a Confederate soldier. Had I expressed that particular sacrilege aloud, some of my family would have been horrified. For the briefest of moments

I contemplated disobeying the next order, whatever it was, and being taken to the stockade. I'd show those bastards. It was the loss of control and personal autonomy and dignity that I resented most. Little did I realize how much I had taken my personal freedom for granted. I had just spent 21 months in a foreign country making every decision for myself, going where I wanted when I wanted; now I couldn't even go to the bathroom without permission. Forced servitude in a nation's military machine is one of the world's oldest quasi-prison environments, but I exaggerated its controlled fury in those first moments of basic training. But even now it is a little sickening to realize how quickly I learned to adjust to the loss of freedom. Though from a part of the country that relentlessly celebrated patriotism, I felt a deep ambivalence about the kind of flag waving that celebrates a mentality of "my country, right or wrong." Courtesy of the U.S. government, I had spent almost two years trying to help people; now, I was supposed to learn how to kill them. Only in America! After about a month into basic training, I wrote in capital letters to Lee and Bruce: "I HATE THE ARMY. The only thing I want when I'm through is to remember how much I hated it." As intended by the Army, I imagined I was losing whatever individuality I had. "I have joined the rest of the other trainees in reducing my vocabulary to about 8 words which include motherfucker, cocksucker, fuckhead, and such standbys [as] son-of-a-bitch, goddamn, bastard and shithead. 90 percent of all sentences must include the word fuck."

Poor baby. I wasn't through whining. I wrote melodramatically, "we are all being reduced to an animal level. It is truly a dehumanizing process...there is nothing in my experience to compare to it." I was fortunate never to have served in the Marines, or I really would have had something to whine about. "Not one of my sergeants can get through a sentence without butchering it grammatically," I moaned as if correct English usage were the key to my survival, but I needed something to help me get in touch with my usual sense of supposed superiority to these people who were constantly telling me what to do and when to do it. I never had any trouble understanding what they meant. I cringe reading these words today. Pathetically, I needed to tell myself I was too good for the Army when the truth was I was barely good enough. There was hardly anybody in my barracks who was a worse soldier. At least they could make up their bunks without getting yelled at.

And yet despite everything, class still mattered and would throughout my tenure in the service. The average draftee in that era was not even close to having a college education, especially if he was black. In my basic training barracks there was a black kid from next door Phillips County named Leroy; we had perhaps a full-blooded Native American who fulfilled the stereotype. Toward the end of basic training when we were given a pass and allowed off base, "Joe" got drunk and had to be brought back by MPs.

That I was not a model soldier didn't seem to matter to our platoon's drill sergeant. It was his last training cycle before he got out of the military, and whatever pleasure or meaning, if any, there had been for him in harassing soldiers in basic training disappeared when he got to our barracks. He took it easy on us and himself. From time immemorial there have been soldiers like me. When we got out on the rifle range, I could barely see the 200 meter targets, much less hit them. Not to worry. The sergeants who stood over us and graded the results saw how poorly I was performing and each began to cheat on my behalf. It wasn't about me. It would have reflected badly on them as teachers and our company and battalion. So many cheated for me that I ended up firing "expert," which was good for a cynical laugh when it was announced in our barracks at the end of our training. I imagined everyone remembered I was the college-educated idiot who needed help in learning to disassemble his rifle and then putting it back together. Though it wasn't complicated, I had to have one-on-one instruction, probably from a kid who had a ninth-grade education. Shades of Will Percy! To further humiliate myself, I had cut my finger on the trigger mechanism and bled on my weapon. What a fighting machine I was!

How many Stockleys does it take to change a light bulb? Don't know, we're still working on the first one. In 1992 my daughter Erin would write me from Harvard that she had called me a "million times" but had never gotten me. "I guess expecting an answering machine would be a lot to hope for, that would be another thing to learn how to work. Oh, well." This was a child who loved her father dearly despite his near total inability to make even the most simple machines "work." My sisters are not much better. But something was left out of my brain. It wasn't as if I didn't try. As a child who was enthralled during the Korean War with America's fabled "Sabre jets" I would try to assemble model airplanes and present them to my parents for their approval. Even they couldn't hide their dismay at the glue-covered mess I made out of any project.

The problem in my case goes deeper. Face recognition is often an impossible task for me. Though without a formal diagnosis, I am convinced I suffer from the condition of *prosopagnosia*, or "face blindness," which makes for some outrageously embarrassing moments. Once picking up Erin from middle school, when the buzzer sounded, I spotted a child I didn't know coming toward the car. I thought it must be a friend to tell me she was going to be delayed. I smiled at the girl only to discover it was Erin who had been with her mother a few days and had a slightly different haircut. I had always known something was "wrong," and it was a relief to read that notables such as the psychologist Oliver Sachs, Jane Goodall, and others, had the same condition.

Despite my ineptness as a soldier, I became friends with the draftee who was in charge of our barracks. A college graduate (I no longer remember his name) he had been through at least some ROTC. On Saturday and Sunday afternoons, as our training over those eight weeks became less intense, we occasionally hung out together to talk about something other than basic training. I had read a lot and so had he. It was this brief friendship that led to me being promoted to Private First Class at the end of basic training since it was his recommendation. There was certainly no other reason. No one else in our barracks came out higher than E2. Class rules!

Temple made sure that I wasn't forgotten in the Army. The girls at Alpha Delta Pi deluged me with letters, so many that at mail call I became a minor celebrity in our company. When I went to visit her on leave, the story made *The Commercial Appeal* in Memphis. I was photographed in my dress uniform surrounded by Temple's girls while reading one of the letters. I didn't tell them how terrible a soldier I was or how much I hated it.

There was increasing suspense and anxiety about where we would be assigned after basic training. Unless you were gung-ho, the last thing you wanted to hear was Advanced Infantry Training which guaranteed a trip to Vietnam. When the top Sergeant read out loud to our training company our next duty stations I was assigned to "Order of Battle" analyst school at Ft. Holabird in Baltimore. I had no idea what he was talking about. Holabird, he explained, was then the Army's military intelligence school. He was impressed, and said I must have some "smarts"— if he had only known!

"Not to worry" said our instructors when I got to Baltimore. "No order of battle analyst has ever been killed in the Vietnam war. You'll probably be assigned to Saigon." All of that was cold comfort when on January 31, 1968, the Viet Cong and North

Vietnam conducted a major push throughout South Vietnam during what became known as the "Tet Offensive." Sappers even managed to penetrate the security of the United States Embassy in Saigon. They were beaten back, but the Vietnam War was never the same afterwards in the minds of the American people. These people were willing to die to reunite their country. The world's greatest military power couldn't stop them unless we were going to "nuke" them back to the Stone Age. Declassified documents show that both the Johnson and Nixon administrations for a time considered using "limited" nuclear devices.[2]

For reasons inexplicable to me, I experienced waves of loneliness at Ft. Holabird even in a crowd of soldiers. Perhaps it was just a rare case of allowing myself to feel sadness, which normally was foreign to me. Or maybe it was just being in the Dundalk section of Baltimore, where a yellowish, chemical haze hung over everything. It was so ugly and depressing that even someone as oblivious to his surroundings as I am, noticed. The highlight of those months in Baltimore was riding over with a couple of guys to hear Susan Sontag speak at Goucher College, an expensive liberal arts school for women. As a public intellectual, Ms. Sontag was intriguing and stayed in vogue for much of her life. In my memory, she either talked about or read from her novel *Death Kit* and kept running a hand through her hair which had a shock of white in it. When I later read *Death Kit* I couldn't make heads or tails out of it—something about a blind woman having sex standing up to the rocking motion of the train.

Far up in a balcony seat, I saw Geraldine Chaplin in "The Little Foxes," in Baltimore with Liz Prestridge, a very nice girl from Marianna who was attending Goucher. Since I had no transportation, I had to take the bus downtown and then transfer to a different one to go out to Goucher. It took about two hours and then the return trip had to be repeated. It was a long way to go for female company but that has never stopped me. We could put away the beer and one night, after trying unsuccessfully to keep up with her, I got on the wrong bus and went out into the country until it was just myself and the driver. I had to pee so bad I thought I was going to die. I filled up the cup I was holding and threw it out behind the last departing passenger. I was lucky not to be arrested, but it may not have been all that uncommon behavior. By the time I got back to Goucher, the buses had quit running. I knocked on the door of a fraternity house at Towson State and was let in. Grateful for the kindness of strangers, I would have spent the night on the floor. I ended up on the couch and repented of my bad thoughts about fraternities. It was my last trip to Goucher.

As "graduation" drew near, the only consolation was that I wasn't going to have to be the one to go into the field and provide intelligence. "Order of Battle" analysts took military intelligence and organized it in a way that helped the commanding officer do his job. Everyone in the school, officers included, had to pass a map reading test before they could graduate. John Fears, whom I had known at Southwestern and was a fraternity brother, had become a friend at Holabird and tutored me in map reading, and I was too proud or too insecure to flunk intentionally. How I passed I have no idea since I have never been able to read a map since. Shortly before our school ended, I found out that a guy in the training cycle ahead of me who had been in the Peace Corps was being dropped from intelligence school. Unbeknownst to most everyone, there was a regulation that prohibited someone who had been in the Peace Corps from being assigned to intelligence and vice versa. Somehow this rule was supposed to protect the Peace Corps from being accused of being an intelligence agency. How that made sense for people like me who had already been in the Peace Corps wasn't completely clear, but that was the regulation. I waited until I got my orders (I wouldn't have spoken up if they had been anywhere but for Vietnam) and then told the instructors I had been in the Peace Corps as well. I was dropped from my class instantly. Thinking I had out smarted the Army, I spent a couple of weeks polishing floors and awaiting new orders. They came all right: truck driving school in Ft. Polk, Louisiana. Wise guys in my barracks shuddered, "That's a one-way ticket to Vietnam. The Viet Cong are mining roads every day." I thought I was a dead-man walking long before the movie came out.

Soon thereafter, the black sergeant who was in charge of my barracks, strolled over to my bunk. I thought he was going to chew me out again. It seemed he was on my case every day about something. I looked sloppy; I didn't get my bed tight so that a quarter would bounce on it. I didn't march like I was supposed to. I couldn't spit-shine my boots to please him. Frankly, I didn't see what the fuss was all about. We weren't in basic training any longer. In my view, we didn't need all the spit and polish, but he was a "lifer," and I prepared myself mentally for more criticism. Instead he said, "Stockley, if I were you, I would go to the Inspector General's office and tell him they screwed up your orders. You've got a college degree. You don't need to be going to truck driving school."

I couldn't believe my ears! Before the day was out, I had an appointment to see the IG. When my turn came, I told the officer (a colonel, not a general) what my sergeant had said and asked him if he could help me. Amazingly, while I was standing there, he called the Pentagon and while waiting for somebody to take the call, asked if there was some other reason (other than a college degree) why my orders should be changed. I told him about my eyesight—that I didn't see 20-20 even with my contact lenses (which was true), and soon, I had been reassigned to the 5th Battalion Combat Engineers in Ft. Leonard Wood, Missouri.

Once again, class came to my rescue. Why those two men hadn't just laughed at me and told me I was getting what I deserved I still don't know. Maybe they had thought I would do more harm than good if I were driving a deuce-and-a-half in Vietnam. Actually, the thought that I could do the Army any good as a "combat engineer" was equally unfathomable. Someone finally pointed out that with my college education I would most likely be a clerk.

The weekend I was to report to Ft. Leonard Wood, Martin Luther King, Jr. was assassinated in Memphis. I had already arranged to stop and visit Temple in Oxford and arrived amid campus demonstrations by the small black contingent on campus. I expressed my condolences to Mildred (despite all my growing liberalism, in time honored white privilege fashion I never knew her last name) Temple's loyal cook and housekeeper at the sorority house. While I was there Temple and I talked about King's murder. I told her that there were far more radical black leaders than Martin Luther King in the United States, and that whatever whites thought about him, he spoke for most black people. In fact, like many others, I had come to regard him as an American hero. His willingness to confront what the United States was doing in Vietnam took great courage. He was right to protest the war. In fact, Temple, I believe, already had begun modifying her views about race. Too, she seemed to have worked through some of the bitterness she had felt immediately after Jake's death. Before he died, she had known who she was—the small-town daughter of a much loved doctor and immediately thereafter the wife of a plantation owner and later business owner. Now she had joined the numberless ranks of women who had once derived much of their identity through father figures and husbands, but now these men were gone. Seventeen when Jake had died, I was not qualified for those roles and no one stepped into it. Temple was going to need a job. Her close friend,

Louise Mixon, who would later get similar employment, had put the idea in Temple's head. Within months she had a job at Ole Miss as a "house mother."

Leaving Marianna during the school year and only coming back during the summer probably had saved Temple's life or at least extended it. Beyond a certain point, sitting in the house alone and mourning Jake was a recipe for disaster. Jim Beam and friends were more than guests; they were permanent boarders in the Wall family. As sad as Jake's death had been, things had soured even further for Temple in Marianna. Since he had committed suicide, Jake's business partner, "Mr. Pee-Wee," couldn't collect on the insurance that he and Jake had taken out on their business. This meant that he had to buy out Jake's interest in Owens and Stockley, a situation that caused financial hardship and some understandable resentment. Despite missing Jake terribly and drinking too much at night when the loneliness got to her, Temple's job as a housemother gave her confidence and truly a sense of doing something useful.

When I arrived at Ft. Leonard Wood, the entire base appeared ready to transport itself to Chicago to do riot duty. All leaves had been canceled. Cities with significant black populations were exploding all across the country, and Army bases like Ft. Leonard Wood were on alert. I would have been part of riot control had the order been given. I would have been one of those guys I saw on television clutching a shield and hoping I wasn't going to have to fend off anything harder than a rock.

Almost immediately after things settled down, I was given the opportunity to become a chaplain's assistant. It was tempting. I hadn't read about any chaplains being killed in Vietnam. I told myself it would be a good fit. My prospective boss was young, an intellectual and conversant with the theologians I had studied in college. I imagined I would have my own tutorial. Grandiosely,

I fantasized our conversations would be like Senior Bible at Southwestern, a rich intellectual experience. I don't recall thinking of it as an opportunity to help people. Obviously, my role would have been clerical and administrative. There was just one hold-up: I didn't believe in God any longer. Even as proficient as I was at rationalizing my behavior, I couldn't fake my loss of faith, and the chaplain and I concluded that he would be better served with a Christian believer.

I didn't think of my Army experience as a way to serve the country. It was still me against the Army, and yet, despite myself, I managed as a company clerk over the next 16 months to work up to Specialist 5th Class. I took a non-credit course at night in international economics taught by some professor. He discovered quickly that none of us could do the math, so we discussed policy. There came a night when people discussed their own personal economic philosophies, including the professor. To a person, including him, they were all conservatives who saw the United States as a place where people were self-made and had endless opportunities if they just worked hard enough. Knowing I wasn't self-made, I told them I had been given most everything and argued for a safety-net for people not so fortunate. I didn't admit at the time that I believed, at least hypothetically, in Karl Marx's maxim, "From each according to his ability, to each according to his need." Given my lifelong miserliness, I didn't really believe that, but I told myself I did.

The Army definitely had a place for bullies, favoritism, and racial discrimination. As company clerk of the 158th Quartermaster Company, I saw it all up close and personal and never said a word, but in my defense it would have done no good to complain. Besides, I was favored, too. The two clerks in our company were not put on KP or guard duty like everybody else. My most vivid memory involved a black sergeant who started complaining in no uncertain terms about racial discrimination to the top sergeant of our company. Our "Top" ordered me and the other clerk out of the building. Top was a banty rooster type, short and rail thin and getting up in years, but he acted more than ready to fight that day. The black sergeant was a big beefy guy much younger than Top. If they had fought, they would have torn the place up, and somebody would have been badly hurt. Nothing happened, and the black sergeant didn't get his promotion. My recollection is that he was allowed to transfer out of our unit. Was Top bluffing? What was said between them? I would never know.

Soon after I arrived at Ft. Leonard Wood, I became friends with Bob Smite (not his real name). A draftee who had graduated from college, Bob was assigned to Battalion Headquarters as a clerk. An assignment to battalion headquarters was a real plum for an enlisted man and obviously carried much greater responsibility than a mere company clerk. Bob was married and had no desire to go to Vietnam. One day he told me that he could change a code that meant the difference between going to Vietnam and not. He said he was going to change the code for himself and asked if I wanted him to do the same thing for me. I said I did. I never knew whether he changed the code for either of us, or whether he actually had the power to do so. But I could have easily been sent to Vietnam for a year in the time I had remaining. He eventually got transferred out of Ft. Leonard Wood (not to Vietnam), and I never heard from him again. I've never regretted not being sent to Vietnam, but I have always felt guilt at how I managed to avoid it, if indeed, that was the case. Had I been sent, the odds were overwhelming that I would have survived without a scratch, given my military occupation specialty as a clerk. As the company clerk I typed up at least half a dozen requests from soldiers who volunteered to go back to Vietnam! I have tried to assuage my guilt by thinking of these people as more than happy to take my place. It has never quite worked.

Vietnam overshadowed everything at Ft. Leonard Wood while I was there. Toward the end of my time in the military, a soldier I worked with claimed he had shot an unarmed woman standing in a field. Was he telling the truth or just trying to make himself look tough? I could never tell. He wasn't the tough type. It wasn't like a confession—just a statement of fact one day while we were talking. If true, he was guilty of murder. Nobody else was around when he told me. I couldn't imagine anybody I knew would try to do anything about it if I told someone. But that was just an excuse to not report him. All this guy had to do was say he was just kidding. I never could look at him again without thinking of what he told me. The My Lai Massacre in Vietnam in which American soldiers murdered over 300 civilians would not become public knowledge until November of 1969, after I was already out of the Army. After what I had heard, I wondered if My Lai was just a drop in the bucket.

Until this point in my life I had never owned a car. I never needed one. Within a couple of weeks I was becoming desperate to get off the base at Ft. Leonard Wood. You needed transportation if you were going anywhere off post. The Peace Corps had deposited in an account for volunteers the sum of $100 for each month of service, so I used the money to pay cash for a new Volkswagen. Each Saturday at noon when we were released from formation I would jump in my car, turn up the radio and start screaming curse words until I got off the base. My epithets were purely a release from the regimentation I had dealt with during the week, as well as the things I could do nothing about.

In many ways Fort Leonard Wood was like a regular job, but every week that crawled by I felt like I was wasting two years of my life. After 5 p.m. the prospect of returning to the barracks for the rest of the evening was hardly appealing. Sure, we could go to the NCO Club and get cheap drinks, but that got old, too. During the spring and summer I played tennis and once got to the finals of the base tournament where I lost 6-1, 6-0 in about 20 minutes to a sergeant in his forties who was a native Hawaiian. His name I've forgotten, but he was one of the nicest guys I met while in the military. Since he knew no one would be watching our match, he had brought a six pack of beer for us to share afterwards in the middle of the court. He was a "lifer," of course. He invited me to a Fourth of July party at his house. He was married and had twin daughters "Cookie" and "Candy." I may have been the only Caucasian present, and I think his guests wondered why I was there. The age and rank difference (they were all E6's or above) made my appearance awkward. I stayed for less than an hour. Still, I truly appreciated his kindness in having me to his house.

Our team won the 5th Army tennis championship at Ft Leavenworth, Kansas, one of the summers I was there. The highlight for me was having my own room for two days while I was on active duty. Since we won the tournament, our team was invited to have our photograph made with the commanding general once we returned to Leonard Wood. I had never been that close to a general and frankly was appalled by how much the junior officers sucked up to him. If that behavior was typical, no wonder we were losing in Vietnam. Of course, had I been in their situation, I would have acted the same way.

I also made some good friends in my barracks at Leonard Wood. They were lab technicians who did some kind of testing with petroleum. They were smart guys and very funny. Later, I would have the opportunity to invite them to a party in St. Louis that would prove unforgettable. A number of them were from Ogden, Utah, and described themselves as "Jack Mormons," backsliders in the Church of Latter Day Saints. My future second wife, Susan (there would be two ex-wives named Susan—both very nice women), and her roommate, a Welsh girl named

Rhian Samuel, who became a successful composer and professor in Great Britain, allowed me to include my Army buddies for a party at their off-campus apartment. Though they later divorced, one of the backsliders would marry the daughter of Harry Cary, the baseball announcer for the St. Louis Cardinals and later the Chicago Cubs. Not everyone distinguished themselves that night. The brainiest of my Army friends vomited on the wall next to the life-size cardboard photograph of the mini-skirted "Dodge" girl who advertised on television. She was not impressed.

I got to know Susan #1 while campaigning for Senator Eugene McCarthy for the 1968 Democratic nomination for president. Whether that was legal for someone in the military to do, I didn't ask. I wasn't in uniform from Saturday at noon for the rest of the weekend. McCarthy had taken on the unappetizing and Herculean task of challenging a sitting, albeit increasingly unpopular president of his own party, and with a great deal of help, had driven Lyndon Johnson out of the race. I was visiting Bruce, who had gotten into graduate school at Washington University in St. Louis. As would become a painful but well-known historical fact in the annals of American patriotism, American men in the Armed Services returning from Vietnam were not receiving a hero's welcome, especially on liberal campuses like Washington University. Despite wearing civilian clothes, my military haircut identified me as the enemy. Sure, I might be against the war and I didn't go to Vietnam, but the unasked question in this era was: what was I doing in the military at all? It was during the time when the folksinger Joan Baez was encouraging women to say "yes" to a marriage proposal from the guys who said "no," and burned their draft cards. Since I no longer had a deferment, I didn't appreciate what I considered the hypocrisy of college students who had gotten deferments and looked down on people like myself who were in the military. My own reasoning was hypocritical to say the least, but for one of the few times in the military I identified with my fellow soldiers.

Along with a Japanese friend of Bruce's by the name of Mitsuo Ohare, Susan, Bruce and I drove to Terre Haute, Indiana, one Sunday and met Lee and Ann, who had driven from Purdue, where they were in graduate school, to campaign for McCarthy. With Lyndon Johnson out of the race, McCarthy was now running against Bobby Kennedy. To motivate the volunteers, the movie star Myrna Loy was at McCarthy Campaign Headquarters. Born in 1905, Ms. Loy, though very nice, was a bit past her prime to someone in his early twenties, and that may have been a clue to how the "Be Clean for Gene" campaign would proceed.

In fact, once Robert Kennedy entered the race, I, like many others, switched my support to him. His brother's assassination in Dallas had changed him. From someone who had functioned as the least impressive spokesman while Attorney General for his brother's administration, Bobby Kennedy began to listen and learn from people who were in touch with the poor and powerless. He lost some of the arrogance which had marked his persona. As a Kennedy he knew only too well that besides hard work, the United States was very much about class, privilege, power, and dumb luck, and he began to speak for those on the margins of American society in a way that resonated for a growing number of my generation who were members of a privileged group. His assassination, coming after his brother's and Martin Luther King's, once again shook the country to its foundations even as some white Southerners were happy that another Kennedy was murdered.

Like other people who were gay but hadn't come out then, Bruce lived as a heterosexual. And perhaps like my roommate at Southwestern, he concealed his sexuality from others and himself by dating girls. Bruce had received both a Fulbright and

Rotary International fellowship and lived abroad in Germany and Austria for most of two academic years. But it was on Washington University's campus in St. Louis in the late 1960s where he became radicalized politically. It wasn't merely that Bruce opposed the war in Vietnam. One of his good friends declared himself to be a Marxist and had spent some time in Cuba and was a fan of Fidel Castro. On the wall in his apartment where we visited, Jeff displayed photographs of Karl Marx and Che Guevara. He said he told his parents they were Walt Whitman and Omar Sharif. Despite his roommate, neither Susan nor I could imagine Bruce as a revolutionary, and, he wasn't, despite writing that he hoped Nixon won the election because it would hasten the "revolution," and saying he would burn his draft card. This was all very heady talk, especially coming from someone as gentle and non-violent as Bruce. The revolutionaries would prove to be the SDS, the Black Panthers and the Weather Underground, not Bruce Whitten.

As a southern, white upper-middle-class privileged male in the 1960s, Bruce's one revolutionary act was to marry an unforgettably sweet and kind black woman from Georgia. Of course, it was doomed from the start. Ira (the only female Ira I've ever known) was a graduate student with Bruce in economics. They were wed at the Ethical Society in St. Louis. Bruce's brother, mother, and father came from Arkansas; however, Mr. Whitten didn't attend the wedding and remained in their hotel room. Some of Ira's family were there, but the "celebration" afterwards was brief. I remember washing cups and saucers afterwards with Susan and Rhian and being glad it was over. It was a stressful occasion. I don't recall Bruce smiling a single time. I shuddered at the thought of the conversation he must have had with his father. If it had been Jake, I don't imagine his reaction would have been any different.

Susan and I got married in May of 1969 while I was still in

the Army. By then I had decided to apply to law school instead of graduate school even though Dr. Likes informed me that the University of South Carolina had upped its offer of a fellowship by a thousand dollars. I was no longer interested in a possible academic career even if I somehow made it through graduate school and obtained a doctorate, which was certainly an iffy proposition. I wanted to do something and not just spend the rest of my life analyzing and commenting on what other people did. What was occurring in American society during my time in the Army began to change my idea of what I wanted to be. But it wasn't only the assassinations of Martin Luther King and Robert Kennedy that made me want to find a more pro-active way to live. Teaching seemed too passive. Lawyers had an impact on society that the average professor didn't have, and I wanted to be in the middle of what I figured was "real life." Ramsey Clark, who was Attorney General between 1967 and 1969, and as close to an honest politician as the country would ever see, would become a hero of mine.

I applied to the University of Arkansas at Fayetteville but did poorly on the law school aptitude test. Not to worry! It was explained to me that Fayetteville merely required that the test be taken but that the University at that time didn't use it to determine whether you would be accepted. That policy would change later, but given my test scores I never would have been admitted. Arkansas's law school in Fayetteville preferred to weed students out the first year. These were still the days when in the first week we were told to look to either side of us because after a year one of us would be gone.

Before starting law school I had set off what was amounting to a stink bomb in the white community in Marianna. Beginning in the winter of 1969 I had begun writing "letters to the Editor" to the *The Courier Index* about race relations and school integration in my home town. Obviously feeling emboldened by my temporary "hero" status, I decided it was my obligation to urge Marianna to accept "total integration," which was fast becoming the only school desegregation plan the Nixon Administration would accept. Federal court decisions and the Department of Health, Education and Welfare (now Health and Human Services) were now pressing the Marianna School District (as it was all other districts) to desegregate once and for all. In the winter of 1969, for the people of Marianna, both black and white, the prospect of full public school integration had finally become an unavoidable reality. All efforts to pretend that it was never going to happen in Lee County, Arkansas, realistically ended with the front page headline in the *The Courier Index* in February that twice went across the entire width of the paper: "HEW Presents Plan for Total Desegregation of Marianna Schools Beginning in 1970."

Though the publisher Marvin Caldwell had been happy to run my articles about my Peace Corps experiences in Colombia, my pieces about race relations in Marianna were not welcomed. Though he never responded, I didn't have to be told I had become a troublemaker. What had gotten into these boys from Marianna? Why, the idea of a white boy from Lee County marrying a black girl and the superintendent's son at that! And now letters from Jake and Temple's son calling for total integration—who was he kidding?

The history of interracial sex could be read on the streets of Marianna in the pigment of its citizens, but marry a black person? Lee's father, Franklin, who was one of the kindest men I'd ever met, asked him if I had "dated" a black girl while I was in the Peace Corps. He wanted to know my "mental attitude." A letter to Bruce and Lee from me, on the typewriter volunteers were provided to write our reports, recounts an outing to a professional tennis match in the city of Barranquilla. I wrote them that "I had my first date with a Negro girl." I explained that she was the Colombian Peace Corps secretary at the Barranquilla office. "There were a lot of rich Americans there and we had a lot of stares." I noted, "She is as black as the majority of our Negroes back home—you know that chocolate color." I added, "I wasn't trying to prove anything. I just asked her because she is a nice girl period. I would appreciate if y'all don't write home about this. I don't think Marianna is quite ready for the news. And if it does get out I want to be there to defend myself."

Why did I feel I needed to defend myself or worry if anyone knew? It was one thing to say that I was free from the prejudices I had grown up with and quite another to have internalized those beliefs and feelings to the point where I didn't care what other people thought and said about me. Of course, I cared. And some of the people I knew best and who cared about me most couldn't understand what had gotten into me.

CHAPTER 8

Talk, Talk, Talk

> *Most people in my family's circle of friends didn't join the White Citizens Council or allow their children to use the "N" word, but at the same time we didn't write letters to the state-wide newspaper denouncing our own behavior.*

Viewed almost fifty years later, my advocacy of "total school integration" in Lee County seemed naïve to say the least. Two letters I received in the winter of 1969 from two high profile individuals with vested interests in the Marianna public school system made it clear to me in no uncertain terms how unrealistic my ideas were to whites. Betty Sue Kell, my former speech teacher, who had been so supportive of me (and still was) pointed out that total school integration would mean a private school and white flight with dire consequences to the town; School Board President Lon Mann wrote a three-page letter that, in part, outlined his hope that he could persuade the Nixon administration to continue to accept Marianna's "Freedom-of-Choice" plan that had resulted in only 200 black children choosing white schools, resulting in a 10 to 1 white/black ratio. In the eyes of a small minority of whites, including Betty Sue, this freedom-of-choice solution would have been acceptable. A token amount of public school integration in the South, of course, was no longer agreeable to the federal judiciary and the Nixon Administration which now was refusing to accept anything less than the abolishment of dual educational systems. The era of delay was over.

Though it appears no copies of my letters to the *The Courier Index* in Marianna or to individuals on the subject of race relations in Marianna have survived, my friend Lee captured the gist and tone of them in a letter he wrote to his parents Agnes and Franklin during this period. In part, it reads:

> ...*if you will permit me a biblical analogy, I think there is a strong resemblance on this matter between Grif's attitude, purpose, style, etc. and that of Paul of the New Testament—at least with my conception of Paul. Grif is convinced totally—as I am—that complete integration is right. In pursuing that goal, he is undiplomatic, impatien[t], completely honest, in fact brutally so sometimes—and generally very rough in his approach. But I don't doubt for one second that his motivation is essentially one of love for Marianna which he still holds very close though the feeling may not be reciprocal and love for the black people that he feels have been too long and too much oppressed. He feels he has a responsibility and an obligation as a citizen of Marianna to do what he can to bring integration about. And believe me he still feels very much a citizen of Marianna. He still speaks with great pride of the plaque the city gave him and the love for the community and his sense of responsibility combined with the rightness and goodness of integration that leads him to his actions. Regarding his efforts to speak with Negroes, he has made efforts both over the phone and by letter to communicate with the black community in Marianna. The letters have gone unanswered and his telephone talks have met with a non-committal response. In addition the The Courier Index no longer prints his letters, which have evidently been several.*

So much for a diplomatic career! I guess I wasn't a pleaser any longer. Another letter that I had written to Mary Ava Burke, who had taught me in three subjects in high school, but to which, in my memory, she made no reply, had been shared with Lee's parents.

In the letter to Lee from his father, Franklin makes reference to an "organization" I wished to start in Marianna to support "complete integration." What I had in mind I have no recollection. Nor do I now remember having written her or called individuals to urge solidarity on the issue of integration. Had it not been for Lee's meticulous record keeping I would have very little record of my actions during this period.

Lee goes on to answer his parents' question about what he thought:

> *The one thing that gives me ever-deepening shame is that I grew up listening to the teachings of Christianity and taking it very much to heart—and yet remained so unaware and immune to the brotherhood of white man with black man existing on the doorsteps of the church and the school. The church need not send missionaries to Africa. These are problems down on Alabama St [in Marianna].*

Notwithstanding my naiveté, Lee's comments about his own feelings bolster my belief that I had not become some kind of disillusioned malcontent who was trying to cause trouble in his hometown just for the hell of it. His acknowledgment that he felt "shame" because he had been "unaware and immune" to the notion of our common humanity with black people in Marianna suggests there were others in our generation who had become acutely uncomfortable with the way we treated black people. If someone with Lee's intelligence, scholarly turn-of-mind and fundamental good sense could feel so alienated from his roots, it was a sign that my own emotions weren't the product of some guilty fantasy. More logical, deliberate, measured, and painstaking on his worst day than I would ever be on my best, Lee's willingness to characterize his emotion as one of "shame" said volumes about the untapped potential to acknowledge the truth of what the past in Marianna had been like. Not given to histrionic emotional outbursts, Lee had worked through all the denial, repression, rationalization and other defense mechanisms that allow humans to make tolerable our fears and anxieties and had confronted his "shame." Had I read his letter to his parents back then (whom I became even more fond of as they aged), I would have felt less of the "lone ranger," than I did.

Reading Lee's description of me more than 40 years later should not have come as a revelation. To those who disagreed with me about race—which so far as I knew was likely every white in Marianna outside of Lee and Bruce, who no longer lived there either—I have no doubt my efforts came off as arrogant, self-righteous, and preachy. At the same time, Lee's letter to his parents underscored the influence of our upbringing in Marianna. As children who had been brought up in the Judeo-Christian tradition, we had been taught morality and ethics by our families, the First Presbyterian Church, and by others who influenced us. As previously acknowledged, an agnostic by the time I was in my twenties, in no way did I think of myself as some kind of twentieth century apostle, and yet like Lee, it was these teachings, beginning and ending with the Golden Rule ("Do unto others as you would have them do unto you"), that we were taught. It was understood, of course, that this unassailable precept didn't apply to roughly half the population in town.

Undeterred by the responses and non-responses from people in Marianna, I continued to stay abreast of the civil rights activity that had begun to come to a boil in the Arkansas Delta in 1971. Readers interested in an overview of the events in Marianna during this period and afterwards (1969-1972) are invited to read my chapter titled "Marianna" in *Ruled by Race: Black/White Relations in Arkansas from Slavery to the Present*, published in 2009. My account in no way contains a "Deep Throat" insider's view of the mind-boggling racial turmoil that involved a business and school boycott by blacks which had devastating and tragic educational, social and economic consequences to Lee County as a whole. Beneath the surface what occurred in Marianna and who did what in those years is still a matter of extreme controversy and dispute and so far remains largely undocumented. In short, the business boycott of over a year was in no manner a non-violent protest in the manner of Martin Luther King, nor was the response to it by whites peaceful. Many questions remain as well about the school boycott and its aftermath. From a broader perspective, what happened in Marianna was a more intense replication of what already occurred in much of the South, including the Arkansas Delta.

* * *

The Army had granted me a routine "early out" of a couple of months so that I could start law school at the beginning of the fall semester in September of 1969 in Fayetteville. Susan and I found the bottom part of a house to rent on Dickson Street. The upper floor was occupied by Terry Hopkins, the starting center on the Arkansas Razorbacks football team, his wife Jeanette and their toddler. Susan found a part-time job in a gift shop called Studio Northwest and would later be hired as a secretary in the university's acclaimed Department of Architecture, home to nationally known Fay Jones. I went back to school on her meager earnings, the G.I. Bill and an unexpected $300 dollar scholarship awarded by the law school that I hadn't applied for but which was much appreciated.

Now that I was out of the Army, I was primed for law school but also some involvement with the Arkansas civil rights movement that went beyond letter writing. It had gotten seriously cranked up again in the Arkansas Delta after the assassination of Martin

Luther King, Jr.[1] As I describe in *Ruled by Race*, until his murder, civil rights advocacy in the Arkansas Delta (as it had in Little Rock) in the 1960s had been fueled in part by the nationally organized Student Non-Violent Coordinating Committee. Though on a national level SNCC ("SNICK") had begun to implode in 1965 as a result of internal debates over whites' involvement in the organization, the "black power" movement never had the same appeal in Arkansas as it had elsewhere. In parts of the Arkansas Delta, civil rights activity had never ended, only slowed down after SNICK lost most of its funding after ridding itself of whites.[2] In Phillips County, for example, black students in 1966 staged a seven-week boycott of classes in Marvell, protesting school authorities' refusal to comply with federal desegregation guidelines. With 1,500 out of 1,800 students staying out of classes, the power of students and their parents to affect changes was formidable. The tactic would become familiar in this new phase of the civil rights movement in Arkansas and very familiar in Marianna.

At the time Susan and I moved to Fayetteville from Ft. Leonard Wood in August of 1969, there were civil rights demonstrations underway in Forrest City just 17 miles north of Marianna. While waiting for law school to begin, I seriously considered driving to Forrest City and joining the demonstrators. Had Martin Luther King, Jr. been alive and leading the protest I would have gone; however, it was then being orchestrated by a group out of Memphis called the "Invaders," not a name that inspired confidence. Their leader, Lance Watson, aka "Sweet Willie Wine," had little credibility after his "March Against Fear" across the Arkansas Delta attracted about as many newsmen as marchers. I was also afraid that I would get arrested, and it would somehow keep me out of law school or would come back to haunt me when I graduated and tried to become licensed. Instead, I wrote a letter to the *Arkansas Gazette* which since the middle sixties had become "the liberal queen" and supported civil rights for blacks. Captioned "The Fear in East Arkansas," it reads as follows:

> I am white and a native of Marianna. I have watched the white community in Marianna and the rest of eastern Arkansas deny black people the right to any equal education, equal job opportunities, equal use of public facilities, and equal protection of this country. I have watched the white community discourage black people from registering to vote. And until the last few months I have watched black people remain passive and hopeless in the face of this incredibly vicious racism, because they had been effectively intimidated by the white community.
>
> Now, when black people are starting to demand certain rights which are supposedly guaranteed by the Constitution of the United States, the white community forms a vigilante group which pledges the riddance of outside agitators.
>
> It would seem to me that in eastern Arkansas there are a few white people, at least, who, in the name of human decency, support the civil rights of black people. It would seem that there are a few ministers who would say that we should try to love black people instead of hate them. It would seem that there might be a few educators who would say we must integrate the schools, so that all children will receive the same education. It would seem that there might be a few housewives who would say that they want the same opportunities for black children as they want for their own children.
>
> If these people do exist, and I am convinced that there are people in eastern Arkansas who support the cause of justice, then why don't they speak out and support the just demands of black people? The reason is obvious to anybody, black or white, who lives in eastern Arkansas. No white person speaks out or does anything, because he is afraid to do so. Fear is the main factor which causes people to remain silent. Fear is the reason why we don't have any "insiders" to stand up for equal justice for all men. Outsiders have only their own lives to lose, but insiders risk their families and property as well. They know they will live and raise their children

in a community where many people will hate them for the rest of their lives.

Until we have some white people inside eastern Arkansas who have the tremendous courage that will be required to face up to the racism in their own communities, we will always be directly or indirectly part of the sickening injustices perpetrated against black people in eastern Arkansas. These people must find each other and stand united against the cancer of racism. [3]

    I signed it, and it ran in its entirety on September 3. I didn't have the guts to tell Temple in advance that I was going to write the letter. I was afraid she would guilt me out of it. As both my sisters let me know soon after it was published, the letter hurt her badly. She had been so proud of her "hero" just two years earlier, and, now, in her estimation I had forfeited all the "good will" that had accumulated as a result of the banquet in my honor two years earlier.

    Though Temple had been a housemother at Ole Miss going on seven years, her most important relationships had been formed in Marianna and were still there. Though she had not gotten along with her mother, and her father had been dead for decades, her sense of herself was still that of a Southern white lady born and bred in Lee County, Arkansas, and as Jake Stockley's widow. She never had a date after Jake's death. We used to tease her about some of the eligible widowers in Lee County, but she would shudder at the thought. Neither her mother and older sister had remarried though they were widowed relatively young.

    Temple still rented a small house for when she returned in the summer and thought of herself as having never left Marianna. Evidence that she maintained her class status were the wedding gifts Susan and I received from the elites in Marianna. As Temple had predicted and Susan noted, people were "generous." Even if the *The Courier Index* had not published my letters about integration, it ran an account of our wedding and photo of the bride despite the fact that the wedding was in Pittsburgh and I was still in the Army and had not lived in Marianna in years. Had we married after I sent my letter to the *Arkansas Gazette*, people might not have been so generous.

Though no family members put it so directly, in their minds I might as well have spit in the faces of people who had gone out of their way to honor me. People were now criticizing me, and I wasn't even there to get as good as I had given. Whatever Temple said about it to me, I can no longer remember, having repressed it, too. If she was told about the letters I had written people in Marianna and said something to me about them, I don't recall that either. I will always wonder if Jake had been alive whether I would have had the courage to write it. Certainly, I wouldn't have had I been living in Marianna any longer. Even now I can't imagine defying Jake. I never did while he was alive.

The letter was an emotional turning point for me. By publicly describing and condemning white supremacy in the Delta I had breached an unwritten code of conduct that was a way of life for people in our social class. Most people in my family's circle of friends didn't join the White Citizens Council or allow their children to use the "N" word, but at the same time we didn't write letters to the state-wide newspaper denouncing our own behavior. Whatever misgivings any of us whites had about the past treatment of African-Americans in the Delta, the notion that these views should be aired publicly by whites was not acceptable. White supremacy was not merely some ideology that we gave lip service to. It was a political and social system that had economically worked well for us since the end of slavery, but now political correctness dictated that it need not be articulated or analyzed publicly any longer. Doing so only attracted criticism. That wasn't the white Southern way of doing things. Besides, blacks were beginning to raise hell. To begin to discuss the past candidly and truthfully in this new environment would only bring demands for more change.

One person from Marianna (obviously white and anonymous) responded in the letters-to-the-editor column in the *Arkansas Gazette*. In effect, the letter challenged me to put up or shut up. "If you really are interested and want to help, come home and teach or work with all of our people. Our actions of good will and understanding speak much stronger than words." The actions of "good will and understanding" the writer spoke of presumably referred to the completion of the construction of the new high school (Lee) and meetings in which both races participated. My critic acknowledged, "Perhaps there are many truths in what he said, but there are many facts he did not say because to my knowledge he has not been in Marianna for seven or eight years for more than a few days at a time."

It may have been the first time I had ever known a white person in Marianna to come close to acknowledging publicly that the past might have been different from how we had portrayed it to ourselves and others. Still in the future, my five books of non-fiction would document "many truths" about Arkansas's racial past, which confirmed the "sickening injustices" alluded to in my letter. No matter. The problems in Marianna supposedly could be worked out if people of "good will" were willing to sit down together and talk, but in any case were not going to be solved by a former white resident shooting off his mouth.

The idea that black people in the Delta had rights that transcended what we whites wanted was not only a non-starter, it was intolerable. This was White Supremacy 101, which had always come before morality and the law. For more than a century what we whites had said and done had been the law in Marianna; when that was no longer possible, we avoided complying with it when it suited us, and when that was no longer an option, we pointed out the hypocrisy of well-paid federal judges and politicians who lived in the North and sent their own children to private schools. Then many of us also sent our children to private schools or moved as far away from blacks as possible.

Years later I would occasionally have the opportunity to return to Marianna and visit people including the Manns and the Kells who were very gracious to me. We almost never talked about race and then only fleetingly. Along with a few other whites, Betty Sue would continue to teach in the public school.

CHAPTER 9

Sexism and Racism —the Law School Way

...[U]nless you were extremely idealistic, [the Legal Aid Bureau of Pulaski County] [in 1972] was a "starter" job for lawyers, most of whom who had not been stellar students. It only paid $700 a month. You made contacts, got a little experience and moved on. I took it more seriously than that and stayed 32 years.

UNDERSTANDABLY, I had no illusions about any natural aptitude I had for law, and I studied hard every day. Our class had some very bright people, one of whom was Mike Beebe, later governor of Arkansas. There were only three women in my class. The sexism they had to endure was outrageous in some courses. We males pretended that it wasn't so bad. After all, some of our professors had the notion that their classes were the appropriate venue to exert maximum pressure on law students. The judge hearing your client's case was not worried whether he had ridiculed you and hurt your feelings. The movie, *The Paper Chase*, depicting pitiful, exhausted first-year law students at Harvard being browbeaten by John Houseman as Professor Kingsfield, came out just a year after I graduated.

During class, I wanted to applaud when, after a humiliating exchange with a professor, one student who was sitting at the back of the tiered classroom, got up, gathered his books and walked slowly down the steps and out the door. In more than one class I chose the fattest student I could find to hide behind. The adage "power corrupts and absolute power corrupts absolutely" is as true in the classroom as it is in any other situation, and would come back to mock me years later when I taught clinical courses at the University of Arkansas at Little Rock law school.

Despite all my studying, by mid-semester it looked like I was destined to be one of the students who would not be around much longer. Al Witte, our freshman contracts professor, gave a "practice" test, and my results were not encouraging. An unnerving percentage of us received D-minuses or F's. Typically, I overreacted, telling Susan that I needed to start looking for a job. That semester, my grades were mostly C's, but one B-minus and an A in the one-hour legal research course saved me from total mediocrity. I was not headed for the Law Review, but I wasn't going to flunk out either.

In the grand scheme of things, my memories of that first semester in law school pale in comparison to the "main event" that fall. What we white Southern males (and many women) really considered memorable took place on a bitingly cold day on campus on December 6, 1969, in the presence of the leader of the "free world." Richard M. Nixon helicoptered onto the practice field next to the Razorback stadium for the "Big Shootout" between number one Texas and number two Arkansas. After Arkansas lost 15-14 in this so-called "game of the century," I recall watching a drunken fan (male, of course) angrily knocking over tiny crosses stuck in the ground outside the stadium which were part of a protest of the Vietnam War. From a civil rights perspective, the game was noteworthy for the fact that neither team had a black player, but for the first time the Razorback band didn't play "Dixie," after protests by the student group "BAD" (Black Americans for Democracy).

In my freshman law school class were two black students I would get to know. Gene Hunt, Darrell Brown and I had joined LSCRRC (Law Students Civil Rights Research Council). Our primary activity was trying to recruit black students to come to law school at Fayetteville, a futile exercise, but our interest resulted in a summer internship in 1970 in Little Rock at the state's first integrated law firm of Walker, Rotenberry, Kaplan, Lavey and Hollingsworth. Ted Goodloe, who was president of our LSCRRC chapter, had been an intern the year before and encouraged us to apply. That summer we mainly followed around John Walker, Phil Kaplan and Jack Lavey, who were then doing the bulk of the civil rights litigation in the state. I knew so little law after the first year of school that my summer internship was largely wasted as a learning experience, but it was rich emotionally in a number of ways. It was a privilege to watch John Walker think on his feet as he cross-examined witnesses. He never let people see him sweat, if he ever did. I would never see anyone better. These guys were very bright with impressive backgrounds. Phil had graduated from Harvard and then Michigan Law School and John had a Master's in education from New York University and his law degree from Yale. Phil and Jack had been lawyers at the National Labor Relations Board in St. Louis.

There were a couple of awkward moments for me and Susan that summer in Little Rock. As a token white, she had been hired to work at the State Capitol on one of Governor Winthrop Rockefeller's projects to find jobs for minorities in state government. We had gotten to be friends with Gene and Mary Hunt. Gene and I had talked about going into practice together. We went to a black bar with them and perhaps Darrell Brown one night on Ninth Street. Told that it was a private party (it was clearly not), Susan and I were publicly asked to leave. We did so. Our friends stayed at the bar. In one way, it was a tiny and insignificant lesson in what black people had experienced throughout their lives; on the other hand, however, it was not an encouraging sign that whites and blacks would someday stand together. Less important but true, our feelings were hurt. The interns and their wives were supposed to go to John Walker's house for a social event later that evening. Susan and I didn't go, and John asked me the next morning why we hadn't come, leading to another awkward moment. I told him what had happened. Understandably, he seemed unimpressed by my account of what occurred at the bar on Ninth Street. Many years later John would say as an aside in a speech he gave at the Clinton Center in Little Rock that because I was from Marianna he hadn't trusted me. As a graduate of Harvard, Phil interviewed my daughter Erin, who was applying for admission in 1991. She was accepted, and at least I hadn't hurt her chances.

I would have much more on my mind than law that summer. Temple died suddenly on May 15 in a hospital in Oxford, Mississippi. She had contracted Friedlander's pneumonia, a form of the disease I had never heard of and have never heard of anyone contracting since. I remain convinced that if the doctor had sent her to Memphis before she became so ill that she might have lived. But I wasn't even there when she died. It was my sister Harriet and Temple's sister Sarah Hope who had first gone to Oxford and let me know how serious her condition was, but I was taking my final exams. Finally, I went before my last exam, but it was too late. She was already dead.

I didn't appreciate how kind Temple could be to others until after her death. Beside the letter from the student from Ole Miss, two others reveal a tenderness I had forgotten. One of the letters to her was from Sally's husband, Voris, who once lettered in four sports in the same academic year at Arkansas Tech University, and had been raised in near poverty by an older sister. In some ways, because he was so much younger than Jake, increasingly

I saw him as a father figure, especially as Jake's health began to decline even before he developed lung cancer. In the letter, written in 1968 while I was serving in the Army, Voris is thanking our mother for an undisclosed gift of money that seems timed to coincide with his birthday. In part, he writes:

> *I have told you before how proud I am to be your son...and how glad I am that my children are your grandchildren. It means so very much to us to have you with us, and we all look forward to your coming.*

He signs the letter to my mother, "I love you."[1] Not every son-in-law can honestly say the same, but my sisters agree that Voris genuinely cared about our mother. As someone who had extreme difficulty expressing his emotions, Voris must have found it difficult to write such a letter. Temple was by no means wealthy but always appreciated her son-in-law's kindness to her and the rest of our family. In turn, he saw our mother especially as part of a family he seldom had experienced.

Another letter is to my mother from Sally Mixon, my childhood playmate. Temple had written to let Sally know she couldn't come to her wedding because of her job. Temple writes in part:

> *I'm proud of you, Sally. I also love you very dearly and wish for you all the joys, happiness and fulfillment that are so rightfully yours. I shall follow your life with interest, prayers and thanksgiving in the years to come.*

Unbeknownst to me, Sally had been close to my mother. Sally writes about Temple:

> *...her very real love and support helped me be a better, more loving person...I always knew she loved me, no matter what. A great gift.*

Since neither Susan nor I had any furniture (the house we rented was furnished), my sisters graciously allowed me to take almost all the furniture from Temple's apartment. Some of it was antique—the spooled bed posts, rocking chair, and other pieces are my physical links to Temple and Jake.

My link to my grandmother would be severed the same year. Effie's last years were marked by fear, even horror, perhaps caused by a memory she never named. Something surely had happened to frighten her badly when she, as a young wife, and my physician grandfather had been living at Raggio. She would mutter the name "Raggio" under her breath. At night, when she was still living alone and before dementia completely overtook her, she would place her crystal on the window sills in her house and wedge knives in the frames to wake her and to discourage an attack. Was she robbed or had someone tried to rape her? I never knew. In the late 1960s I visited her for the last time at Crestpark Nursing Home in Marianna with Bob Blankenship, who would serve as the executor of her estate. I was then living in Little Rock and hadn't seen her for years. I can still hear her shrieking, "Let me die! Let me die!" Her cries that day for some reason I associate now with the high-pitched keening of grief-stricken women in Muslim countries. Ouw! Ouw! Was she in pain? Was it nightmares? Whatever, the horror is old age, but now that it is upon us, all we can do is laugh nervously.

Before being confined in the nursing home at Crestpark, Nannie was shuffled from sibling to sibling, except for Uncle David whose "drinking problem" gave him an iron-clad excuse. When Nannie stayed with us one summer, she would lock us out of the house if we happened to go outside. Her growing deafness, memory loss and fear would up the odds that we would have to break in but it never was necessary. If we pounded hard enough she would eventually hear us and open the door. It was as if an ancient memory had been waiting just for the moment she was alone to terrify her. To us it was maddening, funny and shameful all at the same time. Were we so selfish we couldn't take our turn coping with an old, increasingly addled woman? Aunt Tissie and her family had borne the brunt of her care.

Sadly, a little of Nannie went a long way. She had wanted to live out her life in dignity and usefulness. In her scrapbook there is a newspaper photograph of her at the age of 75 when she was living in Gary, Indiana, with Tissie, who was teaching school. She is paired with another woman, age 64, who had set the record for stuffing envelopes with Christmas Seals in the fight against tuberculosis, still a scourge in the 1950s. Effie was reported to have stuffed "thousands" herself. It has only been in the writing of this memoir that I have wondered, in spite of our differences, how much like her I would become.

With Temple dead, one of Effie's 40-acre farms went to Harriet, Sally and me. It was rented out. The idea of being an absentee landlord in Lee County held no appeal, and we had it sold. In my mind, it was a final step in cutting my ties to the way I had been socialized in Marianna. In fact, I was merely cashing in one of the tangible benefits to having been raised a privileged white male in the South.

It was my second year in law school that I began to write an article or two anonymously for the publication *Many Voices*. In May of 1970, four white former VISTA workers incorporated a civil rights organization headquartered in West Memphis they named Respect, Inc. As VISTAs they had chafed at the restrictions on political activity, but now no longer working for the government, they could serve as staff for the new organization which was funded by private grants. I began to correspond with Earl Anthes, one of the founders. One of them, Gene Richards, would become a famous photojournalist. In the middle 1960s SNCC was active primarily in Forrest City, Helena/West Helena, and Gould in south Arkansas, but now there was civil rights activity in eight counties as blacks came together to protest discrimination in employment, municipal services, the school system, and police misconduct. The black leadership in these counties was homegrown. Respect, Inc. had its own board of directors composed of representatives from each of the Delta counties.

My articles dealt with basic rights of individuals—for example, what to do and say if you were arrested. My plan was to move to West Memphis after the bar exam and go into practice by myself. Susan would keep my books, having taken accounting courses at U of A. I figured I would have a ready-made base of clients in these eight counties. The problem was I didn't know the first thing about practicing law. I didn't know how to try a case. Despite having made a B-plus in the four-hour evidence course, I couldn't have gotten a parking ticket admitted into evidence. The closer I got to graduation, the more I realized how ridiculous it would be to open a law office by myself. There were people in my class capable of succeeding that way, but I wasn't one of them.

I let Earl know that I wasn't coming, and we moved to Little Rock and got an apartment across from the University of Arkansas for Medical Sciences complex. Susan found a job immediately with the Welfare Department. I studied for the bar exam and postponed looking for a job until after it was over. I had only minimal confidence that I could find employment as a lawyer or would even pass the bar exam. Fittingly, it was given in an auditorium at the Arkansas State Hospital for persons with mental illness. The bar exam was an intense experience. Within 30 minutes one person got up and walked out.

While waiting for the results, I looked for a job and also went down to the "casual labor pool" at six one morning, so I could contribute something to the Stockley household. Since I had a car,

I was hired to drive out to west Little Rock and help with some yard work. The woman who had hired me was a large person with an Italian accent who was doing some major lawn repair. I watched her husband drive off in a huge Cadillac. She was bigger and stronger and worked twice as fast as I did. It was close to 100 degrees by noon. Part of the job involved moving sacks of concrete in a wheelbarrow to the back of the house. After three hours my arms were trembling from fatigue. I was so shaky that I couldn't keep the wheelbarrow balanced, and it would tip over. I took break after break. She was barely sweating. I told myself she had been a peasant in Italy who had thrived on manual labor. At noon, afraid that I was going to pass out or worse, she unceremoniously fired me. Though I was shamed and protested that I just needed to rest a bit, I was so grateful that I could have wept. When I got to the apartment, I took my morning's earnings and walked across the street to the liquor store and bought a six pack and went back to the apartment to take a nap. I had to pass the bar exam. I wasn't fit to work.

With what little confidence I had fading fast while I waited for the bar results, I applied for numerous permanent jobs, some non-legal. Somehow, I passed. Fearful that a mistake had been made, like most of my friends were, I didn't go ask to see my exam. A position for a staff attorney was open at the Legal Aid Bureau of Pulaski County, which was funded by the federal government to provide representation to indigents in civil cases. At the time, applicants for attorney positions interviewed with a couple of board members as well as the executive director. My only real selling point was that I had been a member of LSCRRC in law school. To put it mildly, the Legal Aid Bureau was obviously not on a par in terms of prestige with any of the private firms or even state agency jobs in 1972. Arguably, unless you were extremely idealistic, it was a "starter" job for lawyers who had not been stellar students. It only paid $700 a month. You made contacts, got a little experience and moved on. I took it more seriously than that and stayed 32 years.

CHAPTER 10

Legal Services

At Legal Services we were always being asked by our clients if we were "real lawyers." I had wondered that myself on more than one occasion. Because our clients were poor and easily intimidated and had no other place to go, they could be put off. They rarely asked the hard questions, and early in my career I didn't volunteer how few of the answers I knew.

DURING THE FIRST couple of years I was there, the Legal Aid Bureau of Pulaski County seemed more like a "divorce mill" than a law firm charged by Congress with the responsibility of creating access to the American justice system for poor people in non-criminal cases. The emphasis was on keeping the "numbers" up. We staff attorneys primarily did uncontested divorces, name changes, guardianships, adoptions, and other types of cases that moved quickly through the system. We filled in forms and handed them in to our secretaries, and they typed them. Hobson Mahon, our African-American executive director and a licensed attorney, was rarely around. It seemed he was there early in the morning but would soon leave and then return late in the afternoon. He had an excellent secretary who screened his calls. Some of us would later believe that he had outside business interests that occupied his time. The lawyer who supervised the other five or six staff attorneys, including myself, was a friendly, helpful white guy named Bill Isch who was retired military and was trying to get enough experience to open his own practice in the northern part of Arkansas.

When I first began work there in 1972, we were connected administratively to the Economic Opportunity Agency (EOA) of Pulaski County, the local anti-poverty program, which, in turn, was administered by the state Office of Economic Opportunity. At the top of this bureaucracy was the federal Office of Economic Opportunity. As the largest anti-poverty program in the state, the EOA of Pulaski County was a lightning rod for criticism. Articles appeared in the press questioning whether the EOA of Pulaski County was a make-work boondoggle rather than an effective agency that had figured out how to create meaningful job opportunities for the poor and end poverty in the United States. In fact, when I began, our program had a couple of non-attorney employees whose duties I was never certain about.

The debate has never ended over whether the "Great Society" programs would have made a difference had not the Vietnam War intervened. In contrast to the Department of Defense budget, the domestic budget for poverty programs was a pile of sucked-over chicken bones. "Guns and butter" was the shorthand way of describing Lyndon Johnson's dilemma during the Vietnam War. The country was said not to be able to afford to wage a foreign war and fight poverty at the same time. As time has passed, poverty has always seemed like a safe bet, as was noted a couple of thousand years ago. On the other hand, advocates contend a War on Poverty has never been tried in the wealthiest country in the world.

As a federally supported program, Legal Services would survive only because of bipartisan support during the Nixon administration and the steady and high-powered backing of the American Bar Association, whose leaders were convinced there was merit in a federal government-sponsored staff attorney model of providing legal services to indigents in civil cases. In 1974 Congress created the Legal Services Corporation, and it was this crucial move that has kept Legal Services afloat all these years. Not that a legislative amputation from the original War on Poverty programs ended political controversy—far from it. President Ronald Reagan would try to kill Legal Services and came close to doing so, but that was later. Though controversy has routinely centered around the size of its budget—in 2013 funding was just over three hundred million dollars compared, for example, to the defense budget of approximately 716 billion— the most serious opposition has been ideological and political. The United States Constitution doesn't require that indigents have appointed for them free lawyers in non-criminal cases, and here was yet another government program willy-nilly turning on the spigots full blast at the trough of the U.S. treasury.

I don't remember Jake yelling over much of anything. Instead, when angry, in my memory, he usually gritted his teeth and shook his head in disgust. Had he been alive during my legal career, he would have ground his molars down to the gum line. But I didn't hear a single complaint from him about the federal government's subsidies of agriculture and levee projects that benefited our family's social class. We white Southerners took handouts from the federal government at the same time we carped about the federal bureaucracy. The hypocrisy of railing against the government had never fazed me during those years I mooned over Ayn Rand's free enterprise-loving heroines in *Atlas Shrugged* and *The Fountainhead*. The subsidies kept on coming.

As a brand-new lawyer, and all of us staff attorneys were, I was at ground zero as far as knowing the first thing about how to go about the practice of law. I had no clear idea about what I was doing and had no confidence initially that I could teach myself. In the beginning my dominant emotions were fear and anxiety that I was going to humiliate myself and/or commit malpractice. During those early months, I reverted to an infantile way of coping, wanting to be spoon-fed everything. In the beginning, I didn't trust myself to look up the law or understand it even if I could find it. As mentioned, we had no clinical courses at Fayetteville that had prepped us for the practice of law. Nor had I taken any courses in law school that would have prepared me for what was basically a domestic relations practice in the first year or two I was at Legal Services.

Even though in my last year in school I had gotten some sense of how pieces of the law could be made to fit together, it was an intellectual experience that somehow for me at first didn't necessarily translate into practical skills. Fifteen years later when I taught a clinical course at the law school in Little Rock, I remembered how helpless I had felt and guided my students through an exercise in which they were required to take each sentence of a routine legal pleading and document the legal authority for its inclusion. It wasn't rocket science. Much of the needed information could be found in the Arkansas Rules of Civil Procedure. Though nothing more than an elementary confidence builder, it was comforting how much confusion and insecurity began to melt away if you took the trouble to do something so basic to understanding how a lawsuit could be put together. Initially, it was helpful for me to think of the practice of law as a series of traps for the unwary or lazy, a "gotcha" mentality. In fact, the process could be much more creative and consequential for our clients, but that realization was in the future.

By chance I had a great secretary that first year. As disorganized as I was (and still am), it was a relief to know that Barbara Smith could put her hand on every piece of paper in every one of my files in seconds. In the year or so she was my secretary, Barbara, a delightfully warm and kind African-American my age exactly, got visibly annoyed with me just one time, which I still consider a miracle. Certainly, it was a record. Unfortunately for me, the word was out about Barbara's competence and good humor. After a year, she got hired away by federal magistrate Henry Jones and made more money, which she richly deserved. Barbara, I would learn, during the 1960s had been a witness in a federal court case in which blacks overturned Orval Faubus's prohibition of African-Americans eating in the state capitol cafeteria. This was even after the 1964 Civil Rights Act had been passed, but Faubus had been quoted as saying that "if you give in to them on this there will be something else."[1]

Mr. Mahon did one thing for me that made a huge difference in my professional life. He permitted me to drive out to the University of Colorado at Boulder to attend the National Institute of Trial Advocacy (NITA) for three weeks in the summer of 1973. To its immense credit, NITA awarded scholarships to Legal Services attorneys. It was like going through a semester-long clinical program on steroids. We were taught basic trial skills, then taped and critiqued by lawyers and professors who were experts. Though I would never be mistaken for a great trial attorney, I would learn enough to make a record I could take up on appeal, and in some of the cases I would one day handle at Legal Services, this was crucial. The confidence the three weeks in Boulder gave me was a pivotal moment in my legal education and career. I began to feel like I could at least become a "real" lawyer. Had I not been so intimidated I could have gotten on a steeper learning curve. At the same time we had in succession assigned to our office two qualified but young female attorneys from out of state who were funded by the Reginald Heber Smith Fellowship program. At that time "Reggies," as they were called, were then to be given the opportunity to do what would be called "impact litigation" or "law reform." Intimidated by their law school pedigrees (Linda Scholle had graduated from Boston University and Glanetta Miller from the University of Michigan) and fearful I would be over my head in cases brought in federal court, I didn't take advantage of the opportunity to work with them while they were assigned to our program. My own reluctance initially to get involved with federal court litigation was a sign of how little confidence I had in those first few years. At the same time I knew if I were going to get involved in civil rights cases I would have to get over my fear of going into federal court. There is a well-deserved mystique about practice before the federal bench. Appointed and not elected like state court judges in Arkansas, federal judges are generally assumed to be smarter and more scholarly and even more ethical. They make more money and have more prestige. In state court there was occasionally "a good ole boy" feel to the proceedings and once a Little Rock lawyer left Pulaski County to try a case, there was routinely a belief that the local lawyer got home cooking. A three-hour course in law school on federal jurisdiction was available as an elective, but I had never made higher than a C-minus in the two courses I'd had under Professor Al Witte (Contracts and Constitutional Law), so being a coward or perhaps prudent, I had dropped it after about a week. I would have to learn it on my own, an educational process that never ended while I practiced law.

There were members of the bar and Congress who wondered what Legal Services attorneys needed to be doing in federal court anyway. In fact, from its inception there has been a battle royal at both the national and local level over the purpose and direction of Legal Services. Advocates from the National Legal Aid and Defender Association (NADLA) and their allies argue that Legal Services offices should be allowed to represent their clients as vigorously as corporate lawyers. This would mean lobbying, class actions, doing complex litigation in both state and federal courts, appellate work, etc. Conservative opponents contend that this kind of advocacy amounts to social engineering and implementing the liberal agenda. Back and forth the board of Legal Services and Congress went, some years restricting our advocacy and other years allowing us to be full service lawyers depending generally on which administration was in power.

While I was at Boulder the summer of 1973, Susan called the first week to tell me she was pregnant. We were thrilled. We had bought a home in the Oak Forest neighborhood in Little Rock at a time when white flight was well underway in central Little Rock. Real estate agents sent letter after letter to whites trying to frighten them into selling their homes at low prices to escape looming racial integration of their neighborhoods. Such "blockbusting" was a violation of the 1968 Housing Act, but the law was rarely enforced. The Justice Department filed one suit and got a consent decree against one Little Rock real estate company, but it had little effect, if any.[2]

Our idealism apparently knew no bounds. By our decision to buy a home in Oak Forest we thought we would help stabilize the area. We joined the Oak Forest Property Owners Association which had been started by ACORN, which then stood for Arkansas Community Organizations for Reform Now. As an aggressive and sometimes effective advocate for low and middle income people on a number of issues including voter registration, ACORN's influence would grow until 2009 when it would be taken down by conservatives who alleged financial and other wrongdoing.

ACORN's style was confrontational and at the same time secretive. As a member of the Oak Forest Property Owners Association in the early 1970s, I was ever so briefly on the state ACORN Board, but resigned after a few weeks because it was clear that Wade Rathke, who ran things with an iron hand, had no intention of making the organization transparent. It was an organizing tactic—had its opponents known how few members ACORN actually had, its influence would have been substantially less in Little Rock. Still, it felt like the Board members were superfluous, a feeling I would come to know well.

When Susan first felt labor pains on December 20, 1973, we had just taken her mother to the airport. She had flown to Little Rock to be present for the birth of her grandchild, and now had just missed it. Susan was admitted to St. Vincent's and, told our baby would not be born until the next morning, I slept that night on the floor at home in the kitchen by the telephone. It was still the era when fathers weren't allowed in the delivery room. As squeamish as I was, it was probably just as well. When the doctor wheeled them out, I asked if it would be okay to touch my daughter. Given the okay, I carefully put my finger on her arm and immediately withdrew it. Obviously, I had a lot to learn. I had no idea what a joy she would be to me and still is.

The longer I was at Legal Aid, the more dissatisfied I became with what I considered the non-performance of Mr. Mahon. I wasn't the only staff attorney who felt that way. Mike Gorman was the kind of attorney who made you smile and proud to be a lawyer. Sensitive, empathetic, by temperament Mike was as much social worker as he was a lawyer. Had he lived (he would die of cancer way too young) and stayed at Legal Services, I would have driven him crazy. He cared more about people than any lawyer I would ever meet.

Mike and I began to make sure that it wasn't just our imagination that Mr. Mahon was rarely present during office hours. Although I don't remember what we found, if anything, we even went through the trash once to see if we could discover what was taking him out of the office. Significantly, my own dissatisfaction coincided or perhaps was precipitated by a life-long fling with the philosophy of existentialism, or at least my understanding of it. On August 3, 1974, I began a journal that reads, "I was living a life which in existentialist terms was inauthentic and not in good faith...I now consider myself a [sic] atheistic existentialist *a la* Sartre as primarily interpreted by Hazel Barnes who translated *Being and Nothingness* and wrote *An Existentialist Ethic*." *Whew!* With time to read again after law school, I had become intrigued by philosopher Jean Paul Sartre's arguments that to live an "authentic" life one is permitted no self deception of any kind. It assumes that humanity is utterly free but also alone. With this freedom comes the responsibility (if one is to live authentically) of choosing at every moment to exercise freedom to make decisions about one's behavior. To allow others to make one's decisions (society, one's parents, religion, authority of any kind) is to choose an inauthentic existence. I imagined it was possible that I could be open at every moment to the notion that I existed in absolute freedom. Thus, I had the responsibility of consciously choosing at every moment how to exercise this freedom. It was exhilarating for a few weeks. But trying to maintain this level of conscious behavior for even five minutes at a time was hard work. Not only was this impossible for me at least, it didn't make daily living with me a pleasure. In any case, I was one serious dude. Mr. Mahon needed to go.

I note in my journal in 1974 that I wrote (I have misplaced a copy of the letter) two of the board members "asking them to resign from the Board of Legal Aid," if they were not going to exercise what I considered their responsibilities to our clients. To put it mildly, this level of arrogance is not generally appreciated from an employee. As I waited for a response, I alternated between expecting to be fired and somehow believing my rebellion might be appreciated. I recorded in my journal that during this time I was offered a job with the Attorney General's office, but this is misleading. Mike Gorman, who resigned to take a job at the AG's office, said he had been told I would be hired if I wanted a job there, but I never went for a formal interview. I didn't want to.

My journal reflects that Legal Aid board member Bud Whetstone, a successful lawyer still in private practice today, took it upon himself to conduct an investigation. Bud had worked at a legal aid clinic while in law school at the University of Mississippi. I felt he could identify with us in a way others on the Board did not. I told him that I was going to resign if the Board wasn't going to act. In a telephone call in 2014, Bud recalled he had gone to the Board and shared his concerns that more people would be resigning. He volunteered to take off from his practice to determine what was going on. Though friendly with Mr. Mahon, Bud said he told him that he would let the chips fall where they may. According to Bud, Mr. Mahon was satisfied with the fact that Bud would be the one checking on him. Bud said he talked with everyone on the staff and determined that discontent was uniform throughout the program and reported his findings to the board. I wrote in my journal that Mr. Mahon resigned on September 28. Even after I wrote the letter to the board, Mr. Mahon continued to treat me with respect. Perhaps he felt that as long as people showed up for work and the "numbers" were "okay," he was doing the job he was hired to do. If it was cowardly not to confront him directly, I didn't allow myself to understand it that way and probably felt how every whistle blower must feel—that I had no other option.

Was this a sign of the appearance of the *hypogrif*? Would I have written such a letter had the Executive Director been a white male? I hope so. I think the truth had to do with my own arrogance during an extremely idealistic period of my life. Though the turning point for me as a lawyer was my three weeks at Boulder, the 1970s were the beginning of a golden age for legal aid attorneys. We had "back-up" centers such as the National Consumer

Law Center and the Housing Law Center, where all you had to do was pick up the phone and talk to an experienced attorney who was a specialist in the area. These attorneys were so eager to help they could overwhelm you with their knowledge, and I never came away from a phone call without sweating as I tried to keep up. There was also meat-and-potatoes material from a monthly publication called the *Clearinghouse Review* that each staff attorney received free. It contained the synopses of the latest poverty law cases from all over the country and gave a list of the essential pleadings and briefs which you could obtain without costs from the *Clearinghouse* library. Legal Services picked up the tab for out-of-state training involving mock hearings where you had to prepare an argument and argue a motion in front of an experienced attorney acting as a judge. You would be critiqued afterwards as was done at Boulder. Despite the pressure or perhaps because of it, the experience was excellent training.

One resource for us, of course, was the private bar, or at least those lawyers who didn't see us as competition or part of the Communist conspiracy. Though we renamed our program Central Arkansas Legal Services (CALS), convincing lawyers outside of Little Rock they had nothing to fear was not easy. Our two biggest supporters in the private bar then were Wright, Lindsey and Jennings, and the Rose firm, both full of excellent lawyers with big-time reputations in Little Rock.

Rose firm partner Vince Foster was particularly mindful of his ethical obligation to see that indigents received competent legal services and was a hands-on member of our board. One sweltering summer day, he, two employees of the Legal Services Corporation (both lawyers) and I, as executive director of CALS, drove to Pine Bluff in a Rose firm car to meet with Jefferson County bar leaders to convince them that our expansion into their county was no threat to anyone. It was not a message that was well received in the mid-1970s. Their arguments were familiar and would be replicated everywhere I went. Poor people were getting legal services already; the government was trying to socialize legal practice; it was a waste of government money, etc. They weren't going to be able to stop us from coming in, but if we hoped we could convince them that day that Legal Services was needed in their community we were dead wrong. By the middle of the afternoon, all we wanted to do was beat it back to Little Rock, lick our wounds and sip something cool.

Vince personified for me the private bar at its best in his commitment to fulfill the lawyer's ethical obligation to make legal services available to the poor. A brilliant lawyer, he was all business whenever he came over for our board meetings, but that visit to Pine Bluff surely tested even his commitment. To make it a perfectly horrible day, the Rose firm car ran out of gas between Little Rock and Pine Bluff. Well before cell phones, I still can see Vince walking down the side of the highway to find a telephone in what I always called (behind his back) his black undertaker suit, though that day it was too hot and miserable to see the humor in anything.

This was many years before he went to Washington as the Clintons' lawyer. His suicide was a total shock. I was on vacation in Canada when I got the news he had shot himself. We would learn that he suffered from depression and was taking medication, but the unrelenting viciousness of Washington politics could have plunged anyone into clinical despondency. The country had lost somebody truly special and never realized it in the swirl of the ridiculous rumors disseminated by the haters of the Clintons, who were their real target.

Later, Legal Services became an accepted part of the legal community throughout Arkansas. Not only did most attorneys in private practice get it through their heads that we created work for them, many lawyers signed up to take *pro bono* cases from our overflow, thus fulfilling their ethical responsibilities to serve the poor.

One of the highlights for me was that Hillary Rodham talked to me about the job of litigation director at Central Arkansas Legal Services after she and Bill moved to Little Rock for him to become attorney general. She had been the director of the Legal Clinic at Fayetteville. I had been in a meeting with her with two officials from the Legal Services Corporation who seemed hell-bent on ending the corporation's support of Legal Clinics in law school settings. She made such persuasive arguments for continuing the partnership between the corporation and legal clinics in law schools she turned them around before they left Little Rock. It was obvious to everyone she was an extraordinary person. I offered her the job even though she had very little actual litigation experience then. In fact, she was so smart and aggressive she would have been dynamite. She took a job at the Rose Law Firm, and the rest would be history. She would serve during the Carter Administration as president of the Legal Services Corporation. I can at least say I interviewed a future Secretary of State.

Though I have never regretted my role in Mr. Mahon's resignation, it wasn't long before I got my comeuppance and learned how difficult it was personally to navigate the issues of race when two years later I was given his job. By 1976 two executive directors had come and gone when I was offered the position. My opportunity coincided with a time in which Congress was appropriating additional funds to make legal services for indigents more widely available. This allowed us to open two new offices outside Pulaski County and hiring more staff as well as a director of litigation. We were fortunate that a young lawyer with trial experience by the name of Bill Massey came over from the Youngdahl firm in Little Rock. Though I learned right away Bill was laser sharp, little did I suspect he would ultimately go on to an outstanding career at the prestigious Washington, D.C. law firm of Covington and Burling. There were other hires I got to make. Now, five years after I had gotten a job as an attorney, the executive branch of the federal government was pushing hard to make the American workplace more inclusive. Affirmative action had arrived. Though requiring a specific number of African-Americans to be hired was considered a "quota" and deemed illegal by the Supreme Court in 1978, "goals" and "timetables" were acceptable. As important as the bureaucratic efforts of the government have been to make employment opportunities available to minorities, everything depended on the good faith of employers to implement affirmative action. This, of course, sometimes meant telling some excellent white applicants they would not be hired.

As an employer, my most conspicuous and clear-cut failure (but far from my only one) was not offering a job to Davis Moore (not his real name), a black attorney from Pine Bluff for the new office in Jefferson County, 50 miles from Little Rock. When Mr. Moore let us know he wanted to be considered for a position in Pine Bluff, I had already filled two of the three positions with two white attorneys who were graduating from law school with outstanding records. A young lawyer named Jim Cromwell, a graduate of William & Mary law school in Virginia, who had graduated near the top of his class, became a third white applicant. He was then teaching in the legal writing program at the law school in Fayetteville. His interview was impressive. A few years earlier he could have been my professor. I badly wanted to hire him as a staff attorney.

Unquestionably, though, we needed a black attorney in the Pine Bluff office which had the largest African-American population of any town in the state after Little Rock. Bill Massey sat in on the interview with me with Mr. Davis, who was clearly nervous that particular day. He had a weak interview. Instead of checking further and contacting lawyers and others in Pine Bluff to get a better idea of his reputation and ability, I didn't offer him the job and instead hired Jim Cromwell. Had I thoroughly checked Mr. Davis out, I would have found he had a good reputation in both the black and white communities and would have done well as a staff attorney. Years later after he was elected a judge in Jefferson County, I represented a person with mental illness in his court. By his demeanor, it was clear he hadn't forgotten me.

Looking back on this time, unquestionably there was quite a bit of hubris, hypocrisy and ego involved in the decisions I made. In 1969 I had pontificated in my published letter about the lack of equal job opportunities for blacks in eastern Arkansas. But when I was in a position of authority to do something about it, I didn't—not in this particular instance. The fact that I hired mostly black paralegals during this time only accentuated what I had done. I wanted to make Central Arkansas Legal Services as respected for its legal work as some of the programs I read about in the *Clearinghouse Review*. And, in fairness to myself, I was trying. But this was also about my own ego and reputation.

Instead of getting out of my office and going into the black community to try to persuade black attorneys to come to work at Legal Services, for the most part I waited for applicants to come to me. But if affirmative action was to mean more than going through the motions it would require reaching out in ways I hadn't done, even though I then lived in an integrated neighborhood. Though our salaries weren't competitive with nearly anyone, Central Arkansas Legal Services wasn't a divorce mill any longer and offered young attorneys the opportunity to get into court on a variety of issues and develop real skills. That was its real selling point.

It has only been in writing this memoir that I have admitted to myself that my poor decisions as executive director had much to do with my own inferiority complex and class bias. If Mr. Davis from Pine Bluff had expressed himself more articulately that day, I would have hired him. Had I been more secure about myself, I would have made better decisions, but the complaints about my management style went far beyond this one error of judgment.

As the executive director for almost a year and a half, I improved upon the saying, "What can go wrong will go wrong." What I could do wrong I did do wrong. When I became the executive director, we had a bookkeeper who had been there since the program had first opened its doors in the sixties. Try as I might, I could not convince her that as the buck-stopper I needed to be able to look at the books myself and make the decision whether we had the money to hire people and pay the bills. She took it as a personal insult. What was she for? If I needed to know if we could afford to hire somebody, she said she would tell me. It wasn't that I thought she was stealing money from us, nor in fact was she. It was about power, of course, or at a minimum, feeling important. Her job wasn't in danger, but she couldn't accept that she wasn't going to have the influence she had enjoyed under previous executive directors, and I couldn't persuade her that it had nothing to do with her. I had always been told that lawyers made terrible administrators, but I had no idea until I took the job. She finally quit in tears after I hired an office manager. I went through two office managers in my tenure.

I had a complaint from a female attorney of Asian descent (now deceased) I had hired that she wasn't being paid commensurate with her responsibilities as supervisor of the domestic relations unit which now included a number of paralegals. My memory is that she felt she should be paid more than the male attorney who had previously served as the domestic relations supervisor but who had supervised no paralegals. He was now the housing attorney. Insanely, I purported to solve that problem by cutting his salary instead of raising her salary, thus treating two people unfairly. She soon left, but Bill Rahn stayed for years and is a good friend, though no longer practicing law.

Recently, he told me he thought I had "gotten a raw deal," remembering that I had been "encouraging" to him and others. A truly nice guy to this day, he was being charitable in his assessment of my performance. The list goes on. A black secretary was unhappy because she wanted to be a paralegal, and I didn't consider her to be qualified. Ultimately, no one filed suit, but there was always that possibility.

All my pain was self-inflicted. Why didn't I pick up the phone and call the Legal Services Corporation and admit that I needed help? I have no idea other than arrogance on my part. The discontent was so great that our employees soon joined a union affiliated with the AFL-CIO, one of a handful of Legal Services unions in the country (I would eventually join it myself after I was no longer executive director)! As someone who believes in unions, I didn't fight it. I was just embarrassed that everyone felt a need to organize against my management. I had ignored the direction of the Legal Services Corporation to draw up salary scales for positions. Having risen to the level of my incompetence, I stupidly tried to argue that management should set attorney salaries based on one's work product instead of longevity despite knowing that non-profits don't work that way. Nor can I say that I was a warm and fuzzy boss. But whether they believed it or not, I sympathized with our attorneys when Bill and I went through their cases and found they were stuck and had never quite gotten around to making decisions about a case. I knew very well what it was to be stuck and push the hard cases to the bottom of the pile.

The worst humiliation of my 32 years at Legal Services came in 1977 when my board placed me on "probation" for not having offered "meaningful opportunities" to black attorneys. Since I was not allowed to appear before the board to try to defend my actions, I was never certain what that meant, but over the years I came to accept I had not recruited or hired black attorneys in sufficient numbers. By coincidence, I had just completed the draft of the manuscript which many years and dozens of revisions and additions later, became *Ruled by Race: Black/White Relations in Arkansas from Slavery to the Present*. In those days I called it, *Thank God for Mississippi: Race Relations in Arkansas*. "Thank God for Mississippi" was a familiar refrain since in those days we seemed to be able to count on the Magnolia State to nose us out for first place in national poverty statistics and racism.

In the next three months I came up with a salary scale with the help of the Legal Services Corporation and the Board voted to "take me off" probation. I waited until this mark of disgrace was formally lifted and then resigned as executive director the same night. I had told no one except Susan that I was going to resign. After being accused of racism and sexism, it had become obvious to me I wouldn't be able to make a personnel decision without wondering if it would stand up. Bill Massey agreed to be acting executive director, and as soon he agreed to take the job, he looked 20 years older, and I felt 20 years younger. I was allowed to remain as a staff attorney. My real career as a lawyer for poor people was now about to begin.

By chance, an anecdote in a memoir by a former Arkansas Supreme Court justice documents my coming of age as a Legal Services attorney. Though he never advertised the fact in his campaign literature, Tom Glaze had worked for six months in 1966 at the Legal Aid Bureau of Pulaski County before I was ever employed there.

Almost immediately thereafter, he would gain a well-deserved reputation as a fighter for election law reform. *Waiting for the*

Cemetery Vote, published in 2011 by the University of Arkansas Press, is largely an account by Justice Glaze (now deceased) and Arkansas journalist Ernie Dumas of the judge's efforts as a young lawyer to combat the notorious electoral corruption in parts of Arkansas. In part because of the publicity garnered as a result of his efforts, Glaze ran for and won a position as a chancery judge, a job that required a much different temperament than serving as a successful advocate. As he states in the book, he was "sworn in January 1, 1979, but it would be a few months before [he] became a judge for real."

The judge was referring to a custody case he heard in which I appeared as an attorney trying unsuccessfully to persuade him to return custody to the mother of a three-year-old child who had been placed in the care of foster parents:

> *The hearing was contentious and Stockley was a zealous advocate. He argued and argued with my rulings and told me I was just dead wrong. I was on the verge of holding him in contempt. I called a recess and had the chamber to myself. My hands were trembling. I thought to myself: I'm a judge now and not an advocate. If I'm going to be an impartial arbiter I have to listen patiently to everyone, even lawyers who are as contentious as I was, and indulge their zealousness. When the hearing resumed I felt a great relief. That moment came back to me hundreds of times at choleric moments in the courtroom and in conferences the next thirty years. I always felt a little obliged to Stockley who was a young lawyer then and who would spend his life as a tribune for the poor and mistreated and as a chronicler of Arkansas's terrible history of racial repression.* [3]

I have only the dimmest memory of this case but hope I wasn't stupid enough to tell a judge he was "dead wrong." Another cringe moment. But even if I didn't use those precise words, all I had achieved up to that moment was to make a judge angry. I can recall that when the hearing resumed, there was an entirely different tone to the rest of the proceedings. The judge and I were both much calmer, no longer adversarial toward each other, and now I understand why. It was no longer a pissing contest between two males who were convinced the other was badly mistaken. Until reading his book, I had no idea how close I had come to being held in contempt of court.

In retrospect, the upside of this story is that it is comforting to see it documented that I tried as hard as I did in cases that would never make the headlines and mattered only to the litigants. It wasn't an act. Part of my behavior probably had to do with ego. A lawyer is at the mercy of the judge who can humiliate him or her publicly with nothing more than a withering look, and over three decades I appeared before more than one who seemed to make little effort to conceal his or her disdain for me, my arguments, or my clients. In front of these judges whose own arrogance was on full display, I learned to concentrate on simply making a sufficient record upon which to appeal if that proved a viable option—not that I have ever forgotten how they acted, but reversing some of them on appeal to the Arkansas Supreme Court was undeniably sweet.

CHAPTER 11

Due Process

Prudently, the faculty didn't ask to see my grades in school or it would have been too embarrassed to hire me.

SEARED INTO my brain during the 32 years I practiced law at Legal Services in Little Rock were some of the men and women who suffered from mental illness and mental disabilities and were confined at the Arkansas State Hospital and in institutions (Human Development Centers) around the state.

My involvement with this discrete underclass began while I was still executive director with the 1977 federal court case of *Wessell v. Pryor*, which had gotten started with a telephone call to our office by a woman who wanted to be released from the State Hospital in Little Rock. It was a tailor-made situation for our program to challenge the Arkansas involuntary civil commitment statutes which transparently denied elementary due process to individuals who were being confined against their will. At the time we brought the suit, David Knight, then a student at the University of Arkansas law school in Fayetteville, had already written an article for the law review titled, "Arkansas Involuntary Civil Commitment: In the Rearguard of the Due Process Revolution." A number of attorneys from our office, Bill Massey, Leon Marks, and myself, worked on that case, but we also associated Phil Kaplan in private practice whose experience and expertise in civil rights cases were known throughout the state.

Faced with certain defeat, the Arkansas attorney general's office entered into a consent decree with us on behalf of our client and the class she represented. Overseen by federal district judge Thomas Eisele, this agreement addressed numerous constitutional deficiencies in the statute. As a result, persons being subjected to involuntary confinement by the state now had a right to such due process guarantees as notice and right to a prompt hearing, appointed counsel, appropriate standards, etc. Plus, our work resulted in the release of our client.

Contrary to complaints from our detractors, we didn't solicit clients for these cases. The word about Legal Services got around after a headline story in the papers of our successful challenge to Arkansas's mental health laws. Soon, we were receiving calls from patients at Rogers Hall, the fortress-like maximum security unit on the grounds of the State Hospital, where individuals were detained who had been involved with the criminal justice system. When I returned to a staff attorney position, I volunteered to handle these cases. I would learn that in Rogers Hall some individuals had been held for years despite having been found not guilty of a crime by reason of insanity or mental defect. Some of these individuals were dangerous; some no longer were. After litigation by our office, the State Hospital agreed to set up an evaluation procedure which resulted in the transfer of some individuals from Rogers Hall to the more therapeutic environment on the "Open Units," a much less restrictive part of the hospital complex. In some instances it was undeniable that the State Hospital was confining individuals indefinitely without following appropriate procedures and without providing adequate treatment appropriate for their condition and disability.

State hospital psychiatrists and social workers were accustomed to criminal defense lawyers coming out to Rogers Hall to interview their clients. The state was directed to provide forensic examinations to assist the judge in the determination of whether these individuals were competent to stand trial, and if so, whether they should be found not guilty because of mental illness or defect. They weren't at all happy to see an attorney from Legal Services (me) show up repeatedly at Rogers Hall to investigate the conditions, length of confinement, and the validity of the commitment and detention procedures.

As an institutional setting designed to facilitate the treatment and care of persons with mental illness and "mental defects," on a scale of one through ten, Rogers Hall was a minus five. As a secure prison warehouse it was a ten plus. Rogers Hall was oppressively grubby and claustrophobic, beginning with the double set of metal doors at its entrance that opened electronically from the inside. Doctor Diemer (not his real name), one of the psychiatrists, looked uncannily like the patients he was trying to help. A shambling bear of a man whose eyes always seemed troubled, he and I got along well enough, but one of the other psychiatrists detested me and made no secret of it.

What in the hell was a Legal Services lawyer doing out there talking to patients, demanding to see their medical records and charts? His way of dealing with me was to pretend I didn't exist. My own diagnosis of his extreme passive/aggressive behavior I kept to myself. It didn't bring out the best in me. I would almost yell, "Good morning, Dr. Smith!" to try to make him acknowledge me. Perhaps others resented me as much but were too professional to show their disdain.

I could easily imagine going crazy in a place like Rogers Hall. Despite perhaps the best of intentions, some individuals confined at Rogers Hall were being allowed to fall through the cracks. Once their criminal cases had been resolved by a judicial finding of incompetency to stand trial or not guilty by reason of mental disease or defect, at the State Hospital their legal options seemed to dry up. Their cases stopped moving through the legal system. It took sustained litigation to make the system work.

I would later fictionalize these institutions, the patients, and their keepers in the Gideon Page series. Dr. Diemer gave me my own tour of the unit where individuals waited for their court-ordered mental evaluations. Locked in cells were men who were noisily delusional and some who were eerily quiet as they wrestled with voices only they could hear. One was completely naked. It reminded me of the classic 1948 movie *Snakepit*. One of my clients in Rogers Hall was Oscar Carson (not his real name) who I was told had killed a man by setting him on fire. Oscar had been found incompetent to stand trial by reason of mental defect. Though he was diagnosed as "moderately retarded," about 95 percent of the time, so far as I was concerned, he made as much sense as I did, or anybody else, for that matter. Once when I was leaving Rogers Hall, he asked, his voice anguished, "Grif [he called me 'Grif' right away], am I going to have to spend the rest of my life here?"

I promised him I would get him out of Rogers Hall. In November of 1983, I filed a class action in federal court on behalf of Oscar and two other individuals alleging (among other things) that persons with mental disabilities who were in the custody of the state at Rogers Hall were not receiving adequate care, treatment and training. The United States Supreme Court had recently held that individuals with mental disabilities confined by the state had not forfeited their constitutional rights to treatment and training appropriate to their condition. The benefit of separating persons with mental illness from persons with mental retardation for purposes of treatment should have been obvious, for it was clearly not therapeutic to lock up people who were classified as mentally deficient with persons with mental illness. After much litigation, Oscar was transferred to Alexander, one of the state's

Human Development Centers, which devised a special program for people in his situation. Due to the tireless advocacy of John Jones, an employee of the Disability Rights Center, Oscar would eventually be allowed to live out his life in a community placement with 24-hour supervision.

Because the facilities at Rogers Hall were so obviously geared to confinement and not treatment, the state eventually entered into a consent decree with us to construct a new facility on the State Hospital grounds. I was invited to the ground-breaking ceremony. It would be a vast improvement over Rogers Hall. I came to believe that at least some of the doctors and social workers came to regard some of the litigation as beneficial and me as only partly a devil.

During the years I was involved with these issues, three individuals for whom I secured a release died shortly thereafter. One committed suicide days after his release and the other was shot and killed on a Little Rock city bus by the police because he wouldn't drop the machete he was holding. The mother of the suicide, making no attempt to control the fury in her voice, called to let me know her son was dead and that she blamed me. The mother of the African-American man killed on the bus called me after his death to thank me for having gotten her son out of Rogers Hall. She sounded genuinely grateful. Had the police been better trained at the time to deal with these contingencies, my client wouldn't have been killed. Of course, he might still be alive if I hadn't gotten him released.

These cases didn't always involve persons with mental illness or mental defect. I received a telephone call from a social worker at a nursing home in Conway, some 25 miles from Little Rock. I was told the nursing home wanted to discharge one of its patients because the facility was no longer eligible for payments by the federal government on his behalf. A day or two later when

I met him, James Mitchell appeared as healthy and competent as anybody I knew. With his consent, I filed a petition for a writ of habeas corpus and got his case set for a hearing. The lawyer for his family had obtained a temporary guardianship without giving Mr. Mitchell notice of his right to a hearing. In the same order the family had gained control of his estate and had transferred his assets to themselves. A severe alcoholic, my client had not been permitted to drink while in the nursing home and had regained his health. He was told if he continued to drink, it would kill him. After a hearing, my client was ordered released. The judge, who was furious with my client's relatives, let them know in no uncertain terms they were to promptly return his assets to him. Within months my client drank himself to death.

More than once after I got an order from a judge releasing a patient from the State Hospital I would be sarcastically asked by social workers and doctors if I planned to take the patient home with me. They would be infuriated that the patient was being released when they felt the individual wasn't ready and/or that they weren't given the time to plan for his or her release. Should I have taken any of these cases? Is a lawyer ethically required to be "a zealous advocate" at all times and demand that the state prove that all requirements of the statute had been met? And how does the community deal with those people who have been discharged from care but have no place to go or people to take care of them? Our office's reading of the Code of Professional Responsibility was that our ethical duty was to represent the lawful wishes of our clients even if we thought they were not in their best interests. In those instances where I thought clients would be better off staying in the hospital and taking their medication I would advise them accordingly, but if they insisted on a hearing, I would represent them as aggressively as I knew how.

There would come a time when I would be involved personally

in one of these cases, and nothing I did in my career as a lawyer would be as painful and revealing. During a vacation to the east coast Susan and I stopped to visit our friends Bruce and his wife Ira in the Washington, D.C. area where they had gotten jobs after graduate school as economists for federal agencies. Within an hour I knew Bruce was experiencing paranoid delusions. He talked to me about riding a bus and overhearing people whispering about him. He and Ira had visited us for a weekend while I was in law school at Fayetteville. They had seemed happy. Now, he kept bringing up these voices. We didn't know what to do except urge him to see a doctor.

It wasn't too long before Ira let us know they had separated and that Bruce was living in Florida. I wouldn't see or hear from him again until 1979. The delusions continued. He came by my house in Little Rock and held out his hand. He had amputated part of one of his fingers and sent it to President Jimmy Carter. He said that it had a listening device implanted in it. Before then he had paid his way to East Germany to have his teeth x-rayed to look for a microphone. As tragic as these delusions were, they were not in degree any more bizarre than comments I was hearing from clients who had been committed to the State Hospital.

Again, of course, I suggested that Bruce get treatment. I told him that if he did, I would make sure his rights were protected. I went into detail about my litigation on behalf of clients at the State Hospital. He appeared to think about it, but by the end of the conversation I had little hope he would go voluntarily. He was staying at his mother's house in Conway. Shortly, I got a phone call from his younger brother Bill. Bruce was worse and getting sicker by the day. He and his mother were desperate to get him in a hospital. Homeless at times, he had spent months wandering around the country.

During this time he had been arrested like many homeless

persons with mental illness. Would I help get him committed to the hospital immediately so he could get treatment?

I had always liked and respected the Whittens. As the longtime superintendent of the Marianna schools, his father, of course, had occupied an important place in the town's hierarchy. A gentle, kind man with a good sense of humor, Bill, Bruce's younger brother, was employed in Pulaski County as a school counselor and worked with elementary students. Ms. Whitten had been a housewife and moved to Conway after Mr. Whitten's death. I knew how much emotional and financial support Bill and his mother had given Bruce over the years during his illness. I had to help them, but I felt torn. If I helped to commit Bruce after telling him I would protect his rights as a voluntary admission, he would never trust me again. I said I would.

I got permission from Legal Services to take this case while using my vacation time and drove to Conway the next day and found Bruce in his mother's yard watering her plants. He glanced up at me and said, "Grif, you look like a corporation lawyer. Are you here to commit me?" I began to stutter. Still hoping I could persuade him to seek a voluntary admission I began to repeat my pledge to protect his rights. Within moments, he broke for the house and was trying to lock himself in the bathroom when Bill caught up with him and wedged himself in the door. Immediately, I drove to the courthouse and got a judge to sign an ex parte order for a temporary guardianship of the person and estate. With no more than the stroke of a pen, I had stripped Bruce of his freedom and his assets. I took the order to the Faulkner County Sheriff's office and followed officers to his mother's house. The deputies found him clinging to a bed post. They didn't abuse him, but what followed was sickening to watch as Bruce futilely tried to hold on. This was a sensitive, non-violent man who studied two years in Europe on Fulbright and Rotary International Fellowships and was immensely talented in a number of areas. All Bill and I could do was to make sure Mrs. Whitten didn't witness this struggle.

Why did I choose a temporary guardianship when I could have advised Bill and his mother to file a petition for an involuntary commitment through the prosecuting attorney's office? I was afraid he would run off before anything could be done. Because of my work in mental health law, I knew that I was violating Bruce's constitutional rights. In a later case that was decided by the Arkansas Supreme Court, I would bring the challenge that resulted in the temporary guardianship statute being declared unconstitutional because it didn't require a prompt hearing and notice to the proposed ward. In another case that I would litigate with my colleague Jim Cromwell, we persuaded the Arkansas Supreme Court to hold unconstitutional the practice of legal guardians admitting their wards to the State Hospital without going through the involuntary commitment statutes.

In my zeal to make certain Bruce got help, I was far too emotionally involved in the process. I filed a petition for Bruce's involuntary commitment and handled the hearing myself even though the prosecuting attorney's office took these cases as a routine matter. There was no doubt of the outcome of the hearing, so why did I choose a role in which I cross-examined one of my oldest and best friends? I wanted to make absolutely certain the case didn't slip through the cracks but also to ensure the legal proceeding was as non-combative as possible. Of course, Bruce saw me as an enemy, which at that moment I was. His particular condition didn't mean he couldn't think. There was something almost surreal about the hearing. Before he issued the order committing Bruce, Judge Lee Munson told him that he had never had a defendant in his court who was so eloquent. To the judge's credit, he treated Bruce with respect and kindness. In his own defense, Bruce had given an erudite but irrelevant oration on personal freedom in American history.

Fortunately, Bruce was later able to get on medication which finally began to stabilize him. He was eventually employed by the Arkansas Department of Human Services as a grant writer in Little Rock. Years later, we occasionally played tennis together, but our friendship understandably was never quite the same. After his mother died, Bruce took his life. Bill asked me to speak at his memorial service. I spoke about how brilliant and talented Bruce had been. Others who had worked with him spoke glowingly about his qualities as a friend. So much for my high-mindedness about constitutional rights! I had been another lawyer justifying the means to achieve a desirable result. For the first time I came close to getting a taste of what families went through to try to help their loved ones navigate a hideous experience. Was this an example of my own hypocrisy? Undoubtedly. But at the time it seemed the right thing to do.

At the time David Knight published his article analyzing Arkansas's involuntary commitment procedure, the phrase "in the rearguard of the Due Process Revolution" applied to a number of provisions in Arkansas law besides mental health. In part, this was due to the fact that Arkansas's state constitution dates back to 1874 and never has been replaced. Though its provisions have been amended periodically, certain issues escaped attention. One in particular was a section giving "county judges" jurisdiction over juveniles. In Arkansas a county judge is an administrator, not a lawyer. In 1923 the Arkansas Supreme Court had upheld this provision in the case of *Ex Parle King* and it continued as a valid legal precedent. As Legal Services attorneys some of us appeared regularly in juvenile court representing parents who were at risk of losing custody of their child or children as a result of allegations of abuse or neglect. For lawyers, these cases in juvenile court were a nightmare in the extreme because there were no rules of evidence or civil procedure to guide the litigants. There was the oft told story of a county judge deciding a paternity case by examining the ears of a putative father. Even when lawyers were appointed as "referees" in juvenile court, as began occurring in the 1970s, there were still no mandated procedural or evidentiary rules that governed the proceedings despite the fact that the parents' fundamental constitutional right to the care and custody of their child[ren] was at stake.

In 1986, determined to challenge the authority of *Ex Parle King*, I appealed a routine dependency/neglect case in Pulaski County to the circuit court. With the help of the widely-respected organization Arkansas Advocates for Children and Families, fellow staff attorney Bill Luppen and I put on evidence that demonstrated that juvenile issues could no longer be considered "local concerns" that were within the purview of a county administrative official. After we filed a notice of appeal to the Arkansas Supreme Court, Bill left Legal Services and I wrote the brief myself. It would be the biggest case I would ever have before the Arkansas Supreme Court. Never graceful under pressure, I spent part of the weekend before the argument in the bathroom with diarrhea. This case had attracted little attention when we had tried it in circuit court, but the day of the oral argument there was a sizable audience on hand. Since, if successful, this case would change proceedings all over the state, Susan Gill, my second wife, and I took Erin and her step-brother Adam out of school to watch.

My argument went well enough, but it was unclear what the court would do. A week or two later, driving back to the office from the clerk's office with the Supreme Court's decision overturning *Ex Parle King*, I pulled over into a vacant parking lot and burst into tears, which had never happened before or would happen since. That afternoon Max Brantley, then news editor at the *Arkansas Gazette*, asked me to pose for a photograph (Figure 14, p. 118) in front of the Pulaski County Juvenile Court sign.

My picture appeared on the front page the next morning. We had an impromptu party at the house the day the decision was announced. A number of people who were child advocates came by. Someone brought a balloon with the words "World's Greatest Lawyer." That was utterly ridiculous, and I was embarrassed, but I didn't take a pin and pop it.

Procedural and evidentiary rules would not be the only "law reform" that was needed in the juvenile courts of Arkansas. Legal Services offices all over the United States as well as the ACLU began to bring class action cases on behalf of children caught up in state child welfare systems that were severely understaffed and which failed to adequately investigate allegations of abuse and/or neglect. But it was not only the lack of staff and the failure to take action that provided a legal basis for intervention. As the issue of child welfare began to draw national attention and result in federal legislation, taking federal money came with obligations to comply with federal statutes and regulations. Federal law and regulations in most cases required state social service agencies to provide services to attempt to reunite children with their parents who had abused or neglected them before they could try to terminate parental rights.

At the same time, the foster care system in many states, not just Arkansas, was shockingly inadequate. Children were shuffled from placement to placement; in some instances, our clients were children who were dying in foster care as a result of preventable negligence or worse. In time, I and other Legal Services attorneys in Arkansas would become deeply and repeatedly involved in litigation against the Arkansas child welfare agency on a variety of issues. Central Arkansas Legal Services would invite the National Youth Law Center to partner with us to sue the state on behalf of children in the foster care system. Lawyers Bill Grimm and Martha Matthews made numerous trips to Arkansas in the early nineties to mastermind litigation which ultimately resulted in a consent decree known as the *Angela R.* case. It pumped ten million new dollars into the system and required the state to comply with a number of protocols that, when followed, improved the conditions (especially health) of children in foster care. The Arkansas case gained so much notoriety that it became a piece on PBS's *Frontline*. Unfortunately, the quality and quantity of appropriate governmental services in Arkansas, as elsewhere, is always a work in progress.

Throughout this period the Fourteenth Amendment remained the constitutional provision of choice for bringing law reform cases. In 1986 I filed suit in federal district court on behalf of a client whose wages were being garnished by a used car dealer after a judgment had been entered against her. Arkansas statutes at the time did not require that persons whose wages were being garnished be given notice of their right to claim state and federal exemptions which prohibited creditors from taking most of the wages and property from debtors. I argued in a motion for summary judgment that a modern day analysis of due process required the court to weigh the competing interests of the parties. Notice of these rights was essential. Federal Judge William Overton agreed and declared the statute unconstitutional. For garnishments in Arkansas to satisfy the due process clause of the Fourteenth Amendment, they now have to give notice of the above rights. Given the number of garnishments in a given year, it was an important case.

Not every case was a winner. The biggest disappointment was the failure of the Arkansas Supreme Court to declare unconstitutional Arkansas's statute which permitted a judge to fine tenants the sum of $25 for every day they overstayed their lease. Nor could we get a case before the Arkansas Supreme Court to consider whether there is an implied warranty of habitability in landlord tenant cases. Arkansas's strong landlord lobby in the legislature has defeated every attempt of advocates to pass a law giving tenants this right. In every state in the country but Arkansas, either the legislature has created legislation or the state's judicial system has found an implied warranty of habitability.

My colleague, Jim De Priest, and I had the perfect case on track to be heard by the Arkansas Supreme Court alleging there existed an implied warranty in every lease that conditions in rental housing would be minimally adequate, but after we filed a notice of appeal to the Arkansas Supreme Court, the landlord wisely offered our clients the monetary damages we had requested, therefore mooting the issue and forcing us to dismiss our appeal. Thus, no matter how wretched conditions are in rental housing, withholding rent is no defense.

The cases that I was doing at Legal Services prompted an invitation to teach a couple of semesters as a visiting professor in the Legal Clinic at the law school in Little Rock. This was a last minute offer that occurred when the professor who had been hired announced he wasn't going to show up. Prudently, the faculty didn't ask to see my grades in school or it would have been too embarrassed to hire me. They wanted a lawyer, not a legal scholar. Teresa Marks, who was hired to be the clinical supervisor, and today still one of my closest friends, and I immediately dubbed the Legal Clinic the "Vo Tech" Department. Our job was to teach the students who signed up for the course how to practice law, a good thing to know if they were going to become lawyers. The cases that we did were domestic relations cases we took from Legal Services. I was invited to teach a course called Practice Skills as an adjunct for several semesters afterwards. I hasten to add that the clinical program has been considerably beefed up since those days.

Coincidentally, the years that I was most involved with clients who contacted our office from the State Hospital was a time when I felt the strongest religious impulse I have ever experienced. Susan, a cradle-to-grave Episcopalian, took her children, Adam and Carrie, to Sunday School and church while I stayed home with the *New York Times*. Soon, Erin, who was with us half the time, started going with Adam and Carrie, and I started going, too.

If there had ever been an argument about whether a class system existed in Little Rock, it would have ended at St. Mark's in west Little Rock. Its congregants numbered doctors, lawyers, business types, up-scale housewives conversant with Jungian psychology, etc. There were a couple of obviously well-heeled, light-skinned African-Americans, but if there ever were poor people who showed up at the worship service they sat on the back row and left early.

I was open to some kind of spiritual experience, but in my case it was hard going. I couldn't blame St. Mark's, the priests or its congregants, a number of whom I got to know and like and a few whom I truly admired. Neither "high" nor "low" (the priests brought out the incense only at Easter), St. Mark's primary vehicle of worship was, of course, the Book of Common Prayer. When stripped of its sophistication and historical background, St. Mark's was Christianity 101, its traditional beliefs expressed in a liturgical format that dated to the fourth century. I would end up writing a never published book called *The Half-Believers*. My principal lament was the Nicene Creed and Apostle's Creed, the bedrock of the so-called "mainline" churches. When it came time in the service to recite it, I found myself omitting most of it. I simply couldn't make myself believe in the supernatural events upon which everything else was based. So what was I doing in church at all? Reading Elaine Pagel's book, *The Gnostic Gospels*, as research for *The Half-Believers*, I realized I felt more comfortable in the camp of those early seekers who seemed to believe they had experienced the truth of Christianity in their hearts and not in their minds. Susan encouraged me to attend a weekend retreat called "Cursillo." From a journal entry dated October 22, 1986: "Back from Cursillo, and I'm still changed. What happened there? Surrender. I felt it. Never have I felt such joy. I still have it.

Unconditional acceptance and unconditional love. For 25 years an atheist and now a child of God."

I still marvel at what I wrote: "It is the surrendering that has done it. Never have I been able to let go of my pride, my complete and total arrogance of self. I reveled [sic] in it, wearing my ego like a badge of honor..." Everyone, including our "teachers" at Cursillo, acknowledged this mountaintop feeling wouldn't last, and, naturally, it didn't. But while it did: "Yesterday at the North Little Rock jail I told a client I would pray for her! Me praying for anybody!"

Cursillo did have a long term beneficial carry-over effect in one area of my life. At different times in my life I had been a heavy drinker, but listening to one of my teachers at Cursillo chronicle her descent into alcoholism and out of it had a profound influence on me. A deeply spiritual and humble person, her utter sincerity, coupled with her intelligence and accomplishments, woke me up temporarily. The Wall weakness for the grape and other "spirits" is in my genes. At intervals I haven't drunk alcohol at all and thus far no longer abuse it.

For three years I regularly attended a small, predominantly African-American church in Little Rock and was attracted by a number of things at New Millennium—its minister, Judge Wendell Griffen, and our group's commitment to social justice and inclusiveness. My cousin, Mary Fulkerson, a tenured professor of theology at Duke, attends a mostly black church that appears to have things in common with New Millennium. She teaches feminist theology. Would Jake and Temple have understood us? Perhaps a little.

CHAPTER 12

Hypogrif

MY COMING OUT as a confessed *hypogrif* is revealed in a chapter I wrote in 1997 for a University of Arkansas Press book whose director at the time was Miller Williams, already a nationally recognized poet whom President Clinton had asked to read for his second inaugural. Each contributor was asked to write about his or her favorite place in Arkansas. I chose downtown Little Rock because, ever since Bill Clinton had announced he was running for president, the city was on the national map for reasons other than our racism displayed in the Central High Crisis in 1957. (Presumably, I was asked to contribute because of the popularity of the Gideon Page series which incidentally coincided with Bill Clinton's time in the White House.) Though Clinton would be called the nation's "first black President" for his genuine rapport with African-Americans, much of the decade of the nineties in Little Rock was a period of racial free fall. In 1993, a reporter from the *New York Times* called us out: "Little Rock, with a modest population of 177,000, is experiencing a big-city epidemic of gangs, guns, crack and murder." In the preceding two years, our per capita murder rate equaled New York and Los Angeles. Overwhelmingly, the victims and perpetrators were African-Americans.[1] A stroll through downtown Little Rock was not always a pleasant way to spend my lunch hour. I wrote:

> *Poverty (and not the kind liberals and conservatives can argue about) haunts downtown Little Rock like a specter. Capitalism and democracy collide in front of my office every day. My own failures as a lawyer for poor people confront me. At noon, as I walk about the area, the homeless, persons with mental illness, alcoholics, and drug addicts dare me to look at them. Often I try not to, because I know I will often be panhandled unless I hurry by and make no eye contact.*[2]

Was it guilt or resentment or both that made these encounters so uncomfortable or both? One individual, a black male, demanded, "*Look* at me!" I did. All I remember is how angry he was. I didn't give him anything, but he had rightly demanded that I acknowledge that he existed. I don't recall when I read Ralph Ellison's classic *Invisible Man*, but the title has always seemed to encapsulate that moment. I was the same person who had spent 21 months in one of the poorest countries in the world, and yet back home I had tried to avoid looking this man in the eye.

I wanted to have it both ways. In *Somewhere Apart: My Favorite Place in Arkansas*, I applauded the richness of the diversity I experienced in the downtown area of Little Rock in contrast to the uniformity and sameness of the shopping malls and freeways that make the western part of the city and the surrounding suburbs indistinguishable from most anywhere else in the country. I pointed out that:

> *...downtown is practically the only place in Little Rock where we as citizens can determine if the American experience can still be about diversity and not sameness... America is cracking and splitting before our eyes into two contiguous but borderless countries—one an underclass, often African-American, composed of the working poor and the unemployed and spiraling downward into an abyss composed of the homeless, persons with mental illness, alcoholics, derelicts, gangs, and drug pushers and their customers, some of*

whom are prone to violence and all to hopelessness. The other country is predominately white, relatively affluent, and concerned with law and order and property values.[3]

The intersection of race and class in downtown Little Rock dates back to the nineteenth century and is illustrated by the story written by African-American John E. Bush, who with Chester W. Keatts, also black, founded a hugely successful African-American burial insurance company in Little Rock, opening 3,000 "lodges" in 26 states and several foreign countries. One day in 1883, while Bush was engaged in conversation with a white man, a black woman approached them to ask for money to bury her husband. The white man complained to Bush, "'I cannot...understand your race. When they work they throw their earnings away and whenever a Negro dies or needs help the public must be worried to death by Negro beggars—it is a shame!'"[4]

In his book, *History of the Mosaic Templars of America—Its Founders and Officials,* chronicling the success of his company, John E. Bush credited this conversation with being the inspiration for the construction of the black-built, owned and operated Mosaic Templars Building at the corner of Ninth and Broadway, which housed not only the insurance company but provided office space for black attorneys such as Scipio Africanus Jones and other black professionals and businessmen. This building would serve as the cornerstone of the black business community in Little Rock for a number of years. More to the point, the story and the person who told it (Bush) highlight the color and class differences within the African-American community in Little Rock in the nineteenth century. The light-skinned boy, who at the age of six was brought to Arkansas from Tennessee with his slave mother and her master to avoid federal troops, somehow obtained enough education to serve as a school principal of two black high schools for three years. During slavery it was not unheard of for Southern planters to see that their mulatto sons were taught to read and write and in some cases use their money and influence to assist them in obtaining more education and even professional careers.[5]

Today, class differences are alive and well as middle-class blacks are financially in a position to choose to live in west Little Rock and can afford to send their children to private schools or have been accepted in the growing charter school movement, leaving the poor to fend for themselves in ghetto areas.

Like the white man in John E. Bush's story more than a century ago, my first thought at encountering the poorest of the poor, often an African-American who was asking for money on the streets of downtown Little Rock, was to wish he or she would go someplace else and get a job. Any relationship that I had with poor people in Little Rock I wanted to be on a "professional" basis; that is, I wanted them to call our office and get an appointment. If I could help them with a legal problem or at least the legal problems I knew how to deal with, fine.

What had happened to the young man who had spent nights in a hammock in the thatched-roof hut of a *campesino* in Colombia? I supported government measures for greater income equality, but I wanted to be left enough not to significantly disturb my own comfortable middle-class existence in the United States. Like many Americans, liberal and conservative, there have been times during my life when I have served meals to the homeless, participated in brotherhood camps for children, volunteered to read weekly with students in the public schools, and served on boards of non-profits. Yet since I have never moved downtown, arguably, I have put the brakes on my sense of community. Assuming one accepts the definition, I am what my good friend Judith Faust calls, "an institutional racist." By my own choices and action I have accepted the "differential inequities" in opportunities available to many African-Americans. A long time resident of downtown Little Rock, my friend sees great value in living in an environment where there is diversity in income, race and class. My motive in not doing so has been largely fear. That what was occurring to make me afraid was generally black-on-black crime didn't ease my concerns. I didn't want to spend my time looking over my shoulder. I worried, too, if a house downtown would hold its value when I tried to sell it.

At the same time, downtown Little Rock, where so much of the history of the state has been acted out, holds an undeniable fascination for me. It was where I set the action for the Gideon Page series and where I practiced law for so many years. So much history within blocks from our office on West Capitol Avenue: in 1927 the bullet-ridden and mutilated body of John Carter was thrown on a bonfire made up of pews robbed from the African-American Bethel AME church across from the Mosaic Templars Building. This had been carried out at the intersection of Ninth and Broadway during Little Rock's last lynching by a frenzied mob of thousands of whites who insisted on making a point to the city's black community. In 1991, I walked over from our office to hear Bill Clinton announce his first candidacy for president in front of the Old State House on Markham Avenue. Inside that building (now a museum) in 1861, a duly elected convention of white men had voted to secede from the United States. In front of the present State Capitol in 2008 I watched Barack Obama speak on behalf of the candidacy of Governor Mike Beebe shortly before announcing his own successful run for president. Perhaps that day the ghost of six-term governor Orval Faubus was in the crowd with me marveling at this astonishing sight. Over in the Arkansas Delta, Jake Stockley, in particular, surely was turning over in his grave. He would have had the last word, as overwhelmingly, white Arkansans had no intention of casting their votes for a black president and demonstrated their disdain for Barack Obama by a landslide margin in both elections. As I conclude a draft of this chapter I am left with a sense of ambivalence about the past and future. Though much progress has been achieved, the issues of race and class continue to dominate the landscape in the two places in Arkansas where I have lived for most of my life (Marianna and Little Rock). A front page headline in the January 28, 2015, *Arkansas Democrat-Gazette* reported, "State Takes Over LR Schools." After a highly emotional five-hour meeting the day before, the Arkansas Board of Education, in a five to four decision, terminated the authority of Little Rock's majority-black school board, effective immediately, an action generating enormous controversy. Dr. Dexter Suggs, the black superintendent, was given "interim" status and instructed to report to the state education commissioner. Only the year before, the Lee County School District (Marianna) had also been "taken over" by the State Education Department because of its "low-achieving" schools.[6] In the case of Lee County, African-American Estelle Mathis, an Arkansas Department of Education employee, met with the Lee County School District and bluntly said the following: "We have veteran teachers who have been here for 100 years and want to teach what they want to teach...and it's hurting the kids." Mathis explained it was a new day for the teachers. "There are three R's: Retrain, relocate, or retire."[7] No one needed to point out that it had become an almost all-black school district taught by blacks. What was impossible to quantify was the effect of the structural and institutional racism that had been a feature of life in the South since slavery.

    A week before the takeover vote by the State Board of the Little Rock School District, then board member and UALR historian Jim Ross, who is white, was one of the leaders fighting to retain the authority of the Little Rock School Board and argued that the district should be given another chance. "We are not going to defend the white privilege in this city anymore. We are not going to defend middle class privilege anymore. We are going to turn our attention to the 75 percent of the children who are poor, who are black, who are poor, who are Latino, who are poor white..."[8]

At this same meeting of the Little Rock School Board, Ross was also quoted by a reporter as saying "every vote by every board since 1955 'was done to protect middle class white privilege in this city and that is what it is still about today.'"[9] One may argue with Dr. Ross, but in fact his larger point is a matter of historical record. White privilege, whether it operates through business or politics or a melding of the two, has shaped education in central Arkansas just as it has shaped where people live. Historians, as well as federal judges, have documented our white supremacist mentality and the measures that have contributed to the portrait of Little Rock as a city deliberately segregated by race and class.[10]

At the end of the day, I am forced to admit that it is more satisfying to wring my hands than it is to act. Perhaps it is as simple as stating the obvious: that I was provided certain opportunities and advantages that others were not and I am too selfish to share. I, too, "have the genius of not seeing...there is a culture of repression here." How much of it is self-imposed is a question for which I have no answer. Historically, some of these privileges have come at the expense of African-Americans, other minorities, the poor and women. The difficulty for me has been summoning the courage and integrity to act consistently on that knowledge. The question that haunts me is determining what my motives were, what they are now.

I end this chapter in February during Black History Month, having attended this morning a program at the Little Rock Central High National Historic Site. Seven of the first

25 African-American students to desegregate the city's junior high schools in 1961-62 spoke publicly about their experiences. Because of the overflow crowd the event was moved to the Bullock Temple CME Church across the street from Central. Lynn and I agreed afterwards that we, as part of the handful of whites in attendance, felt like voyeurs as they talked about what it had been like, day after day, month after month, to be ignored, heckled, spit upon and hit by their white classmates. But they also remembered what it had been like for them growing up in a more cohesive black community which watched over them, disciplined them if necessary, but clearly cherished them.

Judging by their poise and seriousness, leavened by humor, as well as their impressive accomplishments in life, it is apparent that they are among the least damaged by our white supremacy.[11]

Acknowledgments

I THANK my sisters Sally and Harriet for their memories and support and particularly Sally's permission to quote from her unpublished memoir. I thank Janelle Cranford Arnold for her memories of our mother Temple while she was a housemother at the University of Mississippi. I thank my childhood friend Sally Thomas for her letter describing her close relationship with Temple, "a great gift" she calls it. I had no real appreciation until this book that Temple meant so much to others. Similarly, a note of heartfelt gratitude to Temple from Voris Johnson, a brother-in-law who came to stand in for Jake before and after his death. My fondest memory of Voris is sitting in our kitchen on a red stool talking to Temple while she cooked. Truly a father substitute for me, Voris was a kind, quiet, almost shy man who, by the way, was an outstanding athlete.

Closer to home, I thank Arkansas historian Tom Dillard, whose knowledge, encouragement and example has meant so much.

Finally, I would be remiss if I didn't acknowledge the intellectual impact that *The Mind of the South* by W. J. Cash had on me and many, many others. Ditto Will Percy's *Lanterns on the Levee: Recollections of a Planter's Son*.

Notes

Chapter 1: One of the "Ten Hardest Places"

1 Janelle Cranford to Alpha Delta Pi Sorority, University of Mississippi, Oxford, Mississippi, 1970, in possession of author.

2 Janelle Cranford Arnold to Author, Dec. 28, 2014, in possession of author.

3 https://www.nytimes.com/2014/06/26/upshot/where-are-the-hardest-places-to-live-in-the-us.html, July 3, 2014.

4 *Arkansas Democrat-Gazette*, December 25, 2013.

5 https://encyclopediaofarkansas.net/entries/griffin-jasper-stockley-1053/

6 Grif Stockley, *Ruled by Race: Black/White Relations in Arkansas from Slavery to the Present*, (Fayetteville, University of Arkansas Press, 2009) p.42. Quoting, *Confederate Imprints 1861-1865*, Research Publications, Inc., Reel 34, p.44, Arkansas History Commission.

7 Effie Allison Wall Scrapbook, Marianna (Arkansas) Public Library. A copy is in possession of the author.

8 *Ruled by Race*, p.126.

9 The number of African Americans killed in and around Elaine has never been resolved. As I explain in *Blood in their Eyes: The Elaine Race Massacres of 1919* (University of Arkansas Press, 2000), initially, whites largely accepted at face value the explanation of the Phillips County power

structure that what occurred in Elaine was an attempted "insurrection" by blacks, though there was no credible evidence to support this view as trial transcripts help to demonstrate. See "Grif Stockley Papers" at the Butler Center for Arkansas Studies, Little Rock, Arkansas.

10 Wall Scrapbook. See also Arkansas History Commission for microfilm copies of the Marianna *The Courier Index*.

11 Wall Scrapbook. See also Wall, "Recollection in Brief of Raggio City," *Lee County History* (Dallas, Curtis Media Corporation, 1987), p.62-63.

12 *Lee County History*, p.11.

13 *Lee County History*, p.iv.

14 Quoted in *Ruled by Race*, p.69.

15 Quoted in *Blood in Their Eyes*, p.25.

16 *Lee County History*, p.63.

17 *Lee County History*, p.86.

18 E.J. Friedlander, "The Miasmatic Jungles," Reactions to H.L. Mencken 1921 Attack on Arkansas, *The Arkansas Historical Quarterly*, Vol. 38, Spring, 1979, p.63-71.

19 Wall Scrapbook.

20 Wall Scrapbook. Effie appears to have copied in her own hand the diary entry and included it in her scrapbook.

21 Quoted in *Ruled by Race*, p.66.

22 *Ruled by Race*, p.133

23 Jeff Davis's statements on race are cogently analyzed by Raymond Arsenault, *The Wild Ass of the Ozarks: Jeff Davis and the Social Basis of Southern Politics* (Philadelphia, Temple University Press, 1984).

24 Wall Scrapbook, *Lee County History*, p.62–63.

Chapter 2: Looking for a Family Hero

1 "Lee County," online Encyclopedia of Arkansas History and Culture. https://encyclopediaofarkansas.net/entries/lee-county-783/

2 Grandfather Wall's two nieces, Fredia Alice Wall Brantley and Eva Jane Wall Keeton Dunn, shared personal memories or conversations they had heard about him. Email to author, Feb. 11, 2013, in possession of author.

3 Fourth of July Marianna Heritage Tour brochure (n.d.).

4 Wall Scrapbook. Marianna *The Courier Index*, Sept. 3, 1926, *Lee County History*, p.12. Article written by Effie Allison Wall.

5 Quoted in *Blood in Their Eyes*, p.210-211.

6 Quoted in *Ruled by Race*, p.208.

7 *Lee County History*, p.5.

8 Besides writing for the paper and DAR, four of Effie's own pieces appear in the 1948 *Arkansas Historical Quarterly* in Vol. 8, No. 2 (Summer), p.160-170.

9 Blake Wintory, "Environmental and Social Change in Lee County, Arkansas, and the St. Francis River Basin, 1865-1905." Dissertation, University of Arkansas, p.11.

10 *Early Families of the Memphis Area*, Paul A. Matthews, Ed. (Memphis, Descendents of Shelby and Adjoining Counties, First Edition, 2008) p.343.

11 *Early Families of the Memphis Area*, p.270.

12 *Ruled by Race*, p.211.

13 The irony of black domestics being named for the plantation they labored for never seems to register. *History of Lee County*, p.6, "Whitehall named for a handsome residence of Ferd or Fred Rodgers on the banks of the Mississippi River. The house was white.... In 1880, the home with six hundred acres of land was carried into the river." This entry, under the topic heading "Origin of Names of Places in Lee County," was likely written by Effie. Her scrapbook contains her handwritten notes on the derivation of the names of communities.

14 For anyone wondering why my sister uses the term "Negro," rather than black, African-American or person of African descent, she has deliberately used the term which was appropriate for the time which she is writing about.

15 Sally Johnson, p.19.

16 Percy, p.20.

17 Percy, p.287.

18 Percy, p.285.

19 Percy, p.286.

Chapter 3: The "White" American Century

1 Peggy McIntosh, "White Privilege: Unpacking the Invisible Knapsack," Wellesley College Center for Research on Women, Wellesley, MA. 02481.

2 *The Nation*, Vol. 137, Dec. 27, 1933.

3 "States' Rights Democratic Party," Arkansas Encyclopedia of History and Culture.

4 The platform was passed August 14, 1948.

5 Marianna *The Courier Index*, August 26, 1948.

6 *Race and Ethnicity in Arkansas: New Perspectives*, ed. John A. Kirk, (Fayetteville, University of Arkansas, 181, fn. 26).

7 *Lee County History*, p.145.

8 Sally Mixon (now Thomas) remembers riding over to Memphis in the 1950s with her father, a member of the Marianna School Board, to arrange for the purchase of the construction of two tennis courts at the white high school.

9 Author interview with Olly Neal, May 13, 2014. In possession of the author.

10 *Ruled by Race*, p.239.

11 *Ruled by Race*, p.250. Curious about the disparities while Jake was on the School Board, I asked my friend Lee Brown, who obtained his doctorate in the field of econometrics from Purdue University, to analyze selected fiscal year data archived at the Arkansas History Commission specific to the Marianna school system (Lee County School District "A") for the years 1949 and 1956, which were the years Jake began and ended his service on the Marianna School Board. The data is compiled from photocopies I provided to Lee of the annual reports of the Lee County supervisor of schools, which also included other school districts. He writes, "The average elementary school teacher salary was almost 96 percent higher in the white schools in 1949 compared to Negro schools and was about 25% higher for the White school in 1949 than the same average for the Negro school and was about 46 percent higher in 1956. Between the years of 1949 and 1956 there was attrition in the African American schools in the Marianna school district far in excess of the experience in the White schools. For example, the White Schools experienced an attrition rate of 32 percent (537 in the first five grades in 1949 dropping to 364 in grades 8-12 seven years later). In the

black schools for the same years, the student population in grades 1-5 was 926 students in 1949 and had correspondingly declined 61% to 365 in grades 8-12 seven years later." Lee adds, "Without more data it is impossible to know the causes of these differences in the rates of attrition, but a contributing factor is likely the different transportation practices for the White and Negro systems, chiefly in the respective elementary schools. In 1949 45% of White elementary students were transported to school while 4% of Negro elementary students were transported. For high school in 1949, the percentage of students transported had risen to 49% (White) and 22 percent (African American). In 1956, 57% of White elementary students were transported compared to 11 percent for African Americans. The corresponding percentages in high school were 48% (White) and 63 percent (African American)." Having said the above, Lee suspects there is "an error in the 1956 data whereby some elementary teachers were either reassigned or mistakenly classified as high school teachers in the Negro school system. Otherwise the data is anomalous in that the student/teacher ratio in the Negro elementary schools suddenly jumped in 1956 while the Negro high school student/teacher ratio fell below the corresponding value in the White high school." E-mail from Lee Brown to Author, March 27, 2015. In possession of Author.

12 Author Interview with Donna Grady Creer. Notes in possession of the author (undated). Within months of my interview, Donna, a friendly, delightful woman, and her husband perished in a house fire.

13 *Best of Tales of the South*, Vol. 6, Eds. Paula Martin Morell and Stephanie Trevino Slagle, (Temenos Publishing, 2012) "The Dare," p.7.

14 *Encyclopedia of Religion in the South*, Ed. Samuel S. Hill, (Macon, GA, Mercer University Press, 2005), p.381.

15 Stockley, quoted in *Ruled by Race*, p.129.

16 Stockley, quoted in *Ruled by Race*, p.128-129.

17 Sally remembers one other occurrence of the same behavior.

18 Both friends remember this incident.

19 E-mail from Calvin Smith to Grif Stockley, Aug. 2, 2008. Stockley Papers, Butler Center for Arkansas Studies, Little Rock, AR.

20 E-mail from Calvin Smith to Grif Stockley, Aug. 27, 2008. Grif Stockley Papers, Butler Center for Arkansas Studies, Little Rock, AR.

21 Grif Stockley, "The Negro Boys Industrial School Fire: A Holistic Approach to History," *Pulaski County Historical Review*, 2008, p.56.

22 Johnson, p.38.

23 *Ruled by Race*, Introduction, p.xxi, quoting William M. Adler, *Land of Opportunity: One Family's Quest for the American Dream in the Age of Crack* (New York, Atlantic Monthly Press, 1995), p.21.

Chapter 4: "The All-Pervading Doctrine"

1 James W. Silver, *Mississippi: The Closed Society*, (New York, Harcourt, Brace and Co., 1963), p.6. University of Mississippi history professor James W. Silver's book attracted nationwide attention and was praised outside of Mississippi.

2 On October 23, 2014, Ron May granted me written permission to quote from his memoir.

3 Ronald A. May, *Delta Interlude* (unpublished memoir, 1990), p.56. In possession of the Author.

4   May, p.58.

5   May, p.58.

6   May, p.66.

7   May, p.40.

8   May, p.42.

9   *Arkansas Gazette*, 1961.

10 James A. Banks, *Race, Culture and Education: The Selected Works of James A. Banks*, (London, Routledge Publishers, 2006), p.38.

11 Quoted in *Ruled by Race*, p.377, Marianna: A Sociological Essay on an Eastern Arkansas Town (Jefferson City, MO, New Scholars Press, 1973), p.5.

12 May, p.55.

13 *Crisis of Conscience: Arkansas Methodists and the Civil Rights Struggle*, Ed. James T. Clemons and Kelly L. Farr (Little Rock, Butler Center for Arkansas Studies, 2007).

14 *Crisis of Conscience*, p.2, 5.

Chapter 5: College—Let Me Out of There!

1   Stephen R. Haynes, *The Last Segregated Hour: The Memphis Kneel-ins and the Campaign for Southern Church Desegregation* (Oxford, Oxford University Press, 2012).

2   Stephen R. Haynes, p.77.

3   Stephen R. Haynes, p.64.

4   Stephen R. Haynes, p.64.

5   Since I took it, it is my understanding that the Foreign Exam process is considerably less difficult these days. Someone finally got the idea that maybe diplomats should not all be book smart white boys and girls but that maybe a few should look like the rest of the world.

6 Grif Stockley, *Ruled by Race*, p.326, quoted in Nick Kotz, *Judgment Day: Lyndon Banes Johnson, Martin Luther King, Jr. and the Laws That Changed America*, (New York, Houghton Mifflin, 2005), p.153.

7 Grif Stockley, *Ruled by Race*, p.326, quoted in Josh Gottheimer, Ed. *Ripples of Hope: Great American Civil Rights Speeches* (New York, Basic Civitas Books, 2004), p.278.

Chapter 6: Me Not Talk Pretty, EVER

1 In 1965-67, the total time of service was 24 months. The requirement would later be changed to 24 months in country. It became clear that it took most volunteers a year to learn the language well enough to accomplish anything.

Chapter 7: No Strings to Pull

1 Otto Kerner, et. al., *National Advisory Commission on Civil Disorders*, (New York, Dutton, 1968), p.1.

2 https://nsarchive2.gwu.edu/NSAEBB/NSAEBB195/index.htm

Chapter 8: Talk, Talk, Talk

1 *Ruled by Race*, p.357.

2 I explain in *Ruled by Race* that whites were never completely eliminated from SNICK but that the funding dried up. p.346.

3 *Arkansas Gazette*, September 3, 1969.

Chapter 9: Sexism and Racism—The Law School Way

1 Letter to Temple Stockley from Voris Johnson, June 26, 1968 (Grif Stockley Papers).

Chapter 10: Legal Services

1 *Ruled by Race*, p.340.
2 *Ruled by Race*, p.396.
3 Tom Glaze with Ernie Dumas, *Waiting for the Cemetery Vote, a Memoir*, (Fayetteville, University of Arkansas Press, 2010), p.198. Justice Glaze was terminally ill during the period before publication. His decision to ask journalist and author Ernie Dumas to co-author the book was an inspired, if obvious, choice. Dumas's encyclopedic knowledge of Arkansas and the South is the stuff of legend.

Chapter 12: *Hypogrif*

1 *New York Times*, Jan. 31, 1993.
2 Arkansas Residents Past and Present (compiled by staff of *Arkansas Times*), *Somewhere Apart: "My Favorite Place in Arkansas"*, (Fayetteville, University of Arkansas Press, 1997) p.129.
3 p.124
4 *Arkansas Democrat-Gazette*, Jan. 21, 2015.
5 John E. Bush, P. L. Dorman, *History of the Mosaic Templars of America—Its Founders and Officials* (Little Rock, Central Printing Company, 1924), p.81-82. The best known example of a white father assisting his mulatto son in Arkansas is Dr. Sanford Reamy who fathered a child by his housemaid, Mia. The 1870 census documents that Scipio Africanus Jones was the only literate person in his household. Later, Dr. Reamy saw to it that Scipio read law in the offices of his friends. Jones went on to become a persistent and effective civil rights advocate for African Americans during his career.

6 Arkansas schools are deemed to be "academically distressed" if fewer than half of the students reach "proficient levels" on reading and math exams over a three year period. Lee County came off the distressed list in February of 2015, but just barely. Proficiency levels remained abysmally low as they did for much of the Delta.

7 *The Courier Index*, Feb. 20, 2013.

8 *Arkansas Democrat-Gazette*, Jan. 14, 2015.

9 *Arkansas Democrat-Gazette*, Jan. 21, 2015. Dr. Ross's impassioned language was referenced in the media but ignored. In fact, it was an "Aha!" moment in the history of race relations in Arkansas. Whites in political office do not generally acknowledge publicly that our history has been one of "white privilege."

10 *Little Rock School District v. Pulaski County School District, et. al.* - 584 F. Supp. 328 (E.D. 1984). Judge Henry Woods found "[t]he housing authorities, lending institutions, realtors and others had acted in collusion to create segregated neighborhoods..." Quoted in *Ruled by Race*, p.401. See for example, John A. Kirk, "A Study in Second Class Citizenship: Race, Urban Development and Little Rock's Gillam Park, 1934-2004," *Arkansas Historical Quarterly* (2004), p.262-268.

11 Books about the Little Rock Nine's year at Central High School have become a cottage industry as historians and writers continue to mine this controversial period in Southern history.

Made in the USA
Monee, IL
26 July 2020